Morley, S.

Robert

My Father

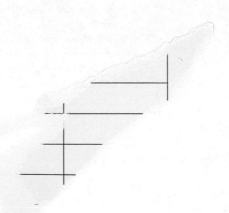

Robert
My Father

by

SHERIDAN
MORLEY

9)382885

WEIDENFELD AND NICOLSON
LONDON

First published in Great Britain in 1993 by
Weidenfeld & Nicolson
The Orion Publishing Group Ltd
Orion House
5 Upper Saint Martin's Lane,
London, WC2H 9EA.

A catalogue reference is available from the British Library

ISBN 0 297 81329 3

382885
920
MOR

Typeset by Create Publishing Services Ltd, Bath, Avon
Printed in Great Britain by The Bath Press, Bath, Avon

For Joan,
his wife, my mother,
who made the best of both of us

Contents

Illustrations

Photographs appear between pages 48 and 49, 112 and 113, and 176 and 177.

With the following exceptions all photographs come from the Morley family collections: portrait by Roddy McDowall (Roddy McDowall), *Hippo Dancing* (Mander and Mitchenson Theatre Collection), portrait by Nicholas Sinclair (Nicholas Sinclair), portrait by Edward St Maur (Edward St Maur), at *Punch* table (Clive Barda). If inadvertently copyright has been infringed in any of the other photographs used, the author and publishers will be happy to make due acknowledgement in subsequent editions.

The following cartoons from *Punch* appear, with permission, within the text: p55, *Pygmalion*; p77, *The Man Who Came to Dinner*; p83, *The First Gentleman*; p129, *Hippo Dancing*; p137, *Fanny*; p153, *Oscar Wilde*; p179, *How the Other Half Loves*; p199, *Banana Ridge*.

Acknowledgements

For quotations used in the preliminary pages, I am grateful to Hugo Williams and Richard Eyre. For the quotation from George Bernard Shaw's *The Doctor's Dilemma* I wish to thank the Society of Authors on behalf of the Bernard Shaw Estate. I am also indebted to Michael Blakemore for the extract from his as yet unpublished memoirs, and to Christopher Matthew for his *Oldie* account of Robert on the lecture circuit.

Sheridan Morley

Author's Note

For most of the biographies I have ever written, from the first of Noël Coward, across twenty years and half a dozen others, to the first of David Niven and James Mason, it has been second nature to interview at least a hundred people as witnesses to the life and the career. For this life of my father, however, written in the immediate aftermath of his death, I seem to have been talking about him only on the typewriter, and to nobody but myself.

Nevertheless I would still greatly like to thank here all his relatives, friends, colleagues and sometimes, indeed, his critics who during the last forty years or so, all over the world, have taught me about the man who was their Robert. I hope, and dare to believe, that they might find him somewhere in here too.

Sheridan Morley,
Chelsea Harbour,
March 1993

Throughout his life, my father struggled to clear a space left unoccupied by his father, and I've made no less an effort in my life. It is a costly operation.
Richard Eyre, *Utopia and Other Places*

Now that he is dead,
Now that he is remembered
Unfavourably by some
For phrases too well cut
To fit their bonhomie,
I wonder what he was like
This stiff theatrical man
With his air of sealed regret.
'I'd have made a first-class tramp,'
He told me once,
'If I'd had more money...'

Hugo Williams, 'Death of an Actor'
from *Writing Home* (1985)

You'll have seen my picture in the papers quite a lot these last few years. When you get home, you can look me up in *Who's Who*, if you happen to have one. It won't tell you everything about me, but there's quite a lot there now, nearly half a page. It will tell you where I was born, and where I went to school, whom I married ... I am telling you all this, not because I want to boast, but because I want to establish some contact with you. Just because you sit in my theatre, it doesn't mean that you have to like me – or I you, for that matter. But it does mean that our lives, like a lot of other people's lives, have already crossed to a certain extent. That is why I should value your opinion; supposing we make a start?

Robert Morley as Arnold Holt in his own *Edward, My Son* (West End, 1947; Broadway, 1948; Australia and New Zealand, 1949–50).

Curtain Down

1992

Robert was always magnificent at exits, but, when he died – shortly before noon on the morning of Derby Day, 3 June 1992, three days after a stroke from which he had never regained consciousness – I was more profoundly shocked than by anything else which had ever happened to me before. At fifty, I suppose I had no right to be; I was already, as Noël Coward had told Clifton Webb on a similar occasion, a little old to consider entering an orphanage, besides which my mother is splendidly alive and thriving. But somehow I had never considered the possibility of Robert being dead, not even in those last few months when his energy levels had been so low that even the resumption of the racing season on television had failed to cheer him.

That unusual and uncharacteristic winter depression should perhaps have been a warning that all was no longer well with him; but his health had never been bad, give or take the 'senile diabetes', a medical term which always infuriated him for its reflection upon his age rather than his well-being, and as recently as December he had been at work on a television commercial for mince pies in which he played a benign Father Christmas. This same role had been his first in a school pageant when he was five, and we were not to know that eighty years later it was also to be his last.

In the immediate aftermath of his death, with my brother home from America and my sister and her family on their way from Australia, and all the other relatives gathering, sheltering for comfort, there was a great deal to arrange, not least the funeral and a response to literally hundreds of letters which came pouring in from around the world. By such means, so I learned, does one hide from death, putting off in all kinds of mechanical, administrative and journalistic ways the moment when one has to face up to the sudden hole in the middle of one's existence.

For me that moment came one night about a month later, in a place where so many of my memories of my father began and belonged. One Saturday in early July, the dozen of us who were his closest relatives gathered at the village church in Wargrave, a mile or two away from the extended cottage where he and my mother had lived since 1940, and where all three of us children had grown up. My sister, her husband and their children had been unable to return from Australia in time for the funeral, and so in the church where Annabel and Charles were married we held another, very private family gathering to put Pa's ashes in the ground against the graveyard wall, beneath a plaque bearing simply his name, and birth and death dates, all tactfully raised just above centre by our local builder and undertaker to leave room, eventually, for the addition of my mother's. 'The great thing about Clifford Maidment', said Ma at the time, 'is that he does plan ahead.'

After that second service, shaken by the finality of seeing Pa's ashes into the earth, but somehow reassured to think that he had achieved a form of permanent billing on the wall of his local church, I drove back to London and to the Whitehall Theatre, where I was, unusually, working on stage. I am by trade a dramatic critic and therefore spend much of my life in the stalls of playhouses. From time to time, however, driven either by some familial folk memory or else by the usual critic's impotent rage at always being the diner in someone else's restaurant, unable to write the menu or choose the wine list, I take to the boards myself, usually as the narrator in an anthology of someone else's songs which I've put together simply for the joy of being around when they are again sung to a live audience.

One of these shows, *Noël and Gertie*, has done me proud around the world these last ten years and a second, *Spread a Little Happiness*, had enjoyed a sold-out Christmas season at the King's Head in Islington shortly before Pa died; it was, in fact, the last show he ever saw in London and he kept his hearing aid in place throughout, always a reassuring sign that he wasn't growing too bored. But we had unwisely decided, just before he died, to try our luck in the West End at the start of what was generally reckoned to have been the worst box-office summer since the war, and we were already closing on the night of that second little funeral. As I went in through the stage door to the matinée, I was thinking, as I had been all through that short Whitehall run, of all the stage doors I had walked through with Pa around the world. The ones along Shaftesbury Avenue, where he was in semipermanent residence for twenty years after the war, in plays which only he ever managed to turn into two-year hits. The ones in Australia, where his fortunes were sometimes less secure: 'My darling boy,' he said once after a bad matinée in Sydney of an Alan Bennett drama called *The Old Country*, in which he gave the last great performance of his life as an exiled British diplomat who had spied for the USSR and was then forced to live there, 'you can have no concept of the vastness of the outback of Australia until you have seen the dress circle of this theatre on a Saturday afternoon.'

Things were much like that at the Whitehall on this particular Saturday afternoon, and after we had played the last two houses to a vociferous but, alas, rather too thin crowd of Vivian Ellis enthusiasts (the show had been built around his classic songbook), I went around the dressing-rooms thanking our small but splendid company and apologising for having involved them in so short a West End stay. Having done that, I went back to dressing-room number five, packed up my dinner-jacket and the telegrams and the few belongings which had managed to gather there in the past month, and walked out across the already darkened, empty stage.

In older and better West End times the set would already have been in the process of being demolished in readiness for next week's coming attraction; but, with the whole theatre going dark like so many others that July, there had been no need to detain any stage management, and I was the last one out to turn off the lights.

I am no believer in ghosts, the paranormal or, indeed, much of an after-life, but on that empty stage I heard my father's voice, just for a moment, as clearly as I could ever remember it. He was talking, as so often, to what I always thought of as 'his' audience: theatregoers who had come out in search not necessarily of a playwright or a director (though they too were often his roles), but in search of Robert himself. From the time of his first great success as an actor/author (*Edward, My Son*, in 1947, which opened and closed with Arnold Holt's speeches to the audience) he had built up a special affinity with his customers almost akin to that achieved by a great head waiter or hotel manager. Night after night, when I was a child, I used to stand in the wings watching Pa peeping through a gap in the curtains as the audience filed into what one always thought of as 'his' theatre, whichever one it happened to be. He would take note of what they were wearing, what sort of age, what sort of people, and that night he would craft his performance, and often those of his cast, to suit them alone.

Disguise was never a part of his art, nor was he ever inclined to 'lose himself' in a performance; because of this, critics often found him and his success bewildering, though no more bewildering than he found them and their lives. In his obituary for the *Guardian*, my old friend and colleague Michael Billington recalled Robert's perpetual astonishment at how Mike and I could continue for so many years to go willingly into theatres and watch plays every night. Somebody in the Garrick club once asked Robert what it was like to be an actor and have a critic for a son: 'Like being head of the Israeli army,' he replied, 'and waking up to find your son is an Arab.'

We were together, my father and I, for fractionally more than fifty years and, in the words of the old vaudeville number, it never seemed a day too long. We quarrelled badly, so far as I can recall, just twice. The first time was when I was seventeen and had won a place at Merton College, Oxford, which I regarded as a rare triumph given my somewhat eccentric and peripatetic previous education around the world, and which he regarded as an unmitigated and potentially disastrous waste of three years. Like many of his ancestors and my children, Pa could never bear to be formally taught things, preferring instead to acquire his considerable education and knowledge in random conversations, often with total strangers on railway trains or across casino tables.

The second time we quarrelled was almost thirty years later, when I left home as my marriage came to an end; 'One falls in love with other people,' was his view, 'but it is generally unwise to leave home for them.' I did, however, and we had a few rather tight-lipped months. Outside of that, I cannot recall a single real argument – not because either of us was especially good-natured or tolerant, but rather, I think, because we were just very adept at avoiding rows. Some would doubtless say this betrays a terrible lack of depth in our relationship; I prefer to think it means that we simply did not enjoy quarrelling, and usually managed to find better ways of spending what time we had together.

It cannot be easy, people used to say, being an actor's son; but then Robert was never that kind of actor, and it was always immensely easy. I got my name by being born on his first night as Sheridan Whiteside in *The Man Who Came To Dinner* at the Savoy in December 1941. By then he had already been an actor for twelve years, having abandoned his original plan for a career in the diplomatic service. Yet his parents were nothing if not hopeful for him. His father had been a soldier and a gambler with a passion for roulette and racing, which was all he ever left his only son. His mother always hoped that her beloved Bobbie might improve upon the family fortunes; acting she regarded as only marginally better than gambling for a living.

There were two children, Robert and his sister Margaret. While they were still babes in arms, they were shown off to one of the many aunts on their mother's Fass side of the family. 'The girl will probably be all right,' said the aunt, 'but I fear the boy is a fool.' Robert never forgot his very first notice and sometimes, indeed, seemed willing to make it his living. But to think of him purely as a light comedian, albeit one of the last and best of that particular stage line, is sorely to underestimate his very real achievement. He was one of the few English boulevardiers, a difficult tradition to sustain in Britain after the war, depending as it did on the actor being in total charge of his surroundings. 'Do sit down, dear boy,' Robert would say to those directors who occasionally ventured to interrupt him in rehearsal, 'and we'll find you something to do in a minute.' John Gielgud once told me that trying to direct Robert was about as useful as trying to alter the sequence on a set of traffic lights.

Playwrights did not fare much better – 'I shall make you very rich and very unhappy,' Robert accurately told Alan Ayckbourn while giving him his first prolonged West End run with *How the Other Half Loves* – unless of course, they happened to be George Bernard Shaw. It was after seeing Esme Percy on a tour of *The Doctor's Dilemma* that Robert decided to act, and Shaw visited him a few years later on the film set of *Major Barbara*, where Robert, Rex Harrison and Wendy Hiller first established themselves and their careers in the most impressive Shavian triumph of their generation.

That was in 1940; two years earlier he had already won an Oscar nomination for his first American film, *Marie Antoinette*, in which he played doomed Louis XVI against John Barrymore, Norma Shearer and most of the best character actors in Hollywood. He was then asked to stay out there for *The Hunchback of Notre Dame*, but declined, having been told that it was a grunting rather than a speaking part. It went instead to Charles Laughton, and I once asked Pa if he had ever regretted having missed the role and, with it, perhaps a different kind of screen stardom. Not at all, he reflected, it was a lucky escape from the kind of life Laughton then spent in Hollywood, forever waiting to be insulted.

In the United States Pa was only truly happy at Las Vegas, which he always reckoned to be heaven on earth. If he understood anything better than acting, it was the pleasure principle: the absolute importance of utter enjoyment. Peter Hall, when he was running Stratford, once asked Robert to play Falstaff and I begged him to do it, if only to disprove the theory of some of my critical colleagues that he was only good at playing versions of himself in essentially lightweight material. Anyone who ever saw him on stage or screen as Oscar Wilde, or as the Beaverbrook figure Arnold Holt in his own *Edward, My Son*, knew well enough that this was not true. But Pa rejected Falstaff, not out of fear or, I think, laziness, but simply because he knew he would not enjoy it and, if he would not, then how could he expect that his audience would? Apart from Shaw and the loosely translated French boulevard comedies such as *The Little Hut* and *Hippo Dancing*, out of which he would regularly get runs of several years where no other actor outside France ever survived more than three months, Robert was happy in Ben Travers and in Kaufman and Hart, but in little else that was not in some way of his own devising. Peter Ustinov once told me he would sometimes sit at the back of the stalls during Robert's long West End run in Ustinov's *Halfway up the Tree*, letting out small whoops of joy whenever he recognised one of his own lines.

Robert and Rex Harrison were of an age, and had started out together in drama school and regional tours – indeed Rex had one of his first leading roles in a shortlived play of Robert's called *Short Story* – but apart from a couple of films, the two men had virtually nothing in common either physically or temperamentally. Fifty years after their start together, they happened to meet in London's Burlington Arcade the morning after Robert had featured in *This Is Your Life* on television. 'So brave', murmured Rex, 'and not a programme I would ever dare to do, not with the two suicides in my life, and the four divorces and all that. But then, Robert, for you life has been so very different: one wife, one family, one home and, if I may say so, one performance.'

In truth I believe it was Rex who really only ever gave the one performance, but the old misanthrope was right about the house and the wife and the family. Sustained across more than half a century by my mother's love, faith and tolerance, Robert was in many ways the happiest man I have ever known. He died, as he had lived, with immaculate timing, regretting only perhaps that he had just missed hearing the result of the Derby.

'I suppose, dear,' cabled Gladys Cooper from Hollywood to her daughter when she heard of her engagement in 1939, 'if you love him, he can't be altogether disastrous,' and that from my grandmother was high praise. If anybody was ever allowed to choose a father, I think most of us would probably have chosen Robert. In these first few months after his death I think about him a great deal; staring into the bathroom mirror in the morning, it is his face I sometimes see staring back at me and I remember, for no very clear reason, a story he once told me about his own father taking him, as an uneasy teenager, around the more scandalously sexy environs of prewar Soho. 'My boy,' said the Major to Robert, 'you won't believe this, but in these very streets are men who paint their faces.' In those very streets Pa spent most of the rest of his life painting his face before going on stage every night, never thinking of his father at all except to wonder sometimes who he really was. I begin, only now, to understand the wonderment: who was my father?

Even as I start to try to answer that question, I am all too aware that it's not going to be altogether easy. If there was a thin, tormented or tortured man inside him trying to escape, he certainly did not make it. With Robert, what you saw was very often what you got, and any analysis of his inner self, either by him or by me, was hindered firstly by our somewhat clenched reluctance, characteristic I think of both our generations, to examine ourselves too deeply for emotional or inherited scars, and secondly by his unspoken but utter belief in the maxim of 'never complain – never explain'.

Our relationship was thus often untroubled by much thought: we took it for granted that nature had cast us, more or less at random, as father and son, and that we had better play the parts as best we could, without getting too far up stage of each other or interrupting each other's best speeches, no matter how often we had heard them before.

As the years went by, people outside the family seemed to take it for granted that we were alike: both large and loud certainly, both desperate to make our names as familiar as possible to total strangers in whatever room or country we happened to find ourselves, both incompetent at financial affairs and very demanding in our personal ones, the principal of those demands being that we should at all times be the centre of attention and the focus of other people's lives, no matter that we were seldom of much help with any of them.

Yet the truth is, I think, that you will find more of my father in my brother, my sister and my children than in me; precisely because he and I were physically and superficially alike in so many ways and ambitions, we often tended to keep a wary distance as if afraid of crashing into each other's headlights. In our own rather inchoate and offhand way we loved each other very much indeed, and in later life took to hugging each other, often to the amazement of passers-by who would look at these two huge men in a bearlike embrace and wonder what on earth was going on.

What was going on, I think, was the realisation, rather late in life, that we were never going to find the words to tell each other how much we mattered to each other's survival, or how glad we were to have ended up in the same family roadshow. Of that he was, of course, always the leader, if sometimes slightly uncertain as to where precisely it was leading us or himself; Robert's career was often a mystery to critics, but never more so than to himself. It was guided not by any theatrical, cinematic or intellectual principle, but by the ring of the telephone and the offer of a job. On the race course he tended to side with the trainers, but to understand the jockeys best; after all they, too, had to get on whatever horse came down the track and ride it as best they could, if not always to victory then at least seldom to total defeat. If his later career did degenerate into a catalogue of minor movies, the trick, as he understood it, was to hang on and keep going. Perhaps at this point we had better go back to the starting-gate and take it from there through to the unsaddling enclosure.

I

Folkestone Follies

1908–1915

Folkestone in 1915: that was the place for me. Mrs Boddam Whettam, Canon Elliott, two brass bands on the Leas and a great big bath for Margaret Morley; besides, if you dug deep enough into the sands, you could reach Australia.

One morning early in 1963 the classical guitarist and lutenist Julian Bream answered a knock on his front door to find my father, whom he had never met, and an entire BBC television crew standing on his threshold. 'I am Robert Morley', the unexpected guest announced proudly as the cameras turned, 'and I have come home at last.'

In a way, of course, it was true. Robert had been born on 26 May 1908 at a house in Semley, Wiltshire, which was later the home of the Bream family. At the time of its occupation by the Morleys, Robert's father had decided, albeit briefly, upon a career as a gentleman farmer. The Major was a man of many careers, mostly disastrous. A compulsive gambler, he lived a life of regular crisis and constant financial adventure, bequeathing to his only son a passion for roulette and the rare ability (duly inherited by my brother, but not by me) to live on the financial edge without serious loss of sleep or nerve. Robert's father had been born in 1886, educated at Wellington College, to which he was later to send an extremely unwilling and unsuited son, and soon became an officer in the 4th Royal Irish Dragoon Guards. The army appealed to him and, indeed, he returned to it after early retirement to fight in the Boer War.

Civilian life was, however, more of a problem. In uniform, serving as he once did on the military staff of the then Viceroy of India, it had been possible to maintain the 'champagne life on a beer income' which the Major always considered his birthright. When there was no war to fight or uniform to wear, he variously found employment as a café proprietor, night-club impresario, club secretary, farmer and creative organiser of a revolutionary 'send for poems by post' scheme, none of which could be said to have made his fortune.

'Father was often a bankrupt,' Robert later recalled, 'and always a gambler, but of all the excitement, happiness and occasional despair he brought me, I remember him best sitting pretending to be asleep, a handkerchief over his face and four or even sometimes five chocolates arranged on his lap, while I, choking with pleasure and the effort of restraining my giggles, tiptoed towards him to seize a sweet while he feigned unconsciousness. Then he would wake, remove the handkerchief, look down with astonishment, count the remaining chocolates and express bewilderment, rage or resignation before once more replacing the handkerchief and pretending to nod off. If there has ever been a better game, I never learnt to play it.'

Except, of course, acting, which rapidly took the place of formal sports in Robert's childhood. His sister and only sibling, Margaret, had been born a year earlier to the Major and 'poor Daisy', as my paternal grandmother was always known. By the time I knew her in the late 1940s she had taken to dressing in a great deal of black and giving a remarkable impersonation of Anna Neagle as the old Queen Victoria. Her life had not been entirely unhappy, and she was a generous dispenser of boiled sweets, which were kept by her bedside in a circular silver box. But there was a curious air of frailty and faint illness always about her, as though life with the Major had just been too much to bear with any sustained energy.

'Poor Daisy' was, in fact, Gertrude Emily Fass, born in 1882, fifth of ten children of a wealthy German adventurer who had made his fortune in South Africa and then brought his large family home to make suitable marriages. They were living in Chalfont St Giles, Buckinghamshire, next door to the Major's parents, when the two households became maritally entwined. The Major had first had his eye on Daisy's elder sister Edith, but, when she became engaged elsewhere, he took up with the younger sister, who thereupon became known as 'poor Daisy' on account of his general un-suitability and impossibility. As this grew worse over the years following their marriage in January 1906, her family name was adjusted from 'poor Daisy' to 'poor, poor Daisy', a role she played forever afterwards.

Their two children could hardly have been more different and maintained throughout their lives a wary, loving, but mutually uncomprehending relationship. Margaret always said that her parents' constant moving during her childhood was what gave her the determination to settle, as she did for much of her life, on a small farm in Kent and seldom to move out of a ten-mile radius of Biddenden. Robert, by contrast, said that the constant moving bred in him a love of adventure and a passion for touring ideally suited to the prewar demands of a struggling actor. Both children were stubborn, loyal and utterly unable to understand what motivated the other: Margaret would reluctantly attend Robert's theatrical outings, vaguely wondering well into their late middle age when he was going to settle down and find himself a proper career, while he took to chalking up on the board outside her farm advertising the sale of eggs and manure the news that 'celebrated actor's autograph' could also be had for a mere two shillings. Needless to say, she always removed his addition from the sign, often before he had even returned with some relief to the bright lights of London. He could never understand Kent, just as she could never understand Shaftesbury Avenue; it remained one of the great divides in our family, handed down from one generation to the next. She was a Fass, he was a Morley.

And so, of course, was the Major. Alas I never knew him, but by all accounts he was precisely the type of eccentric, larger-than-life figure that his son took to playing in later cameo roles on screen. The Boer War had left the Major with very little except a helmet that he rapidly had converted into a biscuit tin, which he would then keep in the halls of his various abodes. He had also been slightly wounded in South Africa, maintaining that the bullet had entered too close to his heart to be safely removed surgically. Thereafter, in times of stress, he would clutch his stomach and cry, 'I feel it moving,' this often being enough to deter creditors. If that failed, however, he would sometimes take to his bed and threaten suicide with his old Boer revolver if his debts were not immediately taken care of by some relative or other.

Often the debts could be taken care of, because the Major's parents had thoughtfully entailed some of their assets for just such a purpose, hoping to keep the money out of direct contact with their spendthrift son. 'There never has been an entail,' cried the Major later, 'through which a good lawyer cannot drive a coach and horses'; and many of my father's earliest memories of childhood concerned his father's various searches for the right coachman.

Family holidays were taken, whenever possible, within the immediate vicinity of the nearest roulette wheel, just as throughout our childhood Robert would take us to the Lido at Venice, which had the twin advantages of an August film festival (expenses could therefore sometimes be met by a well-timed personal appearance) and a casino (expenses could seldom be met at all). I was almost eighteen before I had ever heard of Canaletto or realised that the Lido was not all they had in Venice.

Whenever Daisy and her own despairing family complained of the Major's spendthrift ways, he would sigh and murmur self-sacrificingly, 'Only trying to make a few pennies for you and the children, dear,' before disappearing back into the welcoming gloom of the *salons des jeux*. On the rare occasions when the ball landed in the right socket, he would return to the steps of the casino and thrust thousand-franc notes at his children, enjoining them to 'take this before the rats get it'.

A keen Francophile, since it was the most convenient country for brief but rapid escape when his creditors proved unusually threatening, the Major would from time to time try to import some of its better notions into southern England. One of these was the pavement café; if the French were accustomed to taking refreshment out of doors, why not the residents of W8? A small and derelict restaurant off Kensington High Street was, therefore, acquired by the Major, chairs and tables were placed on the pavement, and Robert and Margaret, aged roughly five and six, were told to sit outside to encourage custom. Thousands of people, the Major had been assured by the restaurant's previous owner, passed the café every day and, indeed, they continued to do so. The sight of two small, shivering children sitting on the sidewalk in early December trying to look as though they were enjoying a continental breakfast did not encourage other customers, and soon enough the Kensington restaurant project was consigned to the list of the Major's other failed businesses. These included a revival of the aforementioned poems-by-post project; for a while the Major was much taken with the notion of life after death and, in fact, wrote a lengthy verse on the subject. He then took a small advertisement in *The Times* which read: 'Is there an after-life? If in doubt, send three shillings to Major Morley at the following address.'

Few did, and the Major considered the alternative possibility of becoming a street singer, or to be strictly accurate an above-street singer: placing an early phonograph record of the great Caruso on a gramophone in the living-room of a flat he was then renting off Fulham Road, he would stand on the first-floor balcony miming the voice of the great tenor to the amazement of passers-by below. The problem with this scheme was that from the balcony he had no way of collecting their money, even had they been disposed to offer him any.

Then again, when Robert was about four, there was the celebrated near-drowning of the boy in the Serpentine. Out for a stroll around Hyde Park with the Major, Robert had asked his father if he might walk fully clothed into the lake. The Major, who like many in our family only ever listened to conversations in which he himself was principal speaker, absent-mindedly agreed that this would be a thoroughly good idea, and Robert, not perhaps always the brightest of small children, was soon up to his neck in several feet of icy water. When rescued by a couple of nervous bystanders, Robert was duly returned by the Major to a near hysterical Daisy at home. 'I have always said', opined the Major as he departed hastily for his club, 'that it does not do to coddle the children.'

It was not until Robert was sixteen that his parents achieved even an informal separation, and they never divorced, but the Major was as tempera-mentally unsuited to marriage as he was to any fixed address and, as a result, Robert's childhood was spent on the move between London and Folkes-tone, to which the family first repaired around the outbreak of the First World War and which was always to be the focus of his happiest childhood memories. 'Folkestone', he once said to me during a television interview about his beginnings, 'was simply the place to be in those days. Two bands on the Leas and an outside lift down the cliff-face to the shore powered hydraulically, so there was always the additional thrill of wondering whether they had put enough water in at the base to stop us hurtling to our death on the beach below.'

Then there were the street names such as Augusta Gardens and Upper Bouverie Road West, and ladies like Mrs Boddam Whettam, a schoolboy joke all by herself, who would give bridge-afternoon teas. Once, when he was about seven, she unwisely invited Robert to deliver her invitations. But, unbeknownst to Mrs Whettam, Robert had a lifelong fear of dogs, which precluded him walking up the long drives of the houses in Augusta Gardens in case any should be lurking in the shrubberies. On the other hand, he could hardly return the invitations undelivered. After some thought, he therefore took the lift down the cliff and stood at the water's edge, hurling the invitations into the waves while murmuring to himself, 'Alas unable to attend, alas unable to attend.'

Then there were the nannies, large numbers of whom came and went as and when the Major could afford to pay them. The best remembered of these nursed a violent hatred of foreigners and would take the young Robert and Margaret on regular walks around Folkestone Harbour whilst the cross-Channel ferries were docking from France. On rougher days passengers would lurch ashore yellow in the face and frequently still being seasick. 'That, Master Bobbie and Miss Margaret,' Nanny would say sharply, 'is what you get for going abroad,' and it was several years before either of them did so.

In these years their time was divided between Folkestone, South Kensington in London and the Fass family home in Chalfont St Giles, to which last they would repair when the Major's fortunes had sunk below the level of any possible rent. Of the three addresses, Robert infinitely preferred Folkestone: something about its already faintly decayed gentility, the roller-skating near the pier, the man selling raspberry sherbet on the beach, appealed to him to such an extent that sixty or seventy years later he could still be brought up short by an evening paper paragraph headlined 'Minor Accident in Folkestone High Street: None Hurt'. As for his sister, Folkestone was simply the place where she first set eyes on the sea: 'What a great big bath for Margaret Morley,' was one of her first recorded utterances.

London held other pleasures, not so memorable, perhaps, unless one counts Mrs Boddam Whettam's only true rival in the gallery of dragon ladies who beset Robert's childhood. She was Mrs Agnes Pope of Courtfield Gardens, the road next to where his grandmother lived, and her claim to fame was a lifelong terror of handkerchieves. These, she believed, were the work of the devil and served only to spread terrible diseases around South Kensington and even, it was reliably rumoured, beyond. Accordingly, she had founded several years earlier a Society for the Abolition of the Handkerchief. This had met with only limited success even among her own relatives, but for Robert and Margaret there was the joy of a weekly tea at Mrs Pope's with her permission to sniff as often and as loudly as they liked. Mrs Pope, on the other hand, never sniffed at all, her nasal passages having been blocked since childhood by an accident to her nose. Her lifelong objection to the handkerchief was, alas, also the cause of her death: when she was very old and ill, a uniformed visitor blew his nose at her bedside; Mrs Pope took it to be the Last Trumpet, and expired.

On the subject of eccentrics, there was also Robert's grandfather on the Major's side of the family, a former chairman of the Parcel Company, forerunner of today's motorcycle messengers and a man who himself would ride coaches around Hyde Park at high speeds until well into his seventies, usually accompanied by gorgeous young ladies he had somehow acquired in the course of his travels. He, too, was more than a little strange about money, however, and although he managed to remain reasonably affluent, at least by the standards of his son, he became convinced late in life that he was no longer solvent. Where other men of similar conviction might have become beggars, he became a philanthropist, accosting total strangers in the street and pressing into their surprised hands a golden sovereign while murmuring, 'Take this, my good man, before the Crash comes.' One of his relatives was then deputed to follow him around, apologising to the surprised recipients of the sovereigns and attempting to retrieve them before the Crash did indeed come.

Courtfield Gardens was the centre of Robert's early London life: both sets of grandparents lived there and only ventured north of the park when it was necessary to purchase chocolates and other essentials at Selfridges. To his dying day, Robert could describe in intricate detail the wrapping used by that emporium for their confectionery and also the noise of a Maxim gun, which could be recreated by tearing off the paper from the outer edge of the box.

Large department stores were a constant fascination, not least because the owners of one of them, Gorringe's, lived next door to one of the grandmothers and actually shared her brougham. When Lady Gorringe lay dying, Robert was hugely impressed by the fact that men came to lay straw in the street outside her door to muffle the sound of the carriages, and was faintly surprised to discover that she died none the less.

The Major, perhaps determined that his son and heir should see more of London life than was available from Courtfield Gardens, took him on more perilous excursions, not only to the Soho where men painted their faces but also on one memorable occasion to Limehouse, which he reckoned was the heart of the drug trade and should therefore be shown to the young Robert as an example of the kind of place to be avoided at all costs in later life. Father and son entered a small Chinese grocery, which the Major had discerned as an ill-disguised opium den. It was July. 'Got any snow, Mother?' asked the Major in what he took to be the colloquial language of Limehouse opium-traders circa 1915. 'Snow?' responded the old lady behind the counter, 'You'd need to come back in December for that.' 'A very secretive lot, these Chinese,' opined the Major as they left to start the long journey back to Courtfield Gardens and a safe tea.

Despite all the eccentric pleasures of London life, Robert's heart was still in Folkestone, where, at the age of five he first managed to paint his face. The local cleric was Canon Elliott, father of the Michael Elliott who many years later founded the 59 Theatre Company and then the revolutionary Royal Exchange Theatre in Manchester. The Canon, too, was a theatrical in the tradition of many clerics of his period, not least the fathers of both Laurence Olivier and Sybil Thorndike. Elliott's performances in his Folkestone pulpit were Robert's introduction to great acting and his command of Folkestone life extended far beyond the church, as Robert later recalled: 'Canon Elliott was the first star I ever knew. In those days he was what they called an Eminent Divine. He wore the most beautiful cassocks, and had the most beautiful voice, and all Folkestone was at his feet. On Sunday evenings, when he preached, you had to be in church an hour before the service or you didn't get in. I remember one Sunday when he climbed into the pulpit dressed in his usual white with the great gold cross on his vestments and flanked on all sides by enormous arum lilies. After leaning forward and surveying us all in silence for over a minute, instead of his usual beginning with "In the name of the Father and of the Son", he said, "I know God will forgive me if I say something quite personal tonight" and then went on to apologise for having been extra busy that week and therefore not completed as many visits to the sick as he, or maybe God, had expected. But you really felt that God was there, in the church and in personal communication with Canon Elliott.'

Suitably enough, it was the Canon who first got Robert into the acting profession. Every Christmas, a highlight of the festivities was the annual Folkestone mystery play, which Robert vaguely expected to be a thriller, but which turned out to be rather more religious. The Canon would always write and direct these himself, sitting at a card table in the church looking apparently very like the director Tyrone Guthrie, to whom Robert was later in life also devoted. One year, Elliott decided, Robert was ready for one of the starring roles:

Here come I, old Father Christmas
Welcome or welcome not,
I hope old Father Christmas
Will never be forgot.

The Canon was not, as Robert later admitted, in the first flight of poetic dramatists, but he forever recalled his first lines and was all for repeating them at the Christmas of 1992, when Sainsbury's employed him to play the same role in his last performance, in a commercial for mince pies. Sadly, they seemed to want their own dialogue.

2

The Message of Art
1916–1926

In one afternoon my whole world was turned upside down: the magic of George Bernard Shaw transformed me from a fat, unlikable, bewildered young teenager into a potential leading man. I never wavered after that from my intention to go on the stage; but of course I was enormously strengthened in my resolve by the implacable antagonism of authority.

Throughout the First World War, Robert's education continued to be a somewhat random affair: the family was forever moving between Folkestone and London and Burnham, depending on the varying fortunes of his father and the willingness of assorted relatives to put them up for longer or shorter visits. On one occasion they ventured as far as Guernsey, where the Major thought there might be money to be made. After a day or two he realised there was not and he caught the next boat back to England, but left his wife and children there to greet and then repack and return the possessions he had had sent from London in the expectation of a longer sojourn.

Sometimes Robert would be sent away for a term or two to what were then known as 'dame' schools, educational establishments for pre-teenagers, which seem to have made remarkably scant impression on him or his reluctance to be taught things. On other occasions, when the Major's fortunes took a brief turn for the better, governesses would be hired and usually despatched in despair a few weeks later, having equally failed to convince Robert or Margaret that a little learning might not be a dangerous thing.

None of the Major's callings occupied him for long and to none did he seem especially well suited, but he continued to press on regardless, convinced, like Micawber, that something better would turn up and commendably unsurprised when it did not. A bankrupt and a gambler, he gave his only son the gifts of perpetual optimism and curiosity, and precious little else.

Towards the end of the First World War Robert and his mother and sister trailed around in the Major's wake, in London sometimes attending the livestock sales at Tattersall's on Knightsbridge Green because he still fancied himself as a racing man despite the fact that he was then club secretary at Boodle's, and would have had some trouble stabling the animals within its portals. But Folkestone was still the favourite home, despite the increasing eccentricity of the aunts, several of whom had already retired more or less permanently to bed, unable to face the rigours of postwar life in a universe which seemed, even from the refuge of the port, to be changing rapidly and not for the better.

By 1921 the thirteen-year-old Robert was actually being educated in Folkestone, at a day school given an entire half-holiday during the summer term in honour and amazement because he had managed to pass into Wellington College. The fact that the Major had taken a house in the college grounds and befriended the headmaster may also have had something to do with this unexpected academic victory. Nevertheless, the half-holiday was declared and Robert used it to wander down to the Pleasure Gardens Theatre, where Esme Percy, the legendary Shavian actor whom Shaw himself considered one of his best friends and interpreters, happened to be starring in a touring revival of *The Doctor's Dilemma*. And that, as Robert later recalled, was it. 'I remember looking at the bills outside the theatre and wondering what the play could possibly be about. But I went in to this rather empty auditorium, because there wasn't much of an audience for Shaw in Folkestone in those days, and all my life I have remembered Percy repeating the affirmation of the artist as he lies dying:

"I know that in an accidental sort of way, struggling through the unreal part of life, I have not always been able to live up to my ideal. But in my own real world I have never done anything wrong, never denied my faith, never been untrue to myself. I've been threatened and blackmailed and insulted and starved. But I've played the game. I've fought the good fight. And now it's all over, there's an indescribable peace. I believe in Michaelangelo, Velasquez and Rembrandt; in the might of design, the mystery of colour, the redemption of all things by Beauty everlasting, and in the message of Art that has made these hands blessed."'

In that one afternoon, during a hot and empty Folkestone matinée, was born Robert's determination to be an actor, his lifelong devotion to Shaw, and his belief in the theatre theatrical as an art which did not merely reflect life, but extended and exaggerated it to the areas of magic. Robert believed Shaw was a saint; I believe that Robert was a conjuror, and that what he understood about the magical possibilities of being an actor he first learnt that afternoon.

Come the autumn, however there was Wellington to face and three of the unhappiest years of his life. He was taken into Wellesley House at a time when the college was going through its most military phase. At the end of each term the boys were lined up by their housemaster and asked what they planned to do in adult life. Almost all chose the army, a few chose the navy, and Robert alone announced from the very outset a determination to go on the stage, which was treated as a sure sign of lunacy by the assembled company. But in nine terms he never changed his answer, and the school never really managed to make him one of its pupils.

Wildly unsuited by flat feet and general temperament to any kind of physical activity, Robert found the army corps and the sportsfield equal torture, and he did not fare much better in the classrooms. Wellington left Robert with a deep, lifelong horror of any kind of orthodox teaching system, one on which he would frequently write and broadcast. He believed quite genuinely that the invention of the ball was one of the worst tragedies ever to befall mankind and that to force small boys on to soggy playing-fields every afternoon to kick or throw or hurl these objects at each other for a couple of hours, before returning the ball to precisely where they had first found it, was a near criminal waste of time, energy and childhood. 'Show me a boy who claims to have been happy at school', he would cry in later life, 'and I will show you a liar and a cheat and a bully.'

Far from making him unpopular, the cry would regularly lead to dozens of invitations to speak at school prize days around the country, several of which he would accept in the hope of getting his subversive message more directly into the hearts and minds of later generations of schoolchildren. The British school system, like many other institutions, has always been careful to welcome its enemies and Robert was, sometimes to his own frustration, always regarded by the educational establishment as a sinner who might one day be persuaded back into the fold. His victory was perhaps in managing never to send any of his own three children to a school which could be considered conventional, and in retaining to the last a fierce distrust of any schoolmaster who believed in any way that he could improve the character or knowledge of any child.

The type of school Robert would have liked Wellington to be was made clear thirty years later when, as a family, we returned from Australia and Pa was searching for a school which might suit or at any rate be willing to take me: 'Father with horrible memories of his own schooldays', he advertised in *The Times*, 'seeks school for son where the catering is given as much consideration as the culture and the standards are those of a really good four-star hotel.' Rather surprisingly, several headmasters replied to the appeal and I ended up at an eccentric establishment in Suffolk which met most, if not all, of Robert's requirements, largely because it was run by a man much like him.

The one school Robert always declined to visit in later life was Wellington itself. 'I shall only come back if allowed to burn the place to the ground,' he replied to one headmaster's speech-day request though, when he died, the college magazine gave him a handsome obituary, noting that Robert was Wellington's 'best-known son', but that the records for his terms there in 1922–24 show 'nothing of note'. However his time there as a free-thinker may not have been easy, with Housemaster Dr Lemmey, who demanded and obtained a rigid discipline.' Slightly optimistically, the magazine concluded that 'by aiding, albeit unintentionally, Morley's non-conformity, the college and Dr Lemmey may have helped to create him as a national treasure, if not a national monument.'

Robert spent as much of his Wellington time as possible in the sick bay, because it was the sole area of the school in which it was possible to achieve any degree of personal comfort, and he was therefore reckoned to be a rather sickly child, though all non-school evidence suggests a constitution as strong as an ox. When, therefore, he was suddenly withdrawn from the college in mid-academic year, at the end of the winter term in 1924, it was vaguely assumed that illness had at last claimed the youth. In fact, it was yet another sudden collapse in the economic fortunes of the Major, leading to local embarrassment about the school fees. Robert was, of course, delighted at the sudden and unexpected freedom, and blissfully unconcerned that he had no academic record of any kind with which to start out in the world. Still determined to be an actor, he saw no need of any qualifications beyond absolute determination.

He was, however, only sixteen and the feeling, even amongst his family (one so laid back as to be positively horizontal in its aspirations for him), was that perhaps he should spend a few more months trying to acquire some form of education elsewhere. Moreover the Major, never averse to sudden travel especially when the creditors were yet again closing in, saw a new role for himself: if he could persuade the family, or at least their trust funds, that Robert needed to complete his education abroad in a miniature version of the Grand Tour round the Continent still ritually undertaken by better born young men, then surely the two of them could set off for the Riviera as soon as the next boat-train would allow?

Robert needed no encouragement: abroad, surely, things would be different. There, instead of finding schoolmasters a shoddy lot of hypocrites who for some reason felt qualified to interfere with children, he began to encounter the more eccentric loners and expatriates among whom he was infinitely happier to further his bizarre education. The Major had by this time vaguely begun to think of a diplomatic career for his ungainly, gangling son and so the two men set off for Deauville to see if France might suit. Not surprisingly the town had a casino, where the Major rapidly succeeded in losing what money he had managed to prise out of the family funds. 'I don't think the boy has a natural aptitude for languages', he said as they returned to Folkestone to face the combined wrath of the aunts.

Once some more money had been made available to him, the Major took his boy to Alassio on the Italian Riviera, where they found a foreign language school run by a retired English army colonel in desperate need of a pupil. Robert was duly installed, and the Major moved on to casinos further up the coast. That arrangement lasted about six weeks, during which time Robert enrolled himself in the local tennis club without any intention of ever playing a game. He found the orange squash in the club room and the sight of well-bred English girls on holiday pleasant enough, and might have stayed longer had not the Colonel, in a rare burst of honesty considering that Robert was his only pupil, announced one morning, 'Morley, you are a fool. You will never manage to learn a foreign language, and I have written to your father to inform him of the fact.'

By this stage even the Major was running out of desirable Riviera gambling resorts, and it was decided that the time had come to try Germany. Accordingly Robert was sent to live with a family in Hanover and enrolled in the university there for German lessons, these being reckoned essential to a career in the diplomatic service as still envisaged by the Major, though never by Robert himself. Germany proved something of a disappointment. Robert, on the verge of his eighteenth birthday, found the Germans hospitable, but boring, and their language impenetrable; attempting to have lunch in a local restaurant, he found he had ordered only bread and whipped cream, and matters did not improve when several weeks later he formed a romantic attachment to a young German girl who kept taking him to smart hotel dining-rooms, ordering the most expensive dish on the menu, and then complaining that she was too much in love with him to eat it.

Robert took a dim view of this, figuring that, if she was that much in love, the least she could do was spare him such constant expense on his meagre student allowance. He also formed a vague dislike for his host, a curious man whose idea of Sunday afternoon outings was either to watch President Hindenburg having his constitutional stroll or else to go and stare down a ravine where a celebrated local mass-murderer had recently hurled several victims.

It is possible that Robert's lifelong passion for detective novels started in Hanover, but precious little else did; and when it was suggested by his host that he might like to take up duelling with a view to acquiring one of the scars locally regarded as badges of honour, Robert decided the time had come to return rapidly to Folkestone, speaking still not a word of German.

So much for the Continent. Robert had not taken against it exactly – in later life he was to become a compulsive traveller with an especial affection for cities well equipped with restaurants and casinos – but at this point Europe did not seem to have much to offer an eighteen-year-old misfit on the run from formal education. The time had come for him to consider finding a job. Acting was still the long-term plan but, eager to make sure that he would not be missing anything else available to him by way of a congenial career, Robert listened to the Major's other propositions.

The diplomatic corps had by now been ruled out by both of them, partly because of Robert's evident inaptitude for languages, but mainly because of their appalled discovery that it was not possible to start straight in as an ambassador. The prospect of his own embassy always rather appealed to Robert, but not the idea of several years as a minor envoy-in-waiting. As a result, thoughts turned first to advertising: the Major, as always, knew a chap who knew a chap who might prove useful, and Robert was duly interviewed by Sir Charles Higham, a pioneer of the slogan, who presented him with a hot water-bottle and asked him to spend a week thinking about how best to advertise it. As it happened, Pa always rather fancied himself at slogans ('Can your Austin Reed? No, but I have Hope Brothers', was one he would occasionally offer the rival chains of mens' outfitters), but the hot water-bottle seems to have defeated him, and he turned instead to the idea of journalism.

This was to form a considerable part of his later career: during the 1960s and 1970s he wrote regular columns for the *Sunday Express* and later (at the invitation of William Davis and Alan Coren) food and wine and travel columns for me when I was arts editor of *Punch*. But his career in journalism did not, in 1926, get off to the most auspicious start. The Major again ransacked his sizeable list of acquaintances, came up with a friend of the then

Lord Astor, proprietor of *The Times*, and within days Robert was being shown into a large office in Printing House Square.

'Curiously enough, that particular interview went off exactly as I had imagined it. Astor appeared delighted to see me. "Why do you want a job on *The Times*?" he asked, and I said because I thought it might be rather nice to be a journalist. He seemed quite taken with me, I thought, and I certainly was with him. He was charming, affable, and seemed to envisage no difficulty at all about my joining his paper. After a while, he pressed the bell for his Managing Editor and, as he appeared, said, "This is Mr Morley, who wishes to join us." The Managing Editor agreed at once that I was precisely the kind of person they were then looking for. It did seem a little odd that I was asked to provide no proof of being able to read or write, but there was no suggestion of any handicap or delay to my being recruited on the spot. After a cup of tea with Astor, and a further brief chat with the Managing Editor about the kind of work I intended to do for them, I left the office happily convinced that I had a job on *The Times* for the rest of my life.'

Wrong. After a few days it seemed strange to Robert that he had received no further communication from the paper of record. After a few more days – for he was never a man to rush things – he phoned the Managing Editor, who apologised for the lack of contact and assured him there would be a letter in the post. After about another week a letter duly arrived from the Managing Editor regretting that there did not seem to be a vacancy on their staff after all, but that a friend of his on the *Islington News* thought there might be a temporary opening there for a court reporter.

So much for journalism. The Major had one final stab at finding his boy a non-theatrical job, this time as a salesman of Pilsner lager, but that collapsed when it transpired that several of the kegs Robert was supposed to be delivering to West End restaurants had mysteriously been filled with salt water instead of beer. It was, Robert and he both agreed, high time to revert to Plan A and apply to a drama school.

3

Move the Fat Boy

1926–1927

In bulk and general untidiness I bore a fleeting resemblance to Charles Laughton, whose recent success had put heart into all us fatties, but I was not an especially promising RADA student. After one particularly terrible performance of mine our teacher, Helen Haye, opened ostentatiously, but not unkindly, a copy of the racing edition of the Evening Standard. *'We must', she said, 'try to find a winner somewhere this afternoon.'*

It was in the autumn of 1926, when he was just over eighteen, that the Major who, as Robert once said, knew everyone slightly but nobody quite well enough, fired off a letter to yet another of his acquaintances. By now he was more or less separated from poor dear Daisy (who had taken up home with her daughter in Kent) and had settled in a room at the Strand Palace Hotel, from where he was still able to carry out his myriad professional and race-course engagements. This time the letter was addressed to the actress Irene Vanburgh, whose brother Kenneth Barnes was the principal of the Royal Academy of Dramatic Art in Gower Street, the oldest established and most distinguished of London's theatre schools.

The Major's letter, as usual, outlined the problems of finding a suitable occupation for a young gentleman with neither means nor the expectation of any, and in due course Robert was summoned to meet Dame Irene, who indicated that there would be no difficulty in getting him a place so long as the fees could be paid. 'They have', she added by way of explanation, 'a great shortage of boys there.'

There was still the formality of the audition, at which Robert decided to give the examiners an extract from Flecker's celebrated *Don Juan*, in fact the speech commencing 'I am Don Juan/Cursed from age to age/By priestly tract and sentimental stage'. Now, it may be that my youthful but already chubby father was not everyone's idea of a natural Don Juan, or merely that his lack of other stage experience of any kind had ill-prepared him for such a difficult debut. In any event, he had got no further than those opening lines when, from the darkness of the stalls, a distinct guffaw was heard, and he was politely asked to leave the stage, convinced that another career opportunity had instantly been closed off.

The next morning, however, a letter arrived at the Strand Palace Hotel from Sir Kenneth, offering Robert a place for the coming term; some time later it transpired that the guffaw had come from Sir Gerald du Maurier, one of the examiners, who, contrite with guilt after such an uncharacteristic breach of his own urbane good manners, had demanded that the lad be given a chance of joining the profession of which gentleman-actor du Maurier was then the acknowledged leader.

RADA in Robert's 1962–28 era had certain distinct advantages: primarily the fact that female students outnumbered the men by at least three to one. This meant that the men were able to play entire roles in the end-of-term productions, whereas the women had to share Portia or Juliet, allowed only an act or so each. But if his sex was in his favour, little else was; indeed one early performance of Robert's, as Shylock, was considered so hilarious by his fellow students that a near riot broke out in the classroom, quelled only by the venerable Sir Kenneth Barnes intoning, 'Come now, fair's fair,' by way of remonstration.

Among Robert's immediate contemporaries at RADA were the character actresses Jean Anderson and Joan Hickson, who became the most celebrated and enduring of television's Miss Marples in later life, and the character actors Brian Oulton and Bruno Barnabe. Theirs was not, by all accounts, a great generation for leading men, though one, Robert Douglas, did head straight for Hollywood, there to make a considerable reputation often as the villain in period swashbucklers of the 1930s and 1940s before becoming a television director.

It was at the Academy that Robert formed the first of his lifelong friendships within the profession, with the actor Llewellyn Rees, later a distinguished secretary of the actors' union Equity, and of the postwar Old Vic, where he briefly replaced the Olivier-Richardson management. 'Lulu', as Rees was always known to Robert, has forever been one of the 'responsible gentlemen' of the business, notable on stage and screen for his judges and doctors in a career of remarkable longevity. He and Robert were best men at each other's weddings and, although they seldom worked together, one of Robert's last semi-public engagements a few months before he died was to make the speech at Lulu's ninetieth birthday.

It was also from the Academy that Robert almost immediately made his first professional appearance as an actor. For the Christmas season of 1926 the actor-manager Arthur Bourchier was directing and starring in *Treasure Island* at the Strand. Bourchier's first wife had been Violet Vanbrugh, the other sister of Kenneth Barnes, and Bourchier had therefore a close attachment to RADA, especially as it could always provide drama students as cheap extras for his crowd scenes. Under this arrangement Robert was duly hired to stand around in the shadow of Long John Silver.

So thrilled was Robert to have thus early and apparently effortlessly entered the profession of his choice that he left the stage door of the Strand after the audition in a daze, only to be accosted on the pavement by a lady of what used to be called easy virtue. 'Doing anything, dearie?' she enquired; 'Yes,' said Robert proudly, 'I'm playing one of the pirates in the winter season of Arthur Bourchier's *Treasure Island* at the Strand.'

From there, however, things went rapidly downhill: Bourchier was not the easiest of stars, and the student-extra sailors and pirates took most of what meagre direction there was from the stage manager. Robert's instruction was to stand menacingly on deck near one of the guns. Come the dress rehearsal, Bourchier's second wife, Kyrle Bellew, was told to watch from the front of the dress circle, taking and giving notes as the evening dragged on. Robert played his big scene as A Pirate, only to hear her shout in ringing tones to her husband on stage, 'Move the fat boy, Arthur, he rather spoils the picture.'

It was not quite the stage debut Robert had dreamed of, and he never forgot the insult; but he did manage not to get sacked and returned for his second term in Gower Street slightly older and wiser in the ways of the profession. As Robert later noted, 'I never really learned how to act at RADA, and perhaps I never have, but I did learn patience and a very little humility. I also learned more useful lessons, such as how to put a spot of carmine make-up in the very corner of each eye to make them look larger and more interesting. Most important of all, I learnt from my fellow students that whether you can act or not is really a matter of personal opinion, and that the opinion which most matters is your own. In my opinion I was a better actor than a good many of the others – theirs may well have been different.'

Back at RADA, Robert realised he was learning something else in the face of the 'fat boy' insult from Kyrle Bellew and the rather unfortunate tendency of some of the other students to giggle at his more emotional highlights in

Shakespeare: he was learning self-confidence as a form of self-defence, and that was perhaps the most useful and invaluable of all the lessons RADA had to teach him over these two years. Clearly he also learnt that he was better at comedy than tragedy, and that even at this early stage he had not much time or enthusiasm for such exercises as mime, fencing or the more advanced European or Russian theories of theatrical training.

'One of my favourite teachers was Elsie Chester, who only had one leg and would simply hurl one of her crutches at me when I failed precisely to imitate her rendering of *Much Ado About Nothing*. That sort of direction I could usually understand, but the mime and movement classes always left me totally bewildered. Indeed, I so depressed our mime teacher that she said I had given her a splitting headache, and would I please mime an aspirin? I think that was when we parted company.'

Then there was the great Rosina Fillipi, who taught breath control by having her students recite Mark Antony's speech to the crowd at the Capitol in a total of three deep breaths. Robert always tested himself on that, and fifty years later reckoned it still accounted for his ability to do almost an entire length of his swimming pool underwater, something he achieved most summer mornings in Berkshire. As for Mark Antony's speech to the crowd, he was never again to find any need for that whatsoever.

One of the happiest lessons he learnt at RADA was, however, entirely self-taught, somewhat suspect, and had rather more to do with the art of theatrical management, which intrigued him nearly as much as acting forever afterwards. Exploring the basement of the school's theatre one day, he happened to open a disused door and found it led up to the back of an old box-office in the foyer which had long since been abandoned because all student performances were given free to families and, hopefully, the occasional agent or producer on the look-out for new talent. Robert waited until about half an hour before that evening's show was due to start, then duly opened up the box-office and announced to the audience on their way in that, as production costs were unfortunately rising backstage, there would now be a charge of half a crown per admission. He then managed to live for a day or two on the proceeds until Sir Kenneth heard of the scam and forced Robert to return what was left of the money to RADA's building fund.

The rest of Robert's RADA stay was unremarkable save in one crucial respect: he had discovered who he wanted to be. He wanted to be Basil Loder. Mr Loder was not a teacher at RADA and is today all but forgotten, except by the most specialist of 1920s' theatre historians. But Basil Loder was the actor most frequently cast as 'hero's best friend' in the drawing-room comedies of the period. His principal function would be to come on early in act one, announcing (as often as not to Sir Gerald du Maurier) that he was 'just tootling off to the tennis court'. Having done so, he would then reappear in act two for a little comic relief, and just possibly in the last act to provide a brief diversion before the final climax. This, Robert saw, as a wholly admirable performance and indeed career. Nothing too strenuous to learn, no special skills required, simply an amiable manner and the willingness to do a bit of light acting before a somewhat heavier dinner. Had there been a Basil Loder School of Acting, Robert would have been its first and perhaps prize pupil.

Even in those days, though, RADA expected rather more solemnity from its pupils and Robert always found it hard to deliver the whole-hearted intensity the Academy required. As a result, there came a parting of the ways just before the end of his last summer term when, one morning, he was sent for by Sir Kenneth Barnes himself. If Robert had been expecting some form of special commendation, he was to be sorely disillusioned. 'Just one question, Morley', said Sir Kenneth from behind his principal's desk. 'Do you by any chance have private means?'

Robert thought for a moment about the Major still gazing into the abyss of perpetual bankruptcy, albeit from the vantage point of a room at the Strand Palace Hotel; about the aunts in Folkestone and dotted along the South Coast in varying states of genteel seclusion; about his mother and sister now settled in Kent. True it was not a background of destitution or desperate poverty, but nor could the family be described as exactly comfortably off, living as they were on a largely unearned and slowly declining income. On the other hand, he was not about to confess this to Barnes, especially as he sensed possible danger in the question. 'Oh yes, sir' was his reply, 'my family have ensured that I am independently wealthy.' Barnes looked at him thoughtfully for a moment, apparently reviewing his career prospects in the years ahead. 'That', he said finally, 'relieves my mind greatly.'

By this time Robert had managed to form strong if even for their time, faintly unorthodox views about his chosen profession. He had already decided, for instance, on the superiority of the actor over the director or the playwright, though he was in fact to make a living as all three. He had also decided, along with many actors of his generation, that directors were in essence only jumped-up stage managers ('Such useful fellows,' said his old friend Wilfrid Hyde-White to me once, 'they take your coat in the morning and hand it back at the end of rehearsal'). In later life he used to give directors the benefit of about the first three days of work on a new play to see if they knew any more than he did; finding that they often did not, he would then take over the production himself.

As for dramatists, I once saw my father after a rather good lunch on an ocean liner being asked by a journalist how an actor judged a really suitable and powerful script. As it happened, one had just reached him at the last port of call. Holding the enveloped contents, Robert announced that the trick was to weigh it in the right hand, check it for size and number of pages, and, if it proved unsuitable on those terms, to hurl it unopened and unread into the nearest ocean, which as it happened was the Indian. The script sank rapidly beneath the waves, and that was how he lost the chance of starring in a long and lucrative West End run of a comedy by Ian Hay.

Thus the principles of his earliest years in the business were to be true to yourself as an actor, not to rely on much help from writers, directors or fellow players, and to try as early as possible to establish a personal relationship with an audience which might encourage them to come back and see you in your next venture.

All these lessons Robert had learned, some by default at RADA, others by simply exploring the West End of the late 1920s, haunting its galleries on student tickets and deciding which of its many attractions most appealed to him. Undoubtedly these were the drawing-room comedies and well-made dramas of the time; if there was a no-go area, it was probably the Old Vic and anywhere which specialised in the classics, all of which were always to have remarkably scant appeal for him unless they happened to be by Bernard Shaw.

By now he had, he reckoned, had the best of RADA, even if it had not had, or managed to find, the best of him. Noticing that he was not being offered anything sizeable by way of a role in his generation's last public performance, Robert quit the Academy on 21 July 1927, not in bitter disappointment or anything more that what might be described as low dudgeon at their failure to recognise his potential. It was time, he had decided, to start making his living as an actor in the real world of the theatre.

4

Do You Have a Harp?

1927–1933

We were perhaps the last generation of actors not to be blindly or blithely dedicated to our chosen career. After we had completed a brief training, all we really wanted was to make some money and have as good a time as possible doing so. If we accepted a part, it was because of the money offered, and if we declined it, that was because the money offered wasn't enough, and we hoped perhaps to do a little better at a rival theatre. We never read plays, because they were never given us to read; all we were given was our 'sides', or parts, with little dots to mark the cue lines.

It was not until nine years after leaving RADA that Robert scored his first major public success; he was to spend the intervening years largely on the road in a long series of regional tours hardly any of which reached London. This was not, for its time, an unusual career pattern. In the late 1920s and early 1930s, before the advent of television and with even talking pictures still a novelty, the touring theatre in Britain was at the height of its powers: a vast network of theatres, through most of which would pass forty or fifty travelling companies in the course of a single year, crossing and recrossing each other's paths, and meeting briefly at Crewe station on Sunday mornings to compare notes, and exchange route and destination warnings, rather in the manner of latterday airline crews at Gatwick or Heathrow.

This prewar touring network had its own stars and managements, and existed totally in its own right. Plays would generally be toured after, rather than before, their London runs, and most companies had no real desire to end up in the West End, where both costs and expectations would inevitably be elevated. Touring was thus an end in itself, one which Robert for the most part hugely enjoyed. Alone, unencumbered by any emotional or familial responsibilities, able to survive on the £5 or £10 a week that was his initial salary, boosted by travelling expenses and the occasional hand-out from the Major or poor dear Daisy, he settled into a routine which perfectly suited both the wanderlust he had inherited from his father and the desire he had discovered to be an actor. He was, in at least that respect, the ideal travelling player – an aptitude he was to hand on to both his younger son Wilton, who was to spend much of his early career as a touring theatre manager in Australia, and to his eldest grandchild, my son Hugo, who at the time of writing largely occupies himself stage-managing exotic tours of the Far and Middle East for Derek Nimmo.

'One of the most curious things about acting,' Robert once said, 'is that either nobody at all thinks you can do it, or else everyone thinks you are brilliant. You just have to be there, ready for when the tide turns.' But for a while it looked as though his tide was never likely to turn an inch. From the outset, Robert had certain advantages and some distinct disadvantages. The advantages were that his was, largely due to his size and shape, a formidable stage presence, which was especially useful for filling up the back of the set in crowd scenes, and for playing very small roles as doctors or lawyers, which still required a respectable-looking 'responsible gentleman' rather than the gawky teenager usually available for the money. His disadvantages were a definitely unromantic manner, which initially ruled out any leading juvenile roles, and a lack of physical dexterity, which ruled out fencing, dancing or anything else more acrobatic than a walk downstage. The work itself, however, was not hard to come by: just as there had been a shortage of young male talent at RADA, so was there in the touring theatre of this period. For this reason, few male drama-school graduates who were willing to work for a pittance and to spend their lives on the road staying in tacky digs actually found it difficult to secure a lowly place in a touring company, and Robert's first engagement was to last him for almost the whole of his first year as a professional actor.

Russell Thorndike, the younger brother of Dame Sybil, was the eccentric of that great theatrical family, a man known frequently to queue up at the box-offices outside wherever he happened to be playing and then announce to an astounded manager, 'I've just come to have a look at this fellow Thorndike, who they all say is so good.' If Sybil was the *tour de force*, in the old backstage joke, then Russell was the one forced to tour; but he took to the road happily enough in a lifelong series of gothic dramas, of which the most famous and successful was his own *Dr Syn*.

Robert spent much of his first year on the road with that and Thorndike's company, playing a variety of very minor roles, while Russell portrayed the Smuggling Parson of Dymchurch, a man who had once been a pirate and in whose character Russell's over-the-top, Victorian barn-storming style found a natural identity. Robert remembered to the end of his life a moment in the play when Thorndike would turn his back on the audience, simulate the sound of sizzling flesh, apparently branding himself, all the while singing at the top of his lungs 'Fifteen Men on a Dead Man's Chest'. Such was the touring theatre of 1928.

A slight but memorable diversion during the tour was caused by Russell's random encounter with a butcher. That particular week they were playing Leamington Spa, and the butcher in question was a man of considerable means who happened to have written a play. Russell, always in search of a backer to help him on with the tour, immediately undertook to have the play produced by his *Dr Syn* company, who would return to Leamington in their first vacant week expressly for the purpose. The play was called *The Eternal Flame*, and large tracts of it consisted of Russell returning as a ghost from the Tomb of the Unknown Soldier to complain about conditions underfoot in the trenches of the First World War. Robert, for reasons which escaped him soon afterwards, was cast as the ghost of Oliver Cromwell.

Things got off to a promising start when a retired general wrote to the local paper in Leamington complaining about the sacrilege of staging a play in which the Unknown Soldier put in an appearance, and for a moment Russell thought his small company might have struck controversy and with it the chance of a London transfer. Unfortunately the first night did not go well, largely because the stage manager, required at one point to play the 'Hallelujah Chorus' off-stage, failed to read the record label with sufficient care, so that a surprised audience heard resonating through Westminster Abbey the strains of 'Hallelujah I'm a Bum.'

The local newspaper critic was unimpressed: 'Nobody need fear that money is being made out of the Unknown Soldier', he wrote, 'because no money will be made by this play at all,' and sure enough the following week the company went scurrying back to *Dr Syn*.

When that particular revival reached its end, Robert moved on to a tour of *And So To Bed*, the ever popular (in its time) bedroom farce about Charles II and Nell Gwynne. Robert's main function here was to appear as the Nightwatchman, who wandered across the stage from time to time chanting, 'Past five o'clock, and a fine windy morning.' He also had to appear briefly as a pickpocket, billed in the programme helpfully as the character Pickpurse, and most important of all double as an assistant stage manager.

In this latter role he was responsible every Saturday night for supervising the stage hands as they loaded the scenery into crates and then on to the night train to their next destination, which would as likely as not be at the other end of the country, since tours were planned up to a year in advance with no thought for geography, simply according to which theatres had vacancies in which weeks. The Saturday-night stage management task was, however, fraught with difficulty: each local theatre in those days, although surviving throughout the year on the weekly arrival of touring companies, was responsible for building and staging its own Christmas pantomime. Theatre managers were then, as now, cautious with money and one of their chief objectives throughout the year was to ensure that sufficient scenery fell out of the back of the touring crates to allow them to construct their own Christmas sets at no extra cost. It was thus not uncommon for Robert to arrive at a new destination on the Monday afternoon, after a brief rest-and-recuperation day in London, to find that his set was missing a door, or several carpets, or, worse still, an entire landscape backing flat.

Compared to that, the acting required of him presented little difficulty or challenge, and he began to settle happily into the routines of touring. Most engagements were for a forty-week period, and it was usual for all the dates in that period to be announced to the company when they first gathered to rehearse, thereby allowing them to write well in advance to favourite landladies around the country reserving their accommodation.

The rituals of touring in this period never ceased to fascinate Robert: how each company would have its own reserved compartment on railway trains, complete with window-stickers announcing the name of their show and its next destination; the way actors would write ahead to their next town, where, if there were two theatres, free seats would be requested for the Wednesday matinée of the rival show; the alibi which had to be prepared in case, upon arrival in a strange town at an alien boarding-house, it was found to be unacceptable even at £3 per week, and something had to be said by way of explanation to the landlady. Robert's regular query in this eventuality was, 'Do you have a harp?' When the landlady replied, as always, in the negative, he would explain that, alas, he had to practise on a harp every morning as part of his professional calling – and then he would beat a hasty retreat to a more comfortable accommodation.

Sometimes there would still be the 'no dogs or actors' sign on the door, but most touring companies had their own lists of congenial digs in each and every town on their map.

As the 1920s turned into the 1930s, Robert became aware that he belonged to a curiously privileged, if still very underpaid, elite:

Being a travelling player meant that you saw everything and had to stay nowhere for too long. But the first thing I noticed as I started to tour was how poor most people outside London really were and how much unemployment there was at that time. I suppose, despite the vagaries of my father's income, I had come from a rather privileged Folkestone background, and I was genuinely shocked by what I saw up north. I would walk to theatres past groups of elderly men lounging at corners, and children playing in the streets, threadbare and undernourished. There was an air of utter hopelessness about some of the towns we played: Sheffield, for instance, and Darlington, where the shops seemed to be full of nothing but postcards of a great train crash which had occurred there. You'd have had to be even more insensitive than I was as a young man not to be aware of the cumulative boredom and misery of provincial England in the early 1930s. How much we ever did to relieve that boredom or entertain the natives is difficult to assess, but we certainly didn't think we were bad, and some of us thought we were very good indeed.

Sometimes, of course, a tour would come to an end with no prospect of further engagement; in one instance it ended rather more rapidly than expected, when bailiffs were seen backstage impounding the scenery on its way to the station. On such occasions, as was customary, Robert would place a small advertisement in the back of *The Stage* announcing his unexpected availability, but that he 'must have terms', a peculiar ritual phrase intended to indicate to employers that he did not come cheap, although naturally he did.

And still he was learning. On one tour he reached Lowestoft, where to his fury a child sat in the front of the dress circle flipping paper pellets whenever Robert made one of his rare entrances as A Butler; finally, able to stand it no more, he hurled a handful of the pellets back at the surprised child and exited to face the wrath of a furious stage manager. 'Never again,' he was told. 'Always remember, Morley, that he is the public and you are not. Once they have paid to come in, they are entitled to do whatever they like.'

Yet Robert relished the life, loved above all the realisation that some management somewhere actually thought it was worth their while to pay his train fare every week from one town to the next, let alone a salary as well. From time to time fellow thespians would even try to teach him how to act: one, Geoffrey Saville, with whom he played for nearly a year in the road company of *Is Your Honeymoon Really Necessary?*, actually invented an elaborate on-stage code. If he clutched his collar, Robert was making an entrance too fast; if he tugged at his tie, the entrance was too slow. If he moved his ankle to the left, it meant that a cross upstage was indicated; if he touched his earlobe, then Robert was speaking too fast – or possibly too slowly. The problem with this elaborate system of visual cues was that my father, like most of my family, had a remarkably brief attention span and found himself utterly unable to remember from night to night which signal meant what.

One of his more frequent employers in these years was the touring management of Parnell and Zeitlin. Mr Zeitlin, it was, who came all the way to Blackpool to inspect one of his shows in which Robert had a small role as usual, only to find the theatre totally and utterly sold out on the Friday night. 'But,' he said to the box-office manager who refused him a ticket, 'I'm Zeitlin, Zeitlin from London.' 'I don't care where you are cycling from, sir,' replied the manager, 'you still can't have a ticket.'

Sometimes, between tours, Robert would join a local repertory theatre, which entailed staying at the same address for more than a week. Early in the 1930s he was, in fact, a founder member of repertory companies at both Bournemouth and York. Of the two, York was marginally the worse: Robert quarrelled early in the first week of rehearsal with the director, who had been unwise enough to give him several notes about his performance. One of the luxuries of being a touring actor, Robert realised, was that after the initial rehearsal period you never had to see, let alone hear, a director again for almost a year. In weekly rep., however, matters were very different, and at York the situation became so bad that Robert decided he would have to appeal over the director's head to the chairman of the board, a member of the renowned Rowntree chocolate family. 'Mr Rowntree,' said my father, having gained admission to his office, 'I fear I can no longer be expected to give my acting best if this director is allowed to stay on a moment longer.' 'Fear not,' said the Chairman, 'the director is leaving this very Saturday. Oh and so, Mr Morley, are you.'

Then it was back on the road again with yet another tour, until the spring of 1933, when Robert joined his first permanent company. This had just been set up in Cambridge by Terence Gray, a curious, visionary figure several decades ahead of his time despite the fact that, as an ex-Egyptologist, he had spent the first half of his career several millenia behind it. Gray was in many ways the forerunner of Tyrone Guthrie: both men believed in passionate naturalism, the avoidance of all Victorian theatrical traditions and flummery, and the abundant possibilities of creating sudden Shakespearian magic on a very low budget with largely untried performers. After a while Gray turned his back on the theatre, which he had only lately taken up, and became a French vineyard owner and then an Irish racehorse breeder. But for a short period he ran a Cambridge theatre festival of considerable, if unacknowledged, brilliance, and Robert was lucky enough to be part of it.

His roles were still small to miniscule, though for one he was required to spend the entire evening behind a mask of thick sponge. 'Do you know,' said one of the loyal aunts coming backstage afterwards, 'you looked, dear Bobbie, just as if someone had stuck a sponge all over your face. I couldn't quite hear what you were saying.'

There was, though, one even less glorious occasion, which occurred when Beatrix Lehmann joined the company as a star guest to play *Salomé* for a week. Robert, to his amazement, was cast as Herod with only a week's rehearsal and not nearly enough time to learn the lines, which he therefore arranged for the actress playing Herodias to carrying within her voluminous costume, allowing ready-reference checks behind the throne. Unfortunately, in her first-night terror, the actress forgot to bring the script on stage and Robert was left to get through the role as best he could, which he decided was very fast. Coming off stage, relieved at having reached the final curtain, he was greeted by a glacial stare from Miss Lehmann. 'All right, was I then?' he asked her eagerly. 'I suppose so,' she said abruptly, 'apart from the fact that you cut the whole of my dance of the seven veils.'

5

A Smile
and a Shoeshine
1934–1936

By the time I joined him 'Pa' Benson was very often inaudible, except of course when we were performing The Tempest. *Then, as Caliban, he had to hang upside down in the tree and, for the only time, his false teeth fitted, so you could hear every melodious word even from the back of the dress circle.*

Sir Frank Benson, 'Pa' to all his companies, was already seventy-five when Robert joined him; he had been touring Shakespeare across the length and breadth of Britain for more than fifty years. The son of a country squire, he had decided to take upon his athletic shoulders the task of 'cleaning up' the English stage after the rogues and vagabonds of preceding generations. An Oxford and Stratford man, he nursed a lifelong passion for cricket, engaging Oscar Asche purely on the strength of his wicket-keeping and the young Robert Donat because he was a good underarm bowler.

The rest of the acting profession of his generation tended to disavow him, rather as they were later to disavow Donald Wolfit: too noisy, too fond of weekly fit-up repertory tours, in a strange way too theatrical for the new intellectuals. Unperturbed at being perennially unfashionable among critics and colleagues alike, Benson simply kept his show on the road, albeit with increasing eccentricity. By the time my father joined him in Birmingham and on tour, Benson was, as Robert recalled, 'no longer in the first, second or even third flush of enthusiasm. The old master was obviously sick of the theatre, and continued to drag his despairing frame through the English provinces because he knew of no other way to make his livelihood and, like all actors, he had failed to provide for his old age. Each week he still performed, for one night each, Caliban, Malvolio, Hardcastle and Sir Peter Teazle, while the bizarre and motley company he had collected around him alternately held its breath and lost its head.'

In his day Benson had been solely responsible for the establishment of regular summer seasons at Stratford, but that day was long gone and Benson's main problem by this time was remembering which day of the week it was. Accordingly, he would regularly get dressed as Caliban only to rush on stage and find himself facing Sir Andrew Aguecheek, while on other nights his appearance as Shylock on stage would amaze a cast already well into act one of *The School For Scandal*.

One of his other frequent problems was forgetting to bring on the bond and the scales for the trial scene of *The Merchant of Venice*; so that, when they reached Portia's line 'I pray you, let me look upon the bond', he would have to sidle towards the wings, hands outstretched behind his back, whereupon the stage manager would thrust the props into his grasp and Benson would carry on with the scene, having miraculously produced them much in the manner of a conjuror at a children's party.

Benson was also extremely economical with his scenery: he had only one flat depicting a sea coast, and naturally this was used for the opening Illyria scenes of Viola's shipwreck in *Twelfth Night*. The only slight problem was that it had several deck-chairs painted on it down by the water's edge, and my father's principal task as the Sea Captain was to stand neatly in front of them, thereby blocking the audience's astonished gaze.

There were, I believe, several lessons that Robert learnt from Pa Benson, few of them to do with acting: he learnt the art of improvisation, he learnt not to believe in the sanctity of any stage text even if it happened to be by Shakespeare and, perhaps above all, he learnt what fun could be had in a theatre company peopled almost exclusively by eccentrics of a high order.

By now Robert had acquired his first agent: the redoubtable Mrs Nelson King, who, rather like Rosalind Chatto in his later life, operated not merely as a job-finder but also as an amazing amalgam of surrogate mother, sister, secretary, friend, dinner companion and general saviour. Like Ros up to this very present, Mrs King in her day performed her balancing act for a small group of specially selected and hugely privileged clients, among whom Robert was soon to find another of his lifelong friends, as well as the only woman to whom he became engaged but not married.

Mrs King seldom demanded her commission from the younger and more impecunious clients, and was in fact frequently willing to lend them money between tours, so that Robert was usually literally as well as figuratively in her debt. But she seemed to have faith that one day he would come good, and she was in no particular hurry; in the meantime she provided, like all good den mothers, a daytime home in St Martin's Lane, where she maintained an office, and a night-time address in Victoria, where it was possible to find a regular bridge and poker school in progress for those resting between tours.

Thanks to a combination of Mrs King's diligence, Robert's enthusiasm for life on the road and a certain amount of luck, he remained almost constantly in work for his first six years in the business and it was not until the beginning of 1935 that prolonged unemployment hit him for the first time. There suddenly seemed an acute shortage of managements willing to continue financing his third-class Sunday rail travel the length and breadth of Britain, and after a few reflective weeks living at home with poor dear Daisy, who had taken up temporary residence in a Chelsea flat while the Major was more or less permanently installed at the Strand Palace, Robert was forced to think of alternative forms of making a living, at least until another tour could be found.

For almost six months he left the stage and occupied himself as a travelling salesman, a job which, he decided, had much in common with that of being an actor. First and foremost he had to give a convincing performance, since he had answered a newspaper advertisement calling for salesmen of vacuum cleaners. His teacher was a man called Murray, who consummated most of his sales on sofas with the lady of the house during quiet afternoons. During these sessions Robert would be left in the car outside, but eventually he was allowed territory of his own in an upmarket neighbourhood where butlers or maids frequently answered the bell. 'I', Robert would announce portentously, 'am Inspector Newstart,' whereupon the terrified servant would rush to announce to Madam that a policeman was at the door.

Once safely inside her living-room, he would explain that there had been an unfortunate misunderstanding: so far from being Inspector Newstart of the CID, he was merely an inspector from the Newstart company, makers of a revolutionary new kind of vacuum cleaner which perhaps Madam would care to try for herself.

Madam, relieved of the terror of a police visit, would usually purchase the cleaner or at least agree to a free trial. Robert learnt as much from these house calls as from Pa Benson about the art of acting and within three months had his own car on the firm and a couple of assistants, whom he would join every Saturday night for a staff meeting which ritually began with the entire sales force singing that well-known hymn 'Onward Salesmen Onward, Selling As We Go'. Half a century later David Mamet in Chicago wrote a play called

Glengarry Glen Ross, which somehow, in the manic intensity of its sales-speak, always makes me think of my father amid the surrogate Hoovers of north London.

Yet life as a travelling vacuum-cleaner salesman was not strictly within the bounds of Robert's career plan, and by midsummer 1935 he was glad to get back on the road in a brief tour of *Late Night Final*, followed by a rather longer one of *Richard of Bordeaux* with Glen Byam Shaw and his wife, Angela Baddeley.

His first prolonged bout of theatrical rejection had taught him a sharp lesson: if he did not wish to end up on a smile and a shoeshine as a door-to-door salesman, it might be wise not to rely solely on his talents as an actor. One period of unemployment could easily lead to another if, for the rest of his life, he was to be at the mercy of directors or casting agents or theatre managers. Suppose, therefore, he tried his hand at playwriting? The work appeared not to be arduous, at least to judge from some of the rubbish he had been playing on prolonged tours, and the life of a dramatist at a comfortable desk seemed vastly preferable to that of an out-of-work actor haunting the casting offices of St Martin's Lane.

As the *Late Night Final* tour was not proving unduly tiring or eventful, he therefore started to draft his first script, a drawing-room comedy initially about a celebrated retired actress who decides to return to the stage to the delight and then gradually to the consternation of the playwright who tempts her back. 'The sort of play I wanted to write', Robert recalled later, 'was the sort of play Frederick Lonsdale was then still writing. I was very innocent in those days, but then so was the theatre itself: plays were full of people who had hardly any troubles, and a great many servants. Later, of course, they were full of people with a great many troubles, but no servants at all. I don't think every line of *Short Story* was what you might call an epigram, but that was what I strove for – a few good jokes which I hoped might pass for wit, a rather vague plot, and a splendid part for a leading lady.'

Since the play bore at least a passing resemblance to another comedy about a celebrated actress debating a comeback to the West End amid domestic mayhem, Noël Coward's *Hay Fever*, it seemed logical to offer *Short Story* to the actress who had made such a success of the original Coward production ten years earlier, Dame Marie Tempest. Not knowing her home address, Robert sent his completed script to her agent, who returned it at once with a sharp note to the effect that it was one of the worst comedies he had ever read.

My father always liked a challenge. Faced with what he considered to be an impertinent rebuke from an underling, he took the trouble to locate Dame Marie's home address and sent the now slightly dog-eared script direct to her. Within forty-eight hours, the miracle occurred. 'Dame Marie's husband rang to invite me to lunch, at which the next day they accepted my play for production. They had two stipulations: it was to be directed by a young man from the Old Vic called Tyrone Guthrie, of whom Dame Marie had heard good reports, and it was to be virtually totally rewritten according to their specifications. Dame Marie then retired for her afternoon nap. Her husband, Willie Graham Browne, casually wrote out a cheque for a hundred pounds, the largest I had ever seen, and handed it to me with my hat. Walking away down Avenue Road, I crashed suddenly and painfully into a pillar-box: I don't think I have ever again felt such overmastering happiness.'

There were, however, problems ahead. The reason why the Dame had demanded a total rewrite was simple enough. In the original draft, the actress in *Short Story* was not and had never been a very good one. It was, said Dame Marie, unthinkable that her public would accept such a notion. The actress had at once to be made into a star, and a very great star at that.

Several rewrites later, the script proved acceptable and Robert was sent to see Dame Marie's impresario, young Hugh Beaumont of H. M. Tennent, for whom Robert was to work as both author and actor for the next forty years, give or take several alarms and diversions along the way. 'Well,' said 'Binkie' Beaumont in that nasal drawl imitated by two generations of his theatrical employees, 'what about Sybil Thorndike then?' 'I rather thought,' said Robert, 'that we had Dame Marie Tempest.' 'Her too,' said Binkie, going on to outline a company which would further consist of Rex Harrison, A. E. Matthews, Ursula Jeans and Margaret Rutherford. It was a dream cast, arguably the best Robert was ever to enjoy in half a century as a writer of comedies for the stage.

Rehearsals were not easy, however: Harrison was commuting from another comedy in Nottingham and could only rehearse in the mornings. Both Rutherford and Matthews had a religious terror of any kind of motorised transport, and insisted on arriving through considerable rain-storms on bicycles. Guthrie rapidly fell out with his autocratic and unyielding star, turning to Robert after one particularly fraught dress rehearsal during which Dame Marie had refused to act on or even accept any of his notes: 'A very common little woman,' said Tony Guthrie; 'Will you tell her or shall I?'

Things were no better between Dame Marie and Dame Sybil, who spent most of their shared time on stage trying to upstage each other with more and more elaborate comic business. 'Such a clever little actress, aren't you?' hissed Dame Marie, after losing one of these battles. 'Not especially,' replied Dame Sybil, 'but clever enough to act with you, dear.'

One way and another the omens for the Edinburgh opening at the end of

October 1935 were not good, though the local press was generous and, when the production reached Manchester, the *Evening News* there announced that 'if ever a play has West End Success stamped on it, then that play is *Short Story* by new young author Robert Morley'. At least one member of the paying public disagreed: awaiting him at the stage door by the end of the week was a telegram which read: 'YOUR PLAY QUITE THE ROTTENEST I HAVE EVER HEARD STOP SO MUCH SO THAT I AM BACK HOME AT 9.30 PM STOP THE STORY IS CHRONIC THE TECHNIQUE IS TERRIBLE THE ARTISTS GARRULOUS STOP WHY MAKE THE UPPER MIDDLE CLASSES APPEAR SUCH FOOLS STOP SIGNED ELSTONE FARROWFIELD.

Having already, on a short pre-London tour, received some of the best and worst reviews he was ever to enjoy, Robert was more or less ready for whatever the West End press had to offer. In the event, they were vaguely undecided about *Short Story*. James Agate for the *Sunday Times*, doyen of the Critics Circle, found it 'moderately novel, though perhaps more witty than interesting and more interesting than new'. 'An evening of pleasant acting' added *The Times* through an almost audible yawn, while Stephen Williams of the *Evening Standard* thought that 'young Mr Morley ought to be permanently on his knees backstage, thanking God for his cast'.

Short Story ran happily enough through Christmas at the Queen's Theatre, but early in January 1936 it became clear that, despite one of the starriest casts in town, the comedy was not to be long for West End life, and H. M. Tennent reluctantly withdrew it at the end of February. Robert and most of the cast seemed to have enjoyed the experience hugely, all save Dame Sybil, who had fared no better in her struggles with Dame Marie. 'I wouldn't go through all that again,' she told Binkie as they closed, 'not for all the money in Howard and Wyndham.' Nevertheless, she remained a lifelong friend of Robert, turning up more than forty years later, shortly before her own death, to acclaim him at the age of seventy on his *This Is Your Life* as still 'such a wonderful and brilliant young man, and sooooo talented'.

Rex Harrison was another matter. He and Robert were to work together again four years later in Gabriel Pascal's film of *Major Barbara*, and towards the end of Rex's life my brother was to tour him around Australia in Lonsdale's *Aren't We All?* But there was a chilly, dry, brittle quality about Rex which, as early as *Short Story*, Robert detected and found somehow unreassuring. The two men thereafter kept their distance around the West End, though Rex did owe Robert's play one of his greatest stage tricks: the habit he borrowed from Marie Tempest of, as he left the stage, himself starting a round of applause in the wings, which it was hoped the audience would duly pick up and echo to the rafters.

On his first, albeit slim, royalties as a dramatist, Robert took himself off to Barcelona for a brief spring holiday: 'Very smelly here', read an unenthusiastic postcard to his mother back in Chelsea. He then returned to the St Martin's Lane office of Mrs Nelson King to consider his future as an unemployed actor or, alternatively, as a very briefly produced playwright.

Among Mrs King's other clients at this time were the actress Meriel Forbes and the actor Peter Bull, to both of whom Robert had become devoted while they all hung around Mrs King's premises waiting for the chance of another tour. Indeed, Robert had become so devoted to Meriel Forbes that he rather tentatively proposed marriage to her, a proposal not viewed with tremendous enthusiasm by the actress's mother, who happened to be Mrs King herself, especially not after he had tried to borrow the money from her for her daughter's engagement ring. Soon after that, Miss Forbes accepted the alternative engagement of a long tour, and some time later still a rather more practical and assured proposal of marriage from Ralph Richardson, whose first wife had tragically died of sleeping sickness.

Robert's friendship with Peter Bull was, however, destined to be considerably stronger, perhaps the most important male relationship of his entire life. 'Bully' was, in 1936, just twenty-four and he could in many respects have been Robert's four-year-younger brother. Both men were chubby, cheery extroverts, and they had a great deal in common: they were actors who believed in the supremacy of the actor, and that the British theatre was already being run by far too many, far too serious directors with no real understanding of the overriding importance of sheer enjoyment on both sides of the footlights.

Like Robert's other best friend, the writer Sewell Stokes, Bully was a lifelong gay, but whereas Sewell, of an older and more conservative generation, was so highly closeted as to be sexually almost invisible, Bully was something of an experimentalist who would veer from stable, live-in relationships, often with younger actors, to occasional ventures into the rough trade. In fact, he was the first man I ever knew, back in the early 1970s, to have been the victim of a gay mugging, a Chelsea experience he characteristically turned into a light-hearted *Punch* article entitled 'Well I'll Be Muggered'.

I was, I think, the eldest of Peter's many godchildren and I loved him very much, largely for the way he constantly reminded me of my father. In the mid-1950s he was the man who first taught me how to travel around London on the Underground (rather suitably, since one of his many distinguished brothers had been a director of London Transport) and where best to dive into the pool beneath the RAC club in Piccadilly, as well as many other survival hints for a stage-struck teenager of the period. He was a marvellous, funny, kind, touching and eccentric man, the most enchanting of godfathers and friends, and, when he died at the age of seventy-two, it seemed to me both strange and a little sad that most people instantly recalled him as the Bully Bear toy inventor or the proprietor of a Zodiac shop in Notting Hill Gate, but not for his other careers on stage and screen, and indeed as the author of a naval war reminiscence hailed by no less a figure than Kenneth Tynan as 'the funniest book ever written by an actor'.

The youngest of the four sons of Sir William Bull, a long-time MP for Hammersmith, Peter had started out briefly as a journalist, but by 1932 had turned to acting. His next three years were spent under Mrs King's guidance on tour, in the West End and even on Broadway, playing small parts in two Elisabeth Bergner hits, *As You Desire Me* and *Escape Me Never*. Early in 1936 he returned to London with Bergner, knowing that at the end of the year they were both to play in J. M. Barrie's *The Boy David*. In the meantime, however, there was the summer to fill in, and Peter had an idea: he would like, he decided, to form a small repertory company of his friends in the Cornish seaside village of Perranporth, and he would like Robert to join him there. Their friendship was already firmly rooted, though it had got off to an uneasy start on the first occasion Robert saw Peter act. This was in a none too triumphant tour of a Nelson play called *England Expects*, in which Bully's sole function had been to hurry on stage and announce the sinking of the *Leviathan*, a crucial plot point. By the time Robert went to see the show, Peter's interest in it had palled to such an extent that, his mind for some reason on the First World War, he rushed on stage to announce to an amazed Nelson the sinking of the *Lusitania*. 'I have, in my short life as a touring player,' said Robert going back stage to Bully's dressing-room, 'seen many bad performances. Yours tonight was, I think, the worst given by any actor on any stage anywhere in the world.'

Performance standards were not to be all that much improved at Perranporth.

6

Wilde Times

1936

It all sounded enchanting: I imagined us inhabiting a large house with lawns sloping down to a creek, rather like Daphne du Maurier's. There would perhaps be some sort of butler to serve tea under the cedar trees. I don't think I have ever been so surprised in my life as when we arrived, after a terrible journey in a very small car over the unspeakable Bodmin Moor, to find the most hideous little village I had ever seen. 'This', said Peter, 'is Perranporth'.

Peter had first happened upon Perranporth during a summer holiday two years earlier and had so fallen in love with the place (as he was later in life to fall in love with the most inaccessible of Greek islands) that he cheerfully agreed in 1936 to take over the local tin-hut Women's Institute and turn it into a summer theatre. Its stage measured six feet by twelve, and the only exit was through a door right in the middle of the set.

The building housed only 200 seats, and they were not seats at all, but deckchairs of a certain age, which Robert and Bully, as the heaviest members of the company, had to test personally at the start of the season to see if they were sufficiently load-bearing. There were to be no salaries, merely a profit share (if any) at the end of the season, but, despite these apparent and considerable disadvantages, Peter's undoubted verve, charm and enthusiasm had managed to recruit a company consisting not only of Robert but also of Frith Banbury, later a distinguished West End director, Roger Furse, who became Olivier's stage and screen designer, Roger's actress sister Judith, and later Pamela Brown, who was just starting her acting career.

In addition, Peter promised to provide his company with board, lodging, haircuts, Cornish cream and the highest teas ever known to mankind, but in return they had to clean the hall and tour the local community borrowing furniture for each of the four plays they intended to rehearse and perform on a weekly turn-around, giving only two performances of each script in rotation.

Robert's training in getting his foot through the door as a vacuum-cleaner salesman came in useful and he perfected the technique not only of borrowing French dressers and dining-room tables but also of suggesting to their proud owners that they might like to purchase tickets to see their furniture starring centre stage in the company's forthcoming attraction.

All went reasonably well with this scheme until one afternoon the actor Richard Ainley, tiring suddenly of Robert's acting and general bossiness, flew into a rage and broke all the stage furniture to smithereens with a cricket stump. After that, the locals were less eager to lend prized possessions.

Despite the deep discomfort, Robert grew to like Perranporth and it became a regular feature of his summers for the next four years. The company gradually expanded to include Pauline Letts, Nicholas Phipps and Richard Ainley. Several members brought loyal relatives to swell the audience: Frith Banbury's mother, slightly hard of hearing, was famous for craning forward with a look of rapt attention to catch his every syllable as A Butler. The rest of the audience gradually took its lead from her, with the result that, by popular acclaim, Frith soon graduated to starring roles.

By the end of these Perranporth seasons Robert had both directed and written for the company, but that first summer he contented himself with playing the detective in *Rope*, whose classic last-act speech arraigning the killers Leopold and Loeb he could still quote in its entirety forty years later, as well as the juvenile leads in a couple of drawing-room comedies, *Springtime For Henry* and *To See Ourselves*, both recent West End hits.

For the last production of the season he was cast as the comic in *Maria Marten or Murder in the Red Barn*, a performance, by all accounts, of such amazing awfulness that Bully had to bribe the audience with boiled sweets to remain in their seats for the last act.

At this point something in Robert seems to have snapped. Whether as a result of his disillusion over life in Perranporth not measuring up to the standards of a Daphne du Maurier novel, or embarrassment at his utter inability to play the villain in a Victorian melodrama, or more possibly horror at the discovery that his personal gain from the profit-share promised by

Peter at the end of an eight-week season turned out to be a total of under £15 – whatever it was, Robert suddenly decided that he no longer wished to be an actor. He even announced his decision to an astounded company and ceremonially threw his make-up box into the sea.

Returning to London, he had barely started to consider the possibility of other professions, notably playwriting and/or journalism, when, by one of those miracles that seem to occur at least once in the career of any leading actor, he was unexpectedly hurled back into his profession and into the role which was overnight to make his reputation.

Two brothers, Leslie and Sewell Stokes, had just written the first play about the life and death of Oscar Wilde. Leslie, the elder, was to go on to become head of the BBC Third Programme; Sewell had already established himself as a journalist and, rather more uncharacteristically, the last lover and first biographer of Isadora Duncan, whom he had met at the very end of her life in the South of France, an encounter which rendered him gay for the rest of his life, but led to a good book about the mad old dancer and also a Ken Russell television film.

Although Wilde had by then been dead for all of thirty-five years and there had already been a considerable number of biographies, the idea of a stage play which dealt, no matter how subtly and tastefully, with his homosexual love for Lord Alfred Douglas was still regarded as a subject for scandal and concern, to such an extent that the Stokes's play was refused a licence by the Lord Chamberlain, then censor of the British theatre.

The alternative was to go for 'private performance' in a club theatre of which the audience were all members, and this the Stokeses and their director Norman Marshall had already agreed to do at the small Gate Theatre, just off the Strand under Charing Cross. The play had originally been written by them for the actor Frank Pettingell; when he had found a more profitable engagement elsewhere, the role had gone to an actor called Gerald Cooper. Now, however, there was a problem: Cooper had proved so bad in the role that he had had to be fired by the director ten days before they were due to open.

Frith Banbury, who had of course just been acting with Robert in Cornwall, was asked if he knew of any actor who might fit the bill and, although he had just seen Robert hurl his make-up box into the sea off Perranporth, it was my father whom Frith recommended for the role. Not, Frith advised Sewell Stokes, that Robert was an especially good or experienced or even talented actor, but he was decidedly witty, had immense charm, and with his natural exuberance would be able to throw off Wilde's epigrams (which the authors had liberally sprinkled through their play) in the manner of Oscar himself.

Accordingly, Robert was approached, though not without several misgivings from the director Norman Marshall, who had unfortunately seen Robert give his Herod at the Cambridge theatre festival and had been as unimpressed by it as was Beatrix Lehmann.

The essence of Marshall's objection was one which was to haunt Robert, albeit not very tragically, for the rest of his career: several directors considered him not quite good enough as an actor to be a star, whereas Robert always maintained, accurately enough, that he was only any good as an actor *when* he was being a star, and this for the stage was always true since, after *Oscar Wilde*, he hardly ever had to give a supporting performance again. The cinema was something else; there he always found it perfectly natural to support, and usually preferable to having to carry a long and difficult film, the failure of which could seriously damage a career.

Marshall was in an extremely difficult position: he could either reluctantly go with Robert and open as planned or else he could close the theatre for several weeks while a new Oscar Wilde was sought. As luck would have it, Marshall was also the manager of the Gate at that time and in no financial position to let his theatre go dark. So he fought back his memory of *Salomé* and offered Robert the role.

Robert went down to the theatre the next morning, took a copy of the script under his arm, and retired to a restaurant in Maiden Lane to read it over a solitary lunch.

Marshall and Sewell waited afterwards at the theatre, convinced that, having read the script, he would be on his bended knees to play the role of a lifetime. 'Robert returned from his lunch smoking a cigar', recalled Sewell of this, their first encounter at the start of a lifetime's friendship, 'and looking like one of those professional gamblers one had started to see in American films of the period. "I have read your little play," he said by way of introduction, "most interesting, but needs a little alteration, don't you think? Not quite right yet, is it?" '

Robert's traditional opening gambit for dealing with directors and/or playwrights who might otherwise have thought they had the upper hand was thus firmly established from the outset, and rehearsals proceeded apace. In fact, given the initial uneasiness of all concerned, they went remarkably smoothly, and the play opened only five days after its original scheduled date, on 29 September 1936.

Oscar Wilde was a star's play, and Robert became a star playing it. *The Times* next morning may still have had its doubts about the suitability of the subject

Robert at ten: 'I was sent to eleven different preparatory schools, mostly named after saints and each with a peculiar nastiness all its own. I was not a happy child, but everything was always better by comparison in later life.'

Robert's parents: 'They separated when I was about sixteen, but mother lived to a ripe old age, bemoaning the loss of a husband and more particularly the family silver, which he had sold early in their marriage at the start of a long and unsuccessful struggle to pay off his gambling debts.'

Early days in seaside rep at Perranporth 1936–9: 'We were not perhaps the best theatre company in Britain, but we were the only one to have food delivered in hampers from Fortnum and Mason.'

At Perranporth with Peter Bull and members of the company, 1936, and thirty years later with Bully again for ITV's *If the Crown Fits*.

As Oscar Wilde on stage in London,
1936; and a Hollywood debut, as
Louis XVI in *Marie Antoinette*, 1938,
with John Barrymore and Norma
Shearer.

Robert and Joan on their wedding day in February 1940.

Above: Rex Harrison, Robert Morley, George Bernard Shaw and Gabriel Pascal in a break during the filming of *Major Barbara* at the Albert Hall on GBS's eighty-fourth birthday, July 26, 1940.

Right: Edward My Son: Robert as Arnold Holt and Peggy Ashcroft as Evelyn in London and on Broadway, 1947–8.

Above left: With his mother-in-law Gladys Cooper on a Honolulu beach in 1949.

Above right: The author and his father unsuccessfully prospecting for gold, Australia, 1950.

Below: At home at Fairmans in 1956: Robert, Annabel, Joan, Wilton and the author.

for staging ('Upon Wilde the artist the play has no real comment of importance to make, and of Wilde the man it merely relates what were best
forgotten'), but Desmond McCarthy in the *New Statesman* was in no doubt of
'Robert Morley's admirable impersonation', while Goronwy Rees, then
drama critic of the *Spectator*, wrote of 'Morley's ability to convey throughout
a sense of Wilde's genius, intelligence and goodness. He even succeeds in
conveying Wilde's extraordinary power of giving happiness to others: the
jokes remain good because Wilde had several practical things to say, and said
them extremely well. And the British public, which was his butt, has not so
changed that these jokes have lost their truth today.'

That, in essence, was the achievement of the play: to bring Oscar back
from the grave to a live audience and remind them not merely of the tragedy
but also of the comedy of his life. Happily for those of us who were not
around to see Robert as Wilde on stage, he made a film version in 1960, but
more of that later; by then, of course, he was rather old for the role, eight
years older than Oscar had been when he died, while John Neville as Alfred
Douglas must have been the oldest undergraduate ever seen at Oxford
University. But the film ended, as did the original play, with a speech of
Wilde's in which my father achieved, in my admittedly biased critical
opinion, a moment of heartbreaking brilliance. Wilde is at a café table in Paris
a few weeks before his death and Alfred Douglas has rejoined him for the last
time:

Quiet, this is a dream. I am telling one of my stories, and the stars have all
come out to listen. When Jesus returned to Nazareth, Nazareth was so
changed that He no longer recognised His own city. The Nazareth where
He had lived was full of lamentation and tears; this city was filled with
outbursts of laughter and song . . . In the street He saw a woman whose face
and raiment were painted, and whose feet were shod with pearls, and
behind her came slowly, as a hunter, a young man who wore a cloak of
two colours. The face of the woman was the face of an idol, and the eyes of
the young man were bright with lust. And Jesus followed swiftly, and
touched the hand of the young man and said to him, 'Why do you look at
this woman in such wise?' And the young man turned round, and
recognised Him, and said, 'But I was blind once, and you gave me my
sight. At what else should I look?'

And Jesus ran forward and touched the painted raiment of the woman,
and said to her: 'Is there no other way in which to walk, save in the way of
sin?' And the woman turned round, and recognised Him, and laughed and
said, 'But you forgave me my sins, and this way is a pleasant way.'

When Jesus had passed out of the city, He saw, seated by the roadside, a young man who was weeping. He went towards him, touched the long locks of his hair, and said to him, 'Why are you weeping?' The young man looked up, recognised Him, and made answer: 'But I was dead once, and you raised me from the dead. What else should I do but weep?'

I perceive that I am drunk. I find that alcohol, taken persistently and in sufficiently large quantities, produces all the effects of intoxication. [*After a pause*]. I have had my hand on the moon: what is the use now of trying to rise a little way from the ground?

He looks up; Lord Alfred Douglas is gone, and the curtain comes down on Wilde's last line: 'Thank you, Bosie, thank you.'

7

Perranporth Perils

1936–1937

'Soon after I first arrived in Hollywood, Norma Shearer gave a dinner for me and asked the stars I most wanted to meet: Janet Gaynor, Carole Lombard, Fred Astaire, Jeanette Macdonald, and, as each entered, I was conscious of a deep feeling of disappointment. They seemed somehow so much smaller than I remembered them on the screen.'

In later Hollywood terms, at the Gate Theatre by Charing Cross for six short weeks Robert Morley *was* Oscar Wilde, the name above the title. His reviews had been ecstatic, but the run was always meant to be a limited one and the play could go no further since the Lord Chamberlain was still not willing to permit the greater British public the sight of the disgraced dramatist on stage, despite the fact that the script was discreet to a fault about Oscar's homosexuality.

The theatre was, however, visited by a number of interested parties including Lord Alfred Douglas himself, who had advised the Stokes brothers on their play and who entered Robert's dressing-room after the first night not at all the willowy, etiolated figure of gossip and legend, but instead a butch, ruddy-faced, rather jocular man, much resembling his pugilist father the Marquess of Queensberry.

Another equally surprising backstage visitor was Sophie Tucker, who decided that she wished to buy the American rights and stage the play on Broadway with the original cast. 'I know real art when I see it', she announced to a surprised company, 'and believe me, this kinda thing could go over big in the States.'

Although nothing came of that, the idea of New York was taking root: as the play could not be staged elsewhere in London, a flight from the jurisdiction of the Lord Chamberlain seemed a good idea. In the event, given the usual contractual and economic problems of transatlantic theatrical production even then, two full years were to elapse between the opening of *Oscar Wilde* at the Gate and its arrival at the Fulton Theatre on Broadway in October 1938. In the meantime Robert had a living to make. The brief *succès de scandale* he had enjoyed as Oscar led, rather as a Hollywood Oscar usually does, to precisely nothing. Agents and managers now knew who he was – the actor who had just scored that little club success as Wilde – but they had not the faintest idea what else to do with him or for him.

As a result, Robert spent several weeks out of work before receiving two offers virtually simultaneously. One was from his old friend Tyrone Guthrie, the director of his play *Short Story*, who wanted him to go to the Old Vic as Claudius to the Hamlet of Laurence Olivier. The other offer, equally intriguing to him, came from Denham Studios, where they were filming a swashbuckler with Conrad Veidt called *Under the Red Robe*, in which Robert was being asked to play a supporting role and help with the dialogue of a rather shaky script.

Naturally enough, Robert leapt at both: he could film at Denham all day, he reckoned, and repair to the Old Vic at night since those rehearsals were due to begin first and it would, therefore, only be a matter of playing by the time the film started. Then, however, his plans were thrown into confusion: the film schedule was brought forward, and Robert was asked after a camera test to play a much larger role in the swashbuckler than had first been offered him. On the principle that he had never much enjoyed Shakespeare on tour with Benson, and that a film career looked both more profitable and more fun than a season with Olivier in Waterloo Road, Robert asked to be released from the Old Vic, a request Guthrie granted with almost suspicious alacrity.

This proved to be a major mistake, possibly on Guthrie's part, but certainly on Robert's. Within a day or two of starting work on his first film at Denham, he had fallen foul of the great Swedish director Victor Seastrom over the utter impossibility of a line like 'The Cardinal's down, he'll hang no more poor fellows.' Seastrom did not brook interference or objection and, at the first sign of trouble from Robert, had him fired from the picture as both actor and dialogue coach.

Robert received a £200 cheque for this brief introduction to the movies, but his pride was distinctly hurt and it was too late to get back into the Old Vic. Out of work again, he decided to start writing a new play for the second of Peter Bull's summer seasons at Perranporth. Called *Goodness How Sad*, it was to be a bitter-sweet comedy about a struggling company of repertory players not unlike the Perranporth team, who are suddenly visited by an actor friend who had left them to make his fame and fortune as a movie star in Hollywood. Towards the end of the play, when he refuses to help them by performing in one of their plays, an actress in the company turns on him with a speech which more or less summarised Robert's feelings about movies at the time:

CAROL: We're the theatre, see; you may have forgotten what that is, but I'll remind you. It's the place where you learned your job, which cradled you, which gave you your first chance, which made an actor out of you, which sent you to Hollywood to make pictures. And just because you don't need us any more, you think you can walk out on us . . . well, you can't. You've got a debt to pay, Robert Mainc, and you're not going to get away without paying it. It's a big debt, too. You're happy now, you're rich, you are doing what you like, you're proud of yourself. Well, everything you've got you owe to us. There wouldn't be any pictures at all if it wasn't for the theatre. The theatre, that's something bigger than you'll ever know in Hollywood, something that was going on hundreds of years before the cinema was ever heard of, and you know and I know it will be going on thousands of years after motion pictures are dead and buried. The greatest author that ever lived once described the whole thing in five words, All the World's a Stage.

Stirring stuff, and how was Robert to know that before the summer was out he would be abandoning the Perranporth season himself for the chance of a Hollywood movie?

In the meantime another off-West End theatre company, not unlike the Gate, came to his rescue: in April 1937 the Repertory Players, a Sunday night group of actors often appearing elsewhere, but dedicated to the staging of new plays, happened upon a script by Jules Eckert Goodman entitled *The Great Romancer*. This was a flamboyant stage biography of Alexandre Dumas *père*, author of *The Three Musketeers* and *The Count of Monte Cristo*. Conceived in much the way that Sartre was later to adapt *Kean* from the Dumas original, the play caught the great novelist at the end of his complex private life, surrounded by relatives and mistresses, in a drama which was in essence an extended character sketch.

Like *Oscar Wilde*, it offered Robert the chance to go spectacularly over the top, and he was again surrounded by a team of strong supporting players, among them Anthony Quayle, Robert Eddison and Coral Browne. The result was another batch of rave reviews, though more for Robert than the play, and this time happily there was no objection from the Lord Chamberlain to a West End transfer. Accordingly *The Great Romancer* opened at the New Theatre with Eric Portman replacing Anthony Quayle, but the rest of the Sunday night cast more or less intact. This time the papers, as if making up for being unable to welcome him to a commercial theatre as Wilde, went wild about Robert himself: there were quite literally headlines in the evening papers reading 'A Star is Born', and several interviewers took this to be his West End debut, having unsurprisingly forgotten his only other appearance there as A Pirate in *Treasure Island* all of eleven years earlier. By now it was June 1937, and Robert was just past his twenty-ninth birthday – not exactly young to have become an overnight sensation, but he was gratified none the less by sudden requests for magazine interviews and stage-door photographs.

One or two critics still had their doubts: Ivor Brown for the *Observer* thought that 'this is a part in which no actor of competence could really fail, though Mr Morley suggests a curious mixture of Billy Bennett and Professor Einstein in the role of the great French romancer', but elsewhere there was considerably more enthusiasm. 'Superb and dominating' thought *The Times*, while the *Telegraph* added: 'Bravura is the word: Mr Morley is an artist of panache whom, if you relish a rich, ebullient performer you must certainly see.' A thoughtful essay in *Time & Tide* from an anonymous critic concluded:

> It is hard to believe that anyone who could present with such uncanny verisimilitude the physical appearance and characteristics of Oscar Wilde would ever be allowed to play anything outside that extremely limited type . . . but in his second big part, Robert Morley shows that he can act in the original meaning of the word. I have not seen anything so exciting since the early days of Charles Laughton . . . both men manage to act with their brains while remaining true to their own characters as well as those of their plays.

All that and the *Evening News* adding: 'Morley is magnificent: he plays the exuberant, pompous, extravagant and yet somehow noble and touching author looking rather like Arnold Bennett, living in the manner of Edgar Wallace, facing tragedy with the courage of Walter Scott, and fighting a duel in the manner of Don Quixote.'

Robert had never had such reviews, even as Wilde, and was seldom to achieve them again with quite such unanimity. There was just one small snag: the play itself ran only twelve performances. Something about the general tenor of the notices seems to have indicated to the public that there was a great performance here, but not much of a play; either that or interest was as limited then in the private life of Dumas the Elder as it has been since outside of France itself. Either way, Robert was out of work again by the beginning of July, except that he had promised Peter Bull he would direct his own *Goodness, How Sad* for the second Perranporth summer season.

This went well enough in its Cornish première, with a cast headed by Bully himself, Frith Banbury, Judith Furse and Pauline Letts, all of whom had parts custom-built for them by Robert, who was making his debut as a director. He then stayed with the troupe to play Chasuble in *The Importance of Being Earnest*, one of the better Perranporth ventures by all accounts, though one he had to leave, for Bully to take over, in mid-run.

Despite the earlier fiasco of his non-appearance in the Olivier *Hamlet*, Robert had been summoned by Guthrie to the Old Vic, this time to play Professor Higgins to Diana Wynyard's Eliza in a revival of *Pygmalion*.

As it turned out, this was to be Robert's sole appearance at the Vic or,

Pygmalion: as Henry Higgins with Diana Wynyard as Eliza Doolittle

indeed, with a classical company of any kind: his reviews were again ecstatic however. 'I do not expect to see a better Higgins' opined Lionel Hale, while the *Telegraph* wrote of 'Morley's splendid Shavian manner, eloquent but offhand, presenting the mannerless pedant very justly'. Twenty years earlier, on the pier at Folkestone, it had been Bernard Shaw who first enticed Robert into the theatre; now he had begun to repay the debt, and would complete the payment a couple of years later as Undershaft in the film of *Major Barbara*.

The Old Vic season was brief, but enjoyable, and by the time it ended something still more exciting was on offer: a Hollywood movie. Some months earlier, the MGM producer Hunt Stromberg had been in London looking for a character actor to play the doomed Louis XVI in a long-planned costume epic about *Marie Antoinette*. Miraculously, he had caught one of the twelve performances of *The Great Romancer*, seen Robert as Alexandre Dumas, and decided that, if he could handle one Frenchman, he could probably handle another.

These things are never that simple, however. First of all Robert had to be tested for the role at a time when he had no knowledge of the script and was still nursing a deep hatred of movies following his dismissal by Seastrom from *Under the Red Robe*. Secondly, there was the small matter of *Oscar Wilde* on Broadway: an American management had by this time taken up an option and it was supposed to be Robert's first priority to hold himself in readiness for a summons to New York once the money had been raised to stage it over there. Thirdly, the limited success of *Goodness, How Sad* at Perranporth that summer had encouraged Robert and Bully to start thinking about setting it up themselves in the West End the following autumn.

Nevertheless, by the time MGM in Hollywood had viewed Robert's test as Louis XVI and decided to offer him the role, it had become clear that this was the option to take. So, in early October 1937, he set sail on the *Bremen* from Southampton, having been bidden a tearful farewell by poor dear Daisy, who was totally convinced she was going to die while her son was abroad. (In the event she lived another quarter of a century, and died with her son at her bedside.)

Peter Bull, initially furious about the enforced postponement of *Goodness, How Sad*, was more than somewhat mollified by the offer from MGM to play Louis's faithful barber in the film, and two portly Perranporth character actors thus set sail to conquer the new world of Hollywood without the faintest idea of what to expect when they actually got there.

While at sea, Robert had one of his few premarital affairs, this one with a married lady who seems to have initiated him into at least some of the mysteries of sex. 'It's a club, you know', he wrote years later,

> and a sort of secret society. Either you are a born member or you are not, and somehow I don't think I ever was. I was scared of disease, conception, involvement, retribution and above all else my own physical incompetence. To be a member of the club one must have no such fears, one must believe in sex as a way of life, just as some people believe in fame or money. I never could, and if it is not your way of life, then it's not the faintest use trying to understand the rules of the sex club. You can either thank God you never joined, or wish to heaven that you could. After a time, you get to the age when there's not much you can do about it either way.

At the dockside in New York he bade a brisk farewell to his shipboard romance, and was almost immediately threatened with a rapid return to England. The port authorities in those days liked to make sure that all immigrants were in the peak of physical health, even if their stay was to be a short one; that way the nation's hospitals would not be cluttered with a lot of Europeans or other undesirables. In the course of his medical check, something Robert made it a rule to avoid whenever possible, the Americans noted that he had a lifelong deficiency in his left eye, though luckily the right one always compensated for it until the time came quite late in his seventies to wear reading glasses.

The immigration officer asked Robert what he did, pondering whether a state of semi-blindness was likely to be an impediment. 'I'm an actor', said Robert proudly, 'on my way to Hollywood.' The officer thought about that for a moment. 'Well', he sighed, 'I guess in that case it won't be a problem. Actors are blind half the time anyway; for you to be half-blind all the time should be OK.'

He was in. His old RADA friend Llewellyn Rees, then playing on Broadway, met him and Peter at the dockside and gave them a lightning one-day tour of New York, before it was time to head for the airport and, unusually for those days, take the plane across country to Los Angeles:

'That same evening I flew for the first time', Robert wrote later,

> and I have never in my life known such excitement. In those days the flight from New York to Los Angeles took sixteen hours and I sat with my nose pressed against the window gazing out at the great moon and down at the limitless land beneath me. A great chain of beacons guided the pilots across

57

the country, and for me the greatest wonder of all was the realisation that men had climbed mountains, crossed deserts, dived down into the great lakes, and with immense labour and courage and ingenuity had seen to it that for 3,000 miles these beacons were all in place and kept alight. We landed to refuel in Omaha, and Dallas, and Salt Lake City, and the sun rose over the Sierras and we came at last back to the ocean.

He and Peter had arrived in lotus-land in ample time for Christmas 1937 and for the start of *Marie Antoinette*, though it has to be said that Robert did not immediately make a firm impression on the most powerful mogul in the land or on the lot, Louis B. Mayer, who had invented the studio slogan 'More Stars Than Are in the Heavens'. 'Oh, yeah' said Mayer, when they were finally introduced in his palatial office, 'you're the guy who's over from London for *Marie Antoinette*. Jesus, how I hate these historical epics.'

Though Robert could not have known it, a studio war was already raging over the making of the film.

8

Hollywood Hopeful

1938–1939

The director of Marie Antoinette was, eventually, 'one-take' Woody Van Dyke who, after sixty films, had learnt a thing or two about getting good performances out of newcomers. He treated me, indeed photographed me, like an errant child: told me to get on with the acting, and he would worry about where to put his cameras so they could see me. He gave me my first screen performance, and probably my best.

The idea of a film about Marie Antoinette had been on the MGM project list for almost five years. In that time a vast range of actors had been considered and some tested for the role of Louis XVI, among them Charles Laughton, for a considerable time the most likely candidate. The others were, in no particular order, Spencer Tracy, Cedric Hardwicke, Ralph Richardson, Maurice Evans, Peter Lorre, Conrad Veidt, Emlyn Williams and Roger Livesey, none of whom proved available or willing or suitable when the moment finally arrived to start the cameras rolling, hence Stromberg's urgent visit to London earlier in the year.

But through all that time there had never been a moment's doubt as to who was to play Louis' unfortunate wife, Marie Antoinette: Norma Shearer had been married to Mayer's deputy at MGM, the 'wonder boy' Irving Thalberg, and together they had made such would-be film classics as *Romeo and Juliet* and *The Barretts of Wimpole Street*.

Thalberg was, by general reckoning, the most talented of all producers; Shearer was a Canadian actress with a versatile screen talent in use since 1920 and a face, as Lillian Hellman noted, 'always splendidly unclouded by thought'. Tragically, however, Thalberg had died of pneumonia at only thirty-seven a year earlier to rather mixed notices. 'The golden bowl is broken' wrote one of his screenwriters, F. Scott Fitzgerald, while Mayer, who had always feared competition from Thalberg, noted merely: 'God is very good to me.'

However, Thalberg's sudden and unexpected death had created myriad problems around the MGM studio, not least for *Marie Antoinette*. It transformed Norma Shearer's position from one of tremendous power, as the wife of the executive producer, overnight to that of the black widow in exile, feared for what she might try to do to preserve the Thalberg supremacy. She was in a strong bargaining position: Thalberg had thoughtfully left her and their two children a sizeable stock option in MGM, which, were she to sell to a hostile bidder, could seriously undermine Mayer's continued tenure of office there.

As a result, relations between Shearer and Mayer were considerably strained: Shearer felt that Mayer had been altogether too quick to remove any trace of Thalberg's presence from the studio, and Mayer felt that she was being disloyal in not offering her shares for sale back to the studio now that Irving was no longer around. A further battlefield was *Marie Antoinette* itself. Had Thalberg remained alive and its producer, Shearer would have had total control over not merely her role but also the entire movie, script, casting, choice of director and all.

But now things were very different. With Thalberg gone, the new producer, Hunt Stromberg, owed his loyalty to old uncle Louis, not to Shearer, and the first evidence of this was an abrupt change of director: the Thalbergs' original choice, Sidney Franklin, was a slow and meticulous 'women's director' in the Cukor mould, but under the new regime he was abruptly fired and replaced by Woody 'one-take' Van Dyke, a man famous for his speed in getting the *Tarzan* and *Thin Man* series out on schedule and under budget.

Franklin had been working on elaborate preparations for the picture for two entire years; Van Dyke, fresh from yet another *Tarzan*, did not appear to have seen the script until the first day of shooting, and seemed to have heard of neither the French nor their Revolution. It was said that for the first week on the set he was so amazed by the size of Miss Shearer's wigs that he thought the picture was called 'Marie and Toilette' and, when one of the numerous historical 'experts' who had been preparing the picture for several months came racing over to inform the director that he had placed the guillotine on the wrong side of the Place de la Concorde, Van Dyke listened for a moment, removed the cigar from his mouth and uttered the immortal line, 'Fine, kid, just fine; that was how it was then, and this is how it's gonna be now.'

Not surprisingly, therefore, relations between Shearer and Van Dyke were more than somewhat strained. Indeed, one of several theories around the set, where local politics were so Byzantine as to make anything going on around eighteenth-century Versailles look positively straightforward by comparison, was that he had been specifically hired to make her look terrible in the movie, thereby undermining her position as the black-widow-in-exile at the studio and so encouraging her to sell her shares back to Mayer and get the hell off his lot forever.

None of this, however, really affected my father, whose memories of the film were almost entirely joyous. 'It was leisurely, and huge, and *de luxe*; we were all treated like visiting maharajahs. Vast cars waited all day outside the sound stages to carry us the 100 yards to our dressing-rooms. On the set there would be a live orchestra to while away the waits – Miss Shearer had it in her contract, believing she always worked better to an orchestral accompaniment – and a *maitre d'hôtel* would take our orders for luncheon, which would be served in the dressing-rooms by a uniformed waiter as soon as we got back there.'

For Robert, on his first prolonged visit outside 1930s England, the luxury of it all was unimaginable. His new agent, Hayes Hunter (there had been an amicable parting with Mrs Nelson King soon after the Meriel Forbes affair), had managed to negotiate him a salary of £200 a week, which was sizeable for the time considering the film was to take six months to shoot. Unfortunately Hunter had only managed to achieve this by claiming, entirely untruthfully, that Robert was a man of independent means who did not need the job and would not take it for less, an illusion somewhat spoiled when he had appeared in MGM's London office the day he was due to sail for New York demanding an advance of £50 so that he could buy his first decent overcoat for the sea voyage.

All was going well, however, until one morning Robert inadvertently arrived late on the set. 'Van Dyke was the kindest of teachers, treating and photographing me like a mad child, but on this occasion he demanded an apology, so I decided to give it to everyone. I spent the next ten minutes climbing and scrabbling around the cat-walks of the overhead gantry, shaking hands and apologising to each of the electricians manning an arc-light. Considering that I totally ruined my white knee-breeches and my ermine train, this wasn't perhaps the most helpful contribution that I could have made towards getting on with the job in hand, but it was, I always felt, the right thing to do in the circumstances.'

On another occasion, bored by the long waits between takes, Robert borrowed a bicycle from a messenger boy and rode it at high speed around the studio streets, dressed in his full Louis XVI coronation robes, before returning the bike to its indignant owner. 'All the stars round here', said the messenger icily, 'think it's funny to do that, but they do it, Mr Morley, just the once.'

Of their producer, Hunt Stromberg, little was ever seen, though Robert was deeply impressed by the way that he would always have his arrival on set announced in advance over loudspeakers and be followed around by a permanent secretary carrying what must have been the first ever portable telephone. As for Louis B. Mayer, he was seen even less, given that he and Shearer were not exactly close. Robert once managed to have a brief conversation with him about his studio. 'We've got them all here,' said Mayer proudly, 'every star who ever mattered to the world. All except one. That damned Mouse over at Disney.'

When the filming was finally complete, Mayer invited Robert to the screening. It ended in total silence, executives apparently terrified to give their verdict until Mayer had given his. 'After a movie like that, LB', one of them finally said to break the silence, 'what more is there to say?' Robert suddenly decided, to his terror, that Mayer was going to ask him for an opinion and realised that, after the effort of the past six months, all he felt was relief that it was mercifully finished and he could return to his comparatively normal life as a London stage actor. So horrified was he at the possibility of being asked to deliver an opinion that he rushed out of the screening-room without a word, and spent the next five hours wandering aimlessly around the darkened streets of Hollywood. 'Nobody ever again ever asked me what I thought of *Marie Antoinette*, which was just as well. I have never been able to watch myself on the screen with any real enjoyment, although I would undoubtedly have been a better film actor if I'd ever managed to bring myself to have the courage to sit through some of my own performances. But the shock of that first sight of myself was absolute, and total.'

The next day was to be his last in Hollywood for almost thirty years, and Mayer took him to lunch at his private table in the MGM executive dining-room. 'It was like eating at Buckingham Palace. Uncle Louis explained that they had spent a lot of money promoting me and that he wanted nothing more than to find new work for me as soon as my commitment to *Oscar Wilde* on Broadway was over. He said I was to call him the moment I was free. A year or so later, after *Oscar Wilde*, I did so, only to be put through to several secretaries. Eventually there came a note from the casting depart-ment: "If", it said, "Mr Mayer should have any suitable employment for you in the future, he will certainly be pleased to get in touch with you. In the meantime Mr Mayer wishes to point out that to avoid any duplication of secretarial effort, it is better not to contact him personally." '

By this time both my father and Peter Bull felt they had been shown the best of Hollywood, and were not eager to hang around for fear it might get rather worse. There was, it's true, the suggestion that Robert might like to be Quasimodo in *The Hunchback of Notre Dame*, but both Peter and my other godfather, Sewell, told him that it was only a grunting role, and that he wouldn't really care for all the make-up required. The part and the hump thus went to Charles Laughton, the actor originally envisaged for Louis XVI.

Robert seems never to have regretted the decision or to have felt he should have had a Hollywood career like that of Laughton, to whom he was forever being compared. He made one or two fleeting returns there after the war, while his beloved mother-in-law, Gladys Cooper, was still in residence, but somehow he never felt it was a place in which to settle down or be happy. At heart he was always first a theatre man, perfectly content to turn up in the movies so long as they were being shot conveniently close to Shaftesbury Avenue or on some sunbaked location preferably equipped with a casino and a few decent restaurants. But the idea of making his life within a purely film community simply never occurred to him as desirable or very practical, given that MGM's love affair with English character actors was already on the wane by the time he first got through its gates.

As for his friend Peter Bull, he too was more than ready for a return to Perranporth and the next summer season there. In California they had happily whiled away the endless hours they were not required on the set by forming a Monopoly school with the journalist John Davenport and the screenwriter Noël Langley, later to be Robert's co-author on the best of his plays, *Edward, My Son*. They had also formed a firm friendship with a young actress called Mary Morris, who was forever being tested for possible Metro roles, so that one morning she would appear in their apartment as a French courtesan and the next as a black slave-girl from the deep South. After a while she grew fed up with the whole system and demanded to be sent back to London via Siberia, which shook the MGM travel department considerably.

Peter's own role in *Marie Antoinette* as the faithful barber ended up entirely on the cutting-room floor, though he did manage to spot one of his ears in a promotional still outside the Empire, Leicester Square, several months later. The money he made from the film, however, went a long way towards financing the next Perranporth season and an eventual London transfer for *Goodness, How Sad* – six months, as Bully noted, well and usefully spent not appearing in a film.

Llewellyn Rees, who had taken over during their last Hollywood months as their company manager, drove them around the West coast and gave Robert his first introduction to the magic of Las Vegas, possibly the only time he ever left there at a profit, Llewellyn having resolutely refused to let him into the casino with more than $20. All other profits were to be saved for *Goodness, How Sad*.

Marie Antoinette was in its time the most expensive production ever made at MGM, coming in at just over $2 million, but it managed to recoup its costs on the back of an immensely starry cast: not only Shearer but also John Barrymore in fine, drunken form as the old Louis XV, and Tyrone Power, like Robert in his first major role. 'A fine, resplendent bore', thought the *New Yorker* of a revival in 1977, but at the time it opened to considerably more critical enthusiasm on both sides of the Atlantic, scoring for Robert his first and only Oscar nomination.

In the meantime, Robert and Bully hastened back to Cornwall for a somewhat truncated summer season as Robert was due imminently to return to Broadway for the American première of *Oscar Wilde*, while Peter was going ahead with his own West End production of *Goodness, How Sad*.

By the time that was in rehearsal, under Tony Guthrie's direction, for the Vaudeville Theatre, where it ran somewhat unprofitably through the winter of 1938–9, Robert was already back in rehearsal with Norman Marshall in New York for the Broadway opening of *Oscar Wilde* at the Fulton on 10 October. This had been arranged by the impresario Gilbert Miller, a flamboyant figure not unlike Robert or Oscar, was a constant source of delight to my father because of his unlimited anglophilia. 'Do you know', said Gilbert to Robert one morning, 'what many members of your very wonderful and delightful Royal Family have been known to call my wife Kitty?' 'No,' said Robert, 'what?' 'Kitty,' said Gilbert proudly.

Miller was a Broadway mogul of the old school, the son of the Henry Miller who had given his name to one of New York's best-known theatres, and, being of Robert's size and character, they were reasonably well matched across the stalls. Once, during rehearsals, Miller asked for a line to be cut from *Wilde*: 'It's the kind of line we've heard in other, I won't say better, but other, plays. I know you have had this tremendous critical success already in London, Robert, and I no way wish to interfere, it's just' – and here Miller waved his hand expansively over an acre of empty auditorium – 'that I'm trying to save them a little agony out there.'

Norman Marshall did not fare much better: he had unwisely laid out the set on the rehearsal floor with a series of chalk marks, even indicating where characters were to stand and sit at certain climactic moments. 'I had no idea', murmured Robert, studying the floor plan intently, 'that *Oscar Wilde* was to open in New York with a cast entirely consisting of midgets.'

But open it did a week or two after *Marie Antoinette* and to equally ecstatic reviews; on the verge of his thirtieth birthday, Robert had achieved the major double of his career. As John Mason Brown, the most distinguished Broadway critic of his day, noted:

What makes *Oscar Wilde* memorable is Morley, best known to American audiences for the historically incorrect but unquestionably commanding halfwit he creates as Louis XVI to Norma Shearer's Marie Antoinette. But his Louis, skilful as it is when once its false premises are granted, is the epitome of the obvious when compared to his Oscar Wilde.

As no actor I have ever seen in any revival of one of Oscar's plays has been able to do, Mr Morley gives point and charm and naturalness to Oscar's epigrams. He purrs with pleasure as, with seeming spontaneity, he rolls them out. He speaks them in the rich, velvet tones of mock innocence with which Mrs Patrick Campbell disguises her most devastating comments; like her, he seems to enjoy playing Malice in Wonderland. But his Oscar is no static creation. It springs from Mr Morley's mind, takes possession of his eyes, and mouth, and hands; and his Oscar changes with the times. At first he is the arrogant *flanneur*; then the amoral decadent; next the witness, witty in his self-defence; then the cornered wretch in a state of sad collapse; and finally the bloated ruin of the last years in Paris. Let there be no mistake about it: Mr Morley's Oscar is an extraordinary performance, which, if you are wise, will command your immediate attention.

Oscar Wilde did something more than make Robert a Broadway star overnight: it introduced him, albeit indirectly, to the woman who was to be his wife for more than fifty years.

9

Major Barbara
Goes to War
1939–1940

*It was in Perranporth, three days before the outbreak of war, that I met Joan
Buckmaster and knew at once that I wanted to marry her; her brother had told me
merely to look her up, and took the view that this was rather overdoing it.*

Oscar Wilde ran on triumphantly at the Fulton Theatre through the winter of
1938–9, much to the relief of Gilbert Miller, who had kept his name off all the
original posters lest the scandal of Oscar's homosexuality do him lasting harm
as a manager or, indeed, at the box-office. In total contrast, Robert and the
play became the talk of the town, and he immensely enjoyed the first of his
only two Broadway runs. In those days to have a huge theatrical success in
New York was also to have a tremendous social success, and Robert was duly
invited everywhere. To the Park Avenue parties of Mrs Cornelius Vander-
bilt, who said she hoped Robert would not mind if she called the King and
Queen of England by their christian names, as that was how she always
thought of them; 'Not at all', replied Robert, 'it's how I always think of them
myself.' To Sing-Sing, where he was solemnly allowed to sit in the electric
chair, though with the current switched off, a macabre tourist attraction of
the time. To the top of the Statue of Liberty, to the World's Fair, and to a
party in Greenwich Village which he managed to convince Beverley Nichols
was in reality a drag ball where all the dancers were men, a theory
unfortunately almost immediately disproved when one of them started to
strip.

Those were the best of times to be a Broadway star and, as with Hollywood, Robert's timing was fortunate; with the war less than a year away, it was already the end of an era, and he had just caught its final curtain.

The Broadway cast for *Oscar Wilde* was inevitably very different to that which had originally opened at the Gate in London two years earlier; indeed the only hold-over was Mark Dignam as Carson. Now playing the fateful Lord Alfred Douglas was a young English actor called John Buckmaster, the only son of Gladys Cooper, who loyally went to see her boy in the role. 'Morley', she wrote to her elder daughter, Joan, back in England, scarcely suspecting that in less than two years she would be his mother-in-law, 'really is surprisingly good in the role.'

He also got on very well with Johnnie, and soon enough the two men were sharing a New York flat occasionally visited by their co-author, Sewell Stokes. 'Sewell and I', recalled Robert later, 'behaved in New York rather like a pair of those bears you used to see in zoos, one forever parading to catch the buns and treacle tins and win applause by turning somersaults, the other only occasionally discernible in the shadows of the artificial lair provided by the authorities.'

Sewell, of course, was 'the other'; he never cared for the limelight, did not much like the air of New York, and never returned. He had not even bothered to look at the Statue of Liberty on the way into the harbour, and his only abiding memory of the entire adventure when, as his intrigued godson, I questioned him about it some years later, was of a literary lunch at which he had been asked by the aging Ford Madox Ford to take him to the lavatory – not by all accounts a very happy experience and apparently enough to put Sewell off America for the rest of his life.

Robert, however, loved New York with an intense passion: 'I even dreamt briefly of settling there and becoming a citizen. I went all the way down to the Battery and took out the necessary papers. I read Winchell and ate hamburgers and drank Coca-Cola. I went to late-night movies, and explored Harlem at breakfast-time, and listened to torch singers in Greenwich Village. John and I rented a pianola for our apartment, and we gave all-night poker parties. I even befriended the local Police Commissioner, Kennedy, who took me on night raids in his police car and kindly introduced me to several leading members of the Mafia. Nowhere in the world is success in the theatre so enjoyable as in that city, where all the head waiters know your weekly box-office takings, and all the cab drivers are out front on your opening night. The sun was on my back, and my coat grew sleek indeed.'

But all good things come to an end and some time during April 1939 the *Oscar Wilde* business began to slacken off, as was traditional even with hits towards what was then the end of the Broadway season. Miller, unable to forecast the events of the following September, decided to cut his losses and take the play off while they were still ahead, with the intention of reassembling his cast for a coast-to-coast tour in the autumn.

This left Robert free to return to his ageing parents in London, to a fourth summer with Bully's Perranporth Rep., and to treat the company of his *Goodness, How Sad* (soon to be filmed by Clive Brook as *Return to Yesterday*) to a slap-up supper at Rule's to compensate for their all too brief stay in the West End. He also had it in his diary to look up John's sister, Joan Buckmaster, to whom Johnnie had asked him to pass on his love and the news that he was doing fine in New York.

The Perranporth season that final summer was not to include anything new by Robert, but he would be playing in such regular repertory standbys as *Dr Knock* and the usual *Springtime For Henry*. There were two main excitements that season – three, if you count the outbreak of war. The first was the arrival at Perranporth's tiny post office of a registered parcel from New York containing the script of a new play by George S. Kaufman and Moss Hart. Entitled *The Man Who Came to Dinner*, it was loosely based on the life and misadventures of the celebrated Algonquin critic Alexander Woollcott, whom Robert had met briefly during his Broadway run. He was the first to be offered it, read it that summer, and declined the title role on the grounds that it did not have much of a last act. He added that, if they could fix one, he would be happy to reconsider. Kaufman and Hart, unaccustomed to such criticism, gave the play instead to Monty Woolley, who achieved a considerable American success in it on stage and screen; luckily Robert was able to retrieve it for a long London run a couple of years later.

The second excitement was the meeting with Joan. Her father, Captain Herbert Buckmaster, the founder of Buck's Club, inventor of the Buck's Fizz and my grandfather, had friends in the Perranporth area and, hearing that Robert had recently been flat-sharing in New York with his son, he arranged a meeting backstage for one of the weekends that Joan would be staying with him.

Their first planned encounter was not a success: Robert entirely forgot they had written to say they were coming round for afternoon tea, and it was not until after the performance that night that they finally all got together for news of Johnnie in New York, and for Robert to be bowled over by his first glimpse of Joan.

With the declaration of war a mere three days away, Robert was among those who still believed it highly unlikely to happen, for which reason he encouraged the Perranporth company to play on regardless. Consequently, they found themselves on the morning of Sunday, 3 September 1939, totally stranded in Cornwall, as all trains to London were jammed. 'I listened to Chamberlain making his speech on the radio that momentous morning,' Robert recalled later, 'and for some reason decided there and then that I'd be a lot safer in the sea. So I hurried down to the beach and swam quite a long way out under water, convinced that the Germans wouldn't be able to get me there. Then, as there seemed to be no sign of them, I swam back again and had lunch with Bully. All in all, it was something of an anti-climax.'

Gradually, though, the company dispersed and, since he was not of call-up age as yet, Robert returned to London to continue his whirlwind courtship of Joan and await news from America of the *Oscar Wilde* tour, which, despite the recent outbreak of hostilities, still seemed to be a reality. Indeed, he planned to take Joan with him on it, so that she might get to see her mother, who had settled in Hollywood and was filming *Rebecca* with Laurence Olivier.

At first they were given to understand that there would be no passport difficulties whatsoever, since Robert was definitely not required for any kind of national service: 'Actors are always a problem in wartime, like head waiters,' he once wrote; 'somehow they don't seem to fit in with anything that's going on. They should probably be deported, or locked up for the duration.' But no sooner had the plans to sail to New York been made than they were rapidly unmade, due to the intervention of an extremely crafty movie producer called Gabriel Pascal.

Like Alexander Korda, his lifelong rival and enemy, Pascal was one of the Middle European emigrés who had been the making of the British and American film industries, and he was now settled in London, where he had brilliantly managed to become the only film-maker liked by George Bernard Shaw. As a result, he had sewn up the rights to all Shaw's plays for the screen, and had already scored a tremendous success, both critical and commercial, by producing the Wendy Hiller-Leslie Howard *Pygmalion* in the previous year. Now Pascal wanted to move straight on to *Major Barbara*, again with Wendy Hiller, but this time he also wanted Robert for her father, the millionaire armaments manufacturer Andrew Undershaft.

Robert was flattered and intrigued by the offer, and would eagerly have taken it, as he explained, had it not unfortunately been for his prior commitment to Gilbert Miller and the American tour of *Oscar Wilde*. Pascal looked suitably regretful and allowed Robert to leave his office thinking that was the end of the matter. Gabby then rang the passport office: was it really true, he enquired, that they were issuing a passport to allow an English actor to leave his country in its hour of need, moreover for the express purpose of going to America and there playing a raging old homosexual poet who was far from the best possible advertisement for his great nation in its aforementioned hour of need, etc?

Within twenty-four hours Robert had a regretful note from the passport office to the effect that his travel permission had been withdrawn – and within forty-eight hours he was playing Undershaft in the film of *Major Barbara*.

Much of this was shot at Denham in Buckinghamshire, where Robert managed to convince Wendy Hiller that Pascal had constructed a personal shelter beneath the lake for his sole use in the event of a sudden air-raid. Relations between the producer and his star were, after that, rather strained, but Pascal had managed to surround her with an amazing cast: not only Robert but also Rex Harrison as his son, and for good measure Emlyn Williams, Robert Newton, Sybil Thorndike and a young Deborah Kerr in almost her first appearance on screen. Pascal himself was directing, with assistance from Harold French and David Lean; Ronald Neame was the cameraman, William Walton had written the score, Cecil Beaton had designed the costumes and Vincent Korda was responsible for the sets. Altogether, not a bad little team.

For wartime reasons, shooting at Denham was protracted. On the strength of his first week's salary, Robert was emboldened to propose to Joan and to marry her at Caxton Hall. By the time the last week's salary had been paid to him, they had been married nine months, had bought a house in the country, he had made another film entirely along the way, and the Second World War had started in earnest.

At the outset of their marriage my parents were living in a rented flat in Arlington House, convenient for the Caprice, when they could afford it, and married life seemed to suit them from the very beginning. The ceremony itself had been a brisk and brief affair, attended by most of Robert's immediate relatives and Joan's father, Buck, who had driven her to Caxton Hall from his club in Clifford Street. Robert's stag night had been spent with Bully, Sewell and Llewellyn Rees at Collin's Music Hall, and, apart from a violent attack of hiccups from one of Joan's friends, the service went well enough until the Registrar had to ask, 'The bride's father, is he alive?' Whereupon Robert heard himself say, 'I'll just pop into the other room and have a look.'

With no time for a honeymoon, since *Major Barbara* was already well under way, Robert returned to Denham and the rampaging of Gabby Pascal, who would alternate shrieks of, 'You're crucifying me with all your acting,' and sudden poetic insights into his own casting. 'That Harrison,' he said once, 'I have him because you see, on screen, he have face of a tortured

Christ.' 'It's his shoes,' murmured David Lean in the background, 'they're far too tight.'

In fact, Harrison was only the third choice, after Leslie Howard had turned it down and Andrew Osborn had been let go during the early shooting. Like Robert, Rex was being paid £10,000 for the picture, though, unlike Robert, he was having to pass most of that on to Alex Korda, with whom he had already signed a long-term contract. The highlight of the prolonged shooting for Rex, as for Robert and others, was the arrival on set of Bernard Shaw himself, come to see his beloved Wendy Hiller and what kind of a mess they were making of his script. In the event Shaw professed himself delighted, leaving Robert with a lifelong memory of 'the only saint I ever met' and of this meeting with the playwright who had first made him want to be an actor.

During the month-long lay off caused by the change over from Osborn to Harrison as Adolphus Cusins, Robert had managed to make another movie. This was *You Will Remember*, a 'biopic' which Sewell Stokes had written rather rapidly with Lydia Hayward about the popular Victorian song-writer Leslie Stuart, composer of *Lily of Laguna* and *Soldiers of the Queen*. Emlyn Williams played his faithful friend, and spent much of the movie wheeling him in a bathchair up and down Brighton seafront whilst Robert, in the role of Stuart, recalled his musical highlights, which were then performed, though not of course by him. As most of Robert's Fass aunts had by this time retired more or less permanently to the wheelchairs of similar coastal resorts along the Channel, he was thoroughly at home in both the convention and the chair.

Then it was back to *Major Barbara* and his new married life. Since the flat at the top of Arlington House was only ever a temporary expedient and likely to suffer in the event of German bombing, Robert and Joan began to hunt around the Home Counties for a cottage not too far from either the theatres of the West End or the film studios clustered around what was then the western fringe of the metropolis in villages like Denham, Pinewood and Shepperton.

After a while they found exactly what they were searching for: Fairmans Cottage, on the upper Henley road out of Wargrave towards Crazies Hill, was a radically undeveloped two-up, two-down gamekeeper's cottage adjoining the Hennerton estate which had been the subject of a very small 'for sale' advertisement in *The Times*. They drove down that very afternoon with Buck, liked what they saw, and offered the local farmer slightly less than the £2,000 he was asking for it, though for an extra £500 he did throw in the four-acre wood and a field at the back of it for which he could think of no agricultural use. Robert always believed he could have bought Fairmans for even less had he really bargained, but the deal was done and, although the cottage required a vast amount of redecoration and (once building permissions were restored after the war) an equally vast amount of enlargement to about three times its original size, Fairmans remained their home for the next fifty years.

With *Major Barbara* and *You Will Remember* safely in the can, Robert had to start thinking rather more seriously about the war, which he had vaguely hoped would have gone away, but clearly had not. At thirty-two, already overweight and with flat feet, he was hardly in the front line for military call-up or action overseas. On the other hand, he would have to do something and duly applied to the RAF, who, being not yet in the last extreme of recruiting desperation, politely but firmly declared him 'unfit'.

He then had to report to an office in Reading, where a civil servant sat behind a desk wearily trying to find suitable wartime occupations for patently unwartime people. He offered Robert a series of options, of which cook appealed to him most, except of course that he could not, owing first of all to his mother's and then Joan's constant coddling; the most he could manage even at the very end of his life was toast and the occasional boiled egg.

Eventually, in some despair, the civil servant asked Robert what else he might like to do to help the war effort. 'I think', replied he with a charming smile, 'I might like to sit behind a desk in a nice warm office in Reading and tell other people what they ought to be doing for the war effort.'

This abruptly put an end to the encounter, and fortunately it was soon afterwards decided, at a higher level, that unless actors were young, fit and agile, they were probably best left to continue with their acting for the entertainment of others with a more military disposition. Thus Equity made it clear that Robert would have more or less permanent deferment from military service provided, of course, he kept on acting and did not insult too many more civil servants.

10

Dinner at the Savoy

1941–1944

For two years at the Savoy Theatre I was Sheridan Whiteside, and we then took The Man Who Came to Dinner *on an ENSA tour of army camps in the Welsh mountains, a curiously haphazard venture as the garrisons we were sent to entertain had often been posted elsewhere just before our arrival, so we would end up performing the play for a few startled cleaners and nightwatchmen.*

In early 1941 it was of considerable importance to Robert, if he were to avoid the vengeance of the man from Reading, that he should remain as permanently and visibly employed in his profession as he could possibly manage to arrange. The problem was that the West End was increasingly given over to wartime musicals and revues, for which he could neither sing nor dance, and the movie situation was no more encouraging. With *Major Barbara* yet to be released, there had been no other offers, and indeed a nasty row over billing was being waged between Robert, who understandably saw himself as one of the stars of the film, and Pascal, who wanted Robert's name firmly placed beneath the title. Robert lost the battle. 'I shall', he told Joan, 'from now on resign myself to being a feature player, which is less worrying and may well prove equally remunerative.'

In the meantime there was very little money coming in and, with the move to Fairmans to be paid for, Robert decided to go back on the road with an Edward Percy thriller about a 'fence' who kills a blackmailer with a poisoned dart and then himself dies of a heart attack. Just the thing, he thought, to take audiences' minds off air-raids, and he duly formed a touring company, which introduced him to a whole new set of post-Perranporth friends. Among these was the director Jack Minster, forever known as 'Jolly Jack' on account of his infinitely lugubrious features and lifelong premonition of theatrical disaster. Robert had first come across him and his wife, Barbara, on their honeymoon, which he had bizarrely shared because he badly needed a lift in their car at a time of acute petrol rationing. It did, however, lead Robert to the belief that all honeymooners should hire a third party to ease the conversation during the most difficult time, and in this case the marriage was (though possibly not thanks to him) a triumph: Jack and Barbara's son Hilary can frequently be found on stage and television as one of the more sinister Nazis in 'Allo, 'Allo, and was to be one of the first of Robert's many godchildren.

Jack was directing the Percy thriller, which Robert had, characteristically, both altered and retitled. As *Play With Fire*, it toured the north of England for several weeks in the spring of 1941 and also served to introduce my father to another lifelong friend, the *grand dame* eccentric Ambrosine Phillpotts, who was still acting with him in his last West End appearance more than thirty years later, largely because she had learnt to treat him, rather as my mother always did, as the eldest and most troublesome of her beloved children.

The tour was not a great success and, by the time they reached Nottingham, Robert had sent for the author to announce that he had done all he could with a doomed piece and was throwing in the towel. Unperturbed, Edward Percy took out all Robert's 'improvements', gave the play back its original title and, as *The Shop at Sly Corner*, it went on to a three-year West End run with Kenneth Kent as the 'fence.' 'You cannot', as Robert memorably wrote of the experience, 'win them all.'

Privately, too, things were going from bad to worse: Fairmans needed much more doing to it than had at first appeared, though, as was to become usual, Joan was in charge of all of that. More seriously, the Major was taken ill and died in the late spring. He and Robert had not been close since the latter's marriage, and his passion for living on the constant borderline of bankruptcy had, at the last, virtually cut him off from the rest of his own and Daisy's family. But Robert's father had still been a considerable, if eccentric, force in his early life and his comparatively sudden death left Robert aware as never before of the passage of time and the changing of the generations, especially as it came within a week or two of the tidings that Joan was pregnant and he himself was to become a father.

'They were alike, Robert and the Major,' mused my Aunt Margaret several years later, 'in many curious ways. After a few hours in family company they would suddenly vanish, as if they couldn't bear being related to any of us for a moment longer. I think what they were both missing was the green baize – gamblers are always like that – but Robert was luckier than Father in that he at least had other interests, some of the time.'

After the collapse of the *Play With Fire* tour, Robert turned back to the cinema and, in a desperate attempt to make some quick money for what was soon to be his own family, he made three minor films in quick succession. All were in a sense wartime propaganda quickies: the first, which seems to have disappeared without trace, was poignantly entitled *This Was Paris*, and Robert played a fifth columnist; for the next, *The Big Blockade* ('a brave attempt to combine entertainment with instruction' – *The Times*), he played an evil Nazi officer in Will Hay's first drama; and in the third, *The Foreman Went to France*, with Tommy Trinder, he was a treacherous French mayor whose opening line, '*Je suis le maire d'Ivry*', used to reduce his more disloyal friends to paroxysms of mirth on account of his never very secure French accent. None of the films can be said to have done him much good and they were, in fact, in some danger of stereotyping him as the 'evil Nazi', a role from which such contemporaries and friends as Peter Bull and Francis L. Sullivan were never really to escape. But the three roles did stave off immediate bankruptcy and, as the latter two were made at Ealing Studios, it is tempting to wonder what would have happened if Robert had somehow managed to take them more seriously or stay around the studios a while longer. Could he have become one of those Ealing comedy regulars who over the next few years were to form a kind of repertory company for such classics as *Whisky Galore* or *The Titfield Thunderbolt*?

Probably not. Robert always had trouble fitting into companies not of his own making, and he never ceased to think of himself as first and foremost a stage actor, albeit one perfectly happy to film in the daytime on his way to Shaftesbury Avenue for the evening performance. And by the time the three films were complete and in the can, the miracle had happened: George S. Kaufman and Moss Hart had come back to him with the offer of the London run of *The Man Who Came to Dinner*, despite his earlier rejection of it on Broadway.

Nothing in Robert's stage career, not even the original *Oscar Wilde*, was really as important as that offer: from his opening line ('I may vomit'), Sheridan Whiteside is one of the gargantuan roles in mid-century American comedy and none the worse for having been fashioned so closely around the personality of Alexander Woollcott. Though these days almost totally forgotten on this side of the Atlantic and barely recalled in America, Woollcott was a giant of his time: in British terms, one would have to imagine a curious amalgam of Malcolm Muggeridge, Gilbert Harding and Godfrey Winn to have some idea of how influential he was in American journalism and broadcasting during the 1930s. Essentially, Woollcott was the man who invented books as a branch of show business; a literary huckster several decades ahead of his time, Aleck, had he lived, would have been one of the first great masters of the television talk show, the author tour and the bookshop signing session. A prolific critic, columnist and guest lecturer, he saw himself as America's chief cultural guide and guru, leading an often recalcitrant general public on to the highways and byways of theatre, music and publishing via a wealth of gossipy anecdotage. But, precisely because his favourite homes were in magazines, newspapers and radio stations, he has left remarkably little behind except on the shelves of second-hand bookshops, where anthologies of his magazine articles can occasionally be found.

Although a wealth of topical references make the play almost unrevivable today, his great monument remains *The Man Who Came to Dinner*. Kaufman and Hart, among his closest friends, simply imagined what would happen if he inadvertently broke a leg and had to billet himself upon an unsuspecting mid-western family for Christmas. Within days their tranquil home has been filled with flocks of nuns, Harpo Marx, Gertrude Lawrence, Noël Coward (or close approximations thereof), as well as several radio engineers intent on broadcasting his seasonal message to the nation. The result is a manic farce celebrating both the showman and the charlatan in Woollcott.

After Robert initially turned down the role for Broadway, it had gone as did the movie to the American actor Monty Woolley and then to Woollcott himself, who had played it not entirely successfully (since he was never an actor, except in real life) on the road. Now, however, he was generous enough to cable Robert from New York – 'At last I am being played by a fine actor' – and rehearsals started in an aura of transatlantic confidence.

Around Robert, the director Marcel Varnel had assembled a strong cast headed by Coral Browne, who had been with him in *The Great Romancer* four years earlier and was at this time living with their impresario, Firth Shephard; as she memorably remarked to Robert, when once backstage he enquired after her fortunes, 'Firth is my shepherd, I shall not want, though he maketh me to lie down in some very strange places.'

After a brief try-out tour in Birmingham and Manchester, from where advance reviews were already enthusiastic, *The Man Who Came to Dinner* opened at the Savoy Theatre on 4 December 1941. I was born a few hours after the curtain came down that night, which, as Robert noted, was an ideal arrangement: 'It made the first night seem comparatively unimportant at the time, but memorable ever afterwards, at least to us.' It was decided that I should be christened Sheridan after the character, though Joan always had her doubts: 'In Gladys's theatre days,' she noted, 'One always named dogs and other pets after stage characters, but never actual children.'

But *The Man Who Came to Dinner* gave Robert something more than a son: it gave him his first huge commercial and critical success. Until this point, despite Oscar Wilde, Alexandre Dumas, Shaw's Undershaft and an Oscar nomination for Louis XVI, he had never quite managed to fix himself in the imagination of the wider public. When he married my mother a year or so earlier, to his chagrin the headlines had all read 'Gladys Cooper's Daughter Marries Actor'. Two years at the Savoy as Woollcott in *The Man Who Came to Dinner* were to change all that, especially as ecstatic notices coincided with those he was receiving for the film of *Major Barbara*. By the time Woollcott came to London early in 1942 to report on the Blitz and to see himself on stage, 'his' play was the hottest ticket in town and had set up a residency for Robert at the Savoy Theatre which was to last through 1943. As for Woollcott, he generously agreed to become my godfather, although, alas, I never met him. Early in 1943, with the play still running to capacity on both sides of the Atlantic, he went into a New York grocery store, ordered a tin of wartime biscuits to be sent to me in Berkshire and then proceeded to his radio studio, where he collapsed and died on the air. He was two weeks away from his fifty-sixth birthday and the most famous pundit in all America.

During the run of the play, Robert went back to the screen for another

The Man Who Came to Dinner: as Sheridan Whiteside

of the many historical costume dramas of the time: he played the wily politician Charles James Fox to Robert Donat's *Young Mr Pitt*, stealing several of Donat's notices and consolidating a reputation for playing real-life historical figures of a certain weight and majesty.

But when he was not filming, the play was really his life; every day he would bicycle from Fairmans to Wargrave station, petrol for a car being strictly rationed, catch the London train, do the show and then hurry back to Paddington for the last train home, before bicycling back up the hill to the house which my mother had already made our home forever. Even when all of us, their children, grew up and married, and made homes of our own all around the world, if anyone ever talked about 'going home', it usually meant to Fairmans.

By now Robert was the talk of the town: gossip columns reported that he would next play Mr Churchill in a film of the great man's life, that he would star in *Hatter's Castle* (the role there went to Robert Newton), and that he would travel back to Hollywood to play the Dauphin in a film of *Saint Joan*, which was in fact not made until five years later and then with Jose Ferrer.

In the event, he continued perfectly happily at the Savoy as Sheridan Whiteside, ensuring only that, when Coral Browne left the cast, she was replaced by his new friend from *Play With Fire*, Ambrosine Phillpotts, who never forgave him for sometimes jamming the brakes on his wheelchair, thereby making it all but impossible for her to push him across the stage.

Robert's only other critic at this time seems to have been my old friend and colleague Dilys Powell, already film critic of the *Sunday Times*, who in her round up of the films of 1941–2 noted: 'It is extraordinary about Mr Morley: whatever historical personage he plays, from Louis XVI to Charles James Fox, all end up looking and sounding uncommonly like Robert Morley himself.' But then, as he always said himself, make-up was never really a part of his art.

It was around this time that Robert took up what became one of his lifelong hobbies – writing letters to the Editor of *The Times*, usually on fairly random topics. Occasionally he and his father-in-law, Buck, used to compete to see who could get the most pointless letter into print, though Robert did at least start with one of reasonable local interest, writing in January 1943 in support of the idea that theatres should, as already in New York, open on Sunday rather than Monday nights. Exactly fifty years later the topic is still being hotly debated in correspondence columns and in precisely the same terms.

As the run progressed, he also found time to return to the typewriter; the outcome was to be a play called *Staff Dance*, a fragile country-houseparty piece somewhere halfway between Frederick Lonsdale and William Douglas-Home. It concerns a housekeeper and butler who take over their employers' premises during a long absence abroad, only to be faced with their unexpected return and its consequent upstairs-downstairs confusions.

Before this could go into rehearsal, however, there was the tour of *The Man Who Came to Dinner* to consider: ENSA, the wartime services' organisation, had indicated to Robert that one of his contributions to the war effort could be providing army bases with their chance to see a hit West End comedy. All did not go well with early ENSA negotiations, though, especially when Robert saw what they were planning to offer him by way of a set. When he complained that it did not even have a carpet, there was an amazed reply from the ENSA official in charge: 'Good Lord', he said apologetically, 'even *Private Lives* gets a carpet.'

Worse was to follow: after several weeks on the road, or more particularly up and down the Welsh hills, a junior member of the company developed chicken-pox. Robert decided it was his duty to phone the station commander of their next venue and alert him to the possible danger of infection. 'Morley,' barked the commander down the Welsh telephone, 'there is a war on, lives are being lost every day, and you are telling me that you actors are so feeble that one little case of chicken-pox stops you playing?'

No, no, Robert meekly assured him, of course they would arrive and play as planned, which they duly did. When the local medical officer of health discovered that one entire army camp had been severely threatened by the possibility of rampant chicken-pox affecting all those who had been to see the play in a small Nissen hut, the *Man Who Came to Dinner* company was sent back to London in some ignominy and that was the end of their tour.

It was time to start thinking about *Staff Dance*: he had written it originally for Ambrosine who, to his deep indignation, but with characteristic critical acuity as it turned out, reckoned that it was not good enough to take her away from her young children even though it might not be for very long. Robert, therefore, looked around for alternative casting and eventually managed to entice Beatrice Lillie, who, as was her wont, tended somewhat to unbalance the rest of the evening.

Staff Dance has the rare distinction of being the only play ever to have been rehearsed in the mortuary of the London Clinic, where Robert happened to be recovering from a brief attack of jaundice; but it was, in other respects, unremarkable, unless one counts the day on the tour when the wardrobe mistress managed to locate a rare rationed tin of treacle and place it in her handbag only to have it leak over all the company's keys. Sadly nothing quite as hilarious as that happened during the play itself, and on the road it soon became clear to the producer, Binkie Beaumont of H. M. Tennent, that the production was not destined for the West End.

Robert himself played the butler opposite Bea, who was in a state of high nervous tension even by her own standards, having recently lost a beloved son in the war; on some nights it was doubtful whether she would appear at all, and Ambrosine Phillpotts loyally stood by the side of the stage in full costume and make-up in case of a sudden collapse. By the time they reached Manchester, however, it was the play which had collapsed. My mother, as was her custom, retired to bed after the performance, there to be joined by my father, Binkie and Bea for a conference of war which started out loftily enough, but ended with Bea screeching that, if they were not going in to the West End, she should at least be reimbursed for several handbags she had purchased on behalf of her stage character. All in all *Staff Dance* was not a success.

II

Prinny and Peace

1944–1947

Churchill came to see me in The First Gentleman *on* VE *Night, and at the curtain call I told the audience that 'the First Gentleman of Europe' was in the stalls. Winston told the theatre manager to thank me afterwards, 'But what,' I asked, 'did he say of my performance?' 'Nothing at all,' said the manager. It is important to remember that Churchill was first and foremost a statesman, not a diplomat.*

After the collapse of *Short Story*, Robert received his call-up papers, a five-shilling postal order and instructions to report to an army camp at Towyn in Wales, though what he was supposed to do when he got there was not divulged. In some panic, he rang his agent, Hayes Hunter. 'My God,' said Hunter, 'perhaps we are going to lose the war after all – they must be scraping the barrel at last. We shall have to see about another deferment.'

This fortunately arrived, complete with instructions to report instead to Totnes in Devon, where he was required by the husband-and-wife team of Herbert Wilcox and Anna Neagle to join them in a weird movie called *I Lived in Grosvenor Square*, later to be translated for American audiences as *A Yank in London*. The stars were Anna herself, Dean Jagger and Rex Harrison, with Robert (who had been Rex's father in the rather better *Major Barbara*) required to play his prospective grandfather in a highly implausible wig. Since Rex and Dean Jagger were also wearing hairpieces, and all three insisted on checking them in the mirror of the hotel bedroom near the location where my parents were staying, Joan said she felt as though she were living in a perpetual barber's shop.

81

The film was not a success, largely because of Wilcox's odd habit of bringing *The Times* on to the set every morning and having anything interesting from its front page incorporated immediately into that day's dialogue. The plot, such as it was, concerned an American soldier (Jagger) falling in love with the grand-daughter (Neagle) of a benevolent old Duke (Robert), while Rex stood around as her other beau. Miss Neagle, encouraged as always by Wilcox to play about thirty years below her true age, was no more unlikely than the rest of the casting, and the film critic of *Punch* took the view that 'there can have been no more painstaking contribution to Anglo-American Understanding; one can almost hear the heavy breathing of those trying to do Good Work for the War Effort. But there is nothing here that wasn't done better, less obviously, less artificially, less snobbishly and with far less apparent self-consciousness in *The Way to the Stars*.'

So much for *I Lived in Grosvenor Square*; by the time shooting in Devon ended, Robert had something rather better on offer. For several months he had been trying to rouse the interest of the impresario Henry Sherek in a play about the young George IV as Prince Regent. It was called *The First Gentleman* and had been written a couple of years earlier by Norman Ginsbury in the vague hope that it might appeal to Charles Laughton, Robert's regular nemesis. But Laughton was firmly settled in California, and Ginsbury had been living in the meantime on various British and Broadway options for the play, which had finally reverted to Henry Sherek, who at last decided to risk it in the spring of 1945.

Like Robert himself and the impresario Gilbert Miller, Sherek was another larger than life, operatic figure, much given to flamboyant backstage rows and compulsively addicted to games of poker in the dressing-room. He was, therefore, an ideal match for Robert, and much of author Norman Ginsbury's and director Norman Marshall's time was spent trying to keep these two great bears off each other's backs and out of each other's hair. As usual, Robert rewrote much of the script on tour, conveniently forgetting that Ginsbury had negotiated a tougher contract than was then usual for an author, one which allowed him to veto any changes to his dialogue or plot.

In construction *The First Gentleman* was a reasonably straightforward historical chronicle of the Prince Regent in middle age, seen around the Brighton Pavilion squabbling with his rebellious daughter Charlotte, for which role Wendy Hiller was cast, about her choice of a husband.

By the time Robert had reworked the piece, however, it had become a marathon tour-de-force for himself as yet another of history's gigantic,

The First Gentleman: as the Prince Regent

lovable misfits, but this was not quite the play its author had envisaged. Ginsbury, naturally slapped on an injunction, leaving Sherek with a dilemma: both Norman and Robert had script approval, and neither would open in London without the text they wanted. In the end a judge ruled in favour of the actor rather than the author, and *The First Gentleman* opened at the New Theatre in July 1945, initially only for a seven-week season during the summer break of the Olivier-Richardson Old Vic company, which was then in residence there.

The overnight reviews were, though, good enough to ensure a rapid transfer back to Robert's old home at the Savoy Theatre, where *The First Gentleman* lasted well over another year. Ivor Brown for the *Observer* later noted that 'Morley passes the first great test of a star, which is that he can play his hand in act one and then replay it in acts two and three without ever losing our interest', while Cecil Beaton, guesting as a critic on the *News Chronicle*, added: 'Whether hanging a necklace around his latest lady-love, drinking pink champagne, being jeered at by the populace or rouged in preparation for Victoria's christening, Mr Morley gives a performance of rare quality and style from the tip of his chestnut curls to the last button of his gourd-like waistcoat.'

It took a rather more dispassionate observer, the drama critic of *Time* magazine over on a London summer visit, to point up the apparent contradiction of a nation which had just returned a Labour Government by a landslide vote flocking to see a play in celebration of 'one of its most dissolute and luxury-loving monarchs, a bully, wit and sot'.

Settled contentedly back into the Savoy Theatre, which he always regarded as his true theatrical home, not least because of the convenience of its adjacent bedrooms for nights when he wished and could afford to stay in town, Robert began to form a kind of backstage salon. Peter Bull, who had returned from a hazardous war in the navy, Sewell Stokes, now a prison visitor within the probation service, Wendy Hiller's playwright husband Ronald Gow and Sherek would all gather in Robert's dressing-room between the shows on matinée days for poker or simply for a gossip about their lives, a tradition Robert was to maintain well into the 1960s.

It was during these sessions that Sherek would urge Robert to write another play of his own, not that he ever required much urging to get back to the typewriter, especially during the repetitious boredom of a long run. The play that vaguely began to take shape in his mind in 1946 would be built around yet another larger-than-life figure, this one drawn not from history or literature, but from the latterday world of international press tycoons. He was to be called Arnold Holt and, although he was to bear a certain resemblance to Lord Beaverbrook, the truth about Holt was simply that he was a media mogul slightly ahead of his time, a man who had willingly sacrificed his own private life and those of all around him, including wife and child, to the apparently greater good of making his fortune by fair means or foul.

Another regular visitor to the *First Gentleman* dressing-room at this time was the dramatist Noel Langley, whom Robert had first met in Hollywood, when Langley was scripting *The Wizard of Oz* and Robert was playing in *Marie Antoinette* nearly a decade earlier. It was with Langley over a weekend at Fairmans that Robert began to map out the drama they first called *My Son, Edward*. They worked in a small wooden hut which Robert had bought from a ready-made catalogue and constructed at the end of the garden, largely because he had read that this was what Shaw had done at his home at Ayot St Lawrence – and it certainly had not harmed his playwriting.

Originally Robert had no intention of playing Holt himself. He had decided to take *The First Gentleman* to America for Sherek and Gilbert Miller on what promised to be a lucrative Broadway and touring afterlife, and the money would be more than welcome as Joan had, on 10 June 1946, given birth to their second child: a daughter named Annabel. Born six weeks prematurely and so tiny that her leg was only the length of one of Robert's fingers, she had to be stored in an airing cupboard for safe keeping.

Years later Robert recalled: 'I'd had the idea for *Edward* at the back of my mind for some time, ever since I had seen my elder son in his bath one night and felt that extraordinary mixture of pride and humility a father feels when he tries to evaluate himself as a parent: a sensation, in my case, of smugness and apprehension. What I wanted to say in *Edward*, and what I think I never managed to say clearly, was that a child who could quote his father when he grew up was likely to be happier than one who couldn't. It was as simple as that.'

But, as the play turned out, we never get to meet Edward at all; Langley's influence on Robert's original and rather romantic idea was to case it within an elaborate plot involving big-business chicanery and the gradual disintegration of Holt's own domestic life, so that the more successful he becomes, the more his wife crumbles into alcoholism until finally he is left alone on stage talking to nobody but the audience. Nobody ever knows, wrote Clyde Fitch once, when they are constructing a play, whether or not they have woven in the golden thread; but somewhere in *Edward* was that golden thread, and Robert was able to spin it in the West End, on Broadway and all across Australia and New Zealand for the next four years of his and our lives. As actor and co-author, this was undoubtedly the play of his career and in a curious way it is a great tribute to him that nobody else, not even Spencer Tracy on film, has ever managed to make it work. Robert, as they used to say on movie posters, *was* Arnold Holt: the name above and below the title were both his, and in the role he was unforgettable.

Nevertheless, Robert only came to play it via a chapter of accidents. When the script was complete, he and Langley and Sherek sent it first to Robert Donat and then to Clive Brook, both of whom politely declined the leading role on the grounds that it was 'thoroughly unsympathetic', a theory Robert was later to disprove for several hundred worldwide performances. By then, in something of a quandary, it was decided to offer it to Ian Hunter, a capable leading man who had spent the last ten years filming in Hollywood. Over lunch the arrangements were finalised and it was not until Hunter departed from the restaurant that Robert realised his mistake: 'I have written this little play,' he said to Sherek, 'and now I have just cut its fucking neck.'

What Robert had recognised, suddenly and almost too late, was that Hunter lacked the charisma and bravado to carry off a role like that of Arnold Holt. 'I suppose', said Sherek wearily, 'this means you'll be playing the part yourself?' – an eventuality he had known for several months was inevitable. Hunter's contract was duly unscrambled, *The First Gentleman* brought to the end of a triumphant fifteen-month run seen by half a million people, and my parents repaired to the South of France for their first holiday since before the war.

Time then to find a director and a cast for *Edward*: their first choice, Norman Marshall, who had steered Robert through *The First Gentleman* without too many headlong clashes, proved unavailable and so instead they turned to a wayward but hugely talented young man, the scion of a wealthy Irish undertaking family called Peter Ashmore and perennially known as 'Pocket' on account of his diminutive stature; his daughter Catherine is today one of our most accomplished theatrical photographers.

Ashmore was an ex-actor who had triumphantly run the Oxford Play-house throughout the war and had recently achieved great London success with a revival of *The Master Builder* at the Arts Theatre. In the thick of the freezing winter of 1946–7 he drove himself down to Fairmans one evening to discuss the play with Robert, departing around midnight, only to return apologetically after my parents had retired to bed asking if he might borrow a torch as he had managed to drive his car into a snowdrift with a flat tyre. Robert handed him the torch and watched him trudge back through the snow: 'If he can get his car out of this,' he said to Joan, 'he'll be the man to get us out of trouble with *Edward*.'

In reality their troubles were only just beginning. For the crucial role of Evelyn, the wife who stands by Holt throughout his rise to power and glory, but is finally reduced to alcoholism by the twin deaths of their marriage and their unseen son, Robert and Peter cast Peggy Ashcroft in her first modern-dress part for many years, and one of her rare West End appearances. But Peggy and Robert were like players from two different planets; for her, after years at Stratford and the Old Vic, and with Gielgud's own company, the theatre was a temple of the arts. For Robert it was still somewhere halfway between a hotel and a casino, a pit-stop for pure pleasure.

It was not that they quarrelled much in rehearsal, and both were undoubt-edly fond of each other; at the very end of her life Peggy once said to me, 'Your father always seemed to be having so much fun in the theatre,' in tones still of utter amazement, as though fun was somehow sinful on those premises. In all fairness, she was also not being allowed to work on a level playing-field: *Edward* was originally a huge and unwieldy affair, running to more than three and a half hours, in which the ambitions of Robert (to write a play about the mystic nature of parenthood) and Noel Langley (to write a chronicle of power politics) seemed at first in very real danger of tearing the whole project apart at the seams. Robert's solution to this in rehearsal was, as ever, improvisational and faintly journalistic: he would rewrite or rip whole scenes out of the script overnight, leaving Peggy, accustomed as she was to the more sacred texts of Shakespeare, flabbergasted at his rough-and-ready methods and unable to comprehend how they would work on the night, as a result of which they very nearly did not. Shortly before the company was due to depart for Leeds and the opening of the play on tour, Peggy announced that, on reflection, she had made a terrible mistake in accepting the role and would really be better off leaving the cast.

Robert already had the ever-faithful Ambrosine Phillpotts standing by in the event of such an emergency, but decided that Peggy's contribution to his play would be invaluable if he could keep her in it, at least until they opened on the road. He therefore equipped himself with a huge and unsuitable pot plant, repaired to the house she was sharing in Hampstead with her third husband, the barrister Jeremy Hutchinson, and proceeded to lecture Peggy severely on the folly of her ways. If she left the production now, he told her with no circumstantial evidence whatsoever, she would never work again: it would be a failure of nerve, an admission of defeat which would be the end of her career altogether.

Peggy returned to the show, and they opened in Leeds early in April 1947. The first performance, to the utter horror of Sherek, who was standing in the wings, still ran over three and a half hours at a time when commercial plays seldom went much over two. 'Good Lord,' said Robert, feigning utter amazement, 'this must be the longest performance I have ever given.'

Drastic on-the-road surgery was called for, and *Edward* was cut by almost an hour. Nevertheless, by immediate postwar commercial theatre standards, it remained a play of substantial range, scope and ambition: three acts, ten scenes, set between 1919 and 1947 for a cast of fourteen. It was, in short, a rare Shaftesbury Avenue epic and also, in its own way, a modern morality tale of considerable dramatic power: *Edward, My Son* was the play of Robert's career – it established him as an actor-author of the first dramatic rank.

12

My Name is Holt, Arnold Holt

1947–1948

Well, Ladies and Gentlemen, that's how it all happened, more or less. I wonder what you would have done if you'd been me on that foggy February morning . . . would you have gone on, or would you have turned back? I know what I did. Well, that's all, Ladies and Gentlemen. Look after yourselves. The way things are in this world, nobody else will.

As the curtain fell on the first night of *Edward, My Son* at what was then His Majesty's Theatre, on 30 May 1947, four days after Robert's thirty-ninth birthday, the critics were by no means convinced of its success: 'Not so much well written as well remembered from other and better plays', noted the *Daily Telegraph* icily, and as late as the second and third night Robert was still tinkering with his speeches to the audience, which were not working even after one of the longest dress-rehearsals in history. At about two on that particular morning, with the second act still in progress, Henry Sherek had been surprised to find Robert beside him in the stalls with his hat and coat on. 'What on earth are you doing?' demanded Sherek. 'Going home,' said Robert, 'some of us have got a first night tomorrow.'

Luckily the Sunday critics came on the second and third nights, by which time Robert had finally got the whole piece into shape, and it was Harold Hobson, newly arrived on the *Sunday Times*, who wrote the review they had dreamed of:

The audience at His Majesty's has one of the most pleasing experiences in the world – that of seeing a round peg driven, with superb assurance and complete success, into a hole as circular as Giotto himself could draw ... Mr Morley is no delicate miniaturist: he has no truck with the half-tone or the subtle gradation. His stock in trade is the ten-league canvas and brushes of comets' hair; when you go to see Mr Morley act in this play, leave your telescopes at home; even if you sit in the back row of the dress circle, you won't need them ... his play is sentimental, it romanticises, its political allusions are surprisingly maladroit, but it is intensely theatrical, and where should one be theatrical if not in a theatre?

By Monday, box-office queues had started to form along the Haymarket and they were to continue for almost two years. Within weeks of opening night, Robert had sold the film rights to MGM for £45,000 (more than £500,000 by modern comparison) and could for the first time put some money in the bank; less than ten years earlier he had received a mere £3 per week for the original London performances of *Oscar Wilde*.

After a few months *Edward* moved to the Lyric in Shaftesbury Avenue, where the cast began to take on family connections: Joan's half-sister, Sally Cooper, Gladys's daughter by her second husband, Neville Pearson, joined the company to play the minor role of Edward's fiancée in the last act, and her association with the play was to continue many years later in America, where on television she played opposite Robert as Holt's mistress.

That role was created for London and New York by actress Leueen MacGrath, then about to marry the great Broadway playwright and director George S. Kaufman, whom Robert would occasionally find standing lugubriously in the wings, whether lovelorn for Leueen or furious that here was one of the few major contemporary hits in which he had not had a hand.

Apart from Peggy Ashcroft and Leueen as the two women in Holt's life, Robert had been wise enough to surround himself with some of the best character actors in the land: John Robinson, as the faithful family doctor hopelessly in love with Lady Holt; D. A. Clarke-Smith as the irascible headmaster, whose school Holt buys up in order to avoid the expulsion of his errant son; James Cairncross as his personal assistant; and Richard Caldicot as the business partner he double-crosses and drives into prison: 'You can put that ruler away now, Holt; you have never drawn a straight line in your life.'

Edward was certainly melodramatic at times, but it was also in the best sense a rattling good yarn and one, in my far from impartial view, long overdue for revival, though it would need a player of Albert Finney's stature and quality to recapture its original vibrant theatricality and emotional intensity.

Clearly it was also an immediate candidate for Broadway, and plans were made to open there under the joint management of Sherek and Miller at the start of the 1948 season, by which time the show could be recast for London, where business was showing no signs of slackening. In the meantime MGM despatched director George Cukor, and Spencer Tracy and Deborah Kerr (then newly arrived in Hollywood) to start immediate work on the film version.

Robert was surprised and more than a mite hurt not to be invited to recreate Holt on screen, especially by MGM, for whom he had won his Oscar nomination in *Marie Antoinette* ten years earlier. But, recognising that Tracy was an infinitely bigger and better movie name, as well as being a Metro contract player, he gave in gracefully and continued with the stage version, knowing he was protected by a contract clause which meant that the film could not be released until the end of his Broadway run.

The truth about the film of *Edward* is that it was not very bad, not very good, not really very anything. Despite the fact that Cukor had already given Tracy some of his greatest hits with Katharine Hepburn (*Woman of the Year*, *State of the Union*), in this film the two men seemed lost without her, and Donald Ogden Stewart's main contribution as screenwriter was to change the name of Arnold Holt to that of Arnold Bolt for no apparent reason. Also, under the then stringent American movie censorship laws, he had to send Holt/Bolt to prison at the final fade-out, thereby considerably weakening a faintly ironic end.

It was Tracy who first realised how far they had got it wrong; although staying close by at the Savoy Hotel for the shooting, he was under strict instructions from Cukor not to go and see the stage version; when the shooting was over, however, on his last night in England before catching the boat back to America, Tracy decided to visit the theatre. After the show there was a knock on Robert's dressing-room door. 'I am Spencer Tracy, Mr Morley,' said a familiar, bear-like figure, 'and I fear I have just made the most terrible mess of your fine script. Nobody ever told me that you were playing it for comedy as well as drama.'

Robert's eyes were now firmly set on Broadway and it was agreed that Peggy Ashcroft would go over to New York with him to open the show there, with Ian Hunter (the original choice for Holt) playing the doctor, a role he had already undertaken for the Cukor film. In London the run was to continue with John Clements replacing Robert as Holt and with his former Perranporth leading lady Pauline Letts stepping into the role of Evelyn.

It was still only midsummer, though, and there was no need to begin rehearsing for Broadway until the start of the autumn season in a couple of months. Meanwhile my parents decided it was high time that their two children should be introduced to their grandmother, Gladys Cooper, in Hollywood. She had been resident there since 1939, when she had gone out with her third and last husband, Philip Merivale, to make the film of *Rebecca*, in which she was cast as Laurence Olivier's sister. Gladys had fallen instantly in love with Californian life and sunshine. They had both managed to obtain character-acting contracts with MGM and had bought a modest house in Pacific Palisades.

At first times were certainly not easy; for Gladys, in particular – who had been one of the first picture-postcard beauties of the First World War, who had run the Playhouse Theatre early in the 1920s and who had been a considerable West End stage star for the best part of thirty years – relegation to small character parts while stars like Bette Davis were above the title in *The Letter* (originally a play written by Maugham for Gladys) was not entirely what she had in mind. But she survived, as she always had, graduating to better and better MGM roles, and indeed to an Oscar nomination for *Now, Voyager* (1942).

Philip, too, began to get distinguished work in Orson Welles's *The Stranger* and opposite Rosalind Russell in *Sister Carrie*, but his Hollywood recognition had, sadly, come too late; in March 1946, a few months before his sixtieth birthday, he died of a heart ailment in the Good Samaritan Hospital in Los Angeles. Though she would seldom talk about it afterwards, there is no doubt that the loss of Phil after only nine years of marriage was the greatest sadness of Gladys's long life; she remained his widow for another quarter of a century, until her own death at eighty-two.

All the more reason, therefore, in the summer of 1948 for us to go and remind Gladys that she had another family. Her younger daughter, Sally, and her wayward, beloved, disturbed son John had been much with her in the immediate aftermath of Phil's death, but now we too could be there in the Santa Monica sunshine, a plan I inadvertently ruined by developing a severe case of chicken-pox shortly before we were due to depart from Fairmans. My mother thought quickly: given the incubation period, my sister would start showing her spots in about three weeks' time and we would then be forbidden to travel for a couple of months, at which point New York would be looming. But, if Annabel and a nanny could be flown directly to Los Angeles before her spots started to come through, then Ma and Pa and I could catch the *Queen Elizabeth* only one sailing later than planned, and the summer could still be saved.

Accordingly my parents and I set sail for the New World sometime in June, a transatlantic crossing I seem to remember we shared with Carol Reed and Graham Greene, who were going out to organise the American screenings of what would become their classic, *The Third Man*. If there were anything Graham Greene hated more than children, it was children's games; spotting immediately this chink in his armour, Robert had him for five days organising deck-tennis for several of us under-tens. I have never seen a man so unhappy in mid-ocean, and things did not improve when we landed: Greene had somehow managed to mislay his passport and was summarily sent to Ellis Island with other undesirables until some proof of the great novelist's identity could be established to the satisfaction of the immigration authorities. My first and abiding memory of the United States, apart from the usual dawn glimpse of the Statue of Liberty through the mists of the harbour, is of Graham Greene being led away while my father unreassuringly promised to send him food parcels and several more small children to haunt his incarceration.

Then, for us at least, it was a night at the Waldorf-Astoria and the unimaginable luxury of unrationed food, notably bananas which, like many wartime British children, I had to have carefully explained to me for the first time. The following morning we hastened to Grand Central Station and caught the *Super Chief*, a magnificent train with an all-glass observation car at the rear which took five days and five nights to cross America in the most wondrous journey I have ever experienced.

In those days there was one major stop in Chicago, where, as I recall, the gauge changed and some hours had to be spent. MGM thoughtfully provided a resident minder (the only reason, Katharine Hepburn once told me, that she had ever signed on for a twenty-year contract with that, rather than any other, Hollywood studio) who, having sorted out the baggage, then took his guests on a short tour of the city, before it was time to re-board and travel on across the Rockies. I arrived breathless with excitement; not so all the other passengers. Deborah Kerr, then newly signed to a studio contract at MGM, had sent for her children and nanny from London and was on the platform to meet them. 'Well, Nanny,' she enquired as they disembarked, 'what did you think of it?' 'It, Madam?' 'Well, yes, you know, the Grand Canyon, the Rockies, the Mid-West ... ' 'Ah, Madam,' replied Nanny, 'you must mean America. We did not care for it.'

We *did*, however. Gladys had by this time built herself an enchanting poolside cottage in the garden of 750 Napoli Drive and had moved into that, leaving us to invade the larger house she had originally bought with Phil. We arrived at a moment of high local drama: Rex Harrison had been having an affair with Carole Landis, who had recently taken her own life in apparent despair at his refusal to leave Lilli Palmer and marry her; and another old friend, the English actor Roland Culver, who had also been staying with

Gladys, was the one deputed to hide Carole's last cache of love letters and generally try to ensure Rex did not end up with a body in his bedroom and a career in total ruins. They managed it, but only just; Rex departed rapidly for Broadway and a play about Henry VIII, allowing a few years to elapse before successfully resuming his Hollywood life with other partners, yet another of whom (Rachel Roberts) was later also to take her life in that city on one of his *My Fair Lady* first nights.

But, by the time we came off the train, life was returning to comparative calm around Napoli Drive. Gladys would head off to work at MGM each morning, often unsure which film she was making, but certain that it would only require a few days as Gregory Peck's mother or the faithful old housekeeper in yet another literary classic. We lay around the pool, unable to believe the weather or our luck at having landed just this side of paradise, if not actually in it, and Robert, with no work to do until the autumn, began to forge a firm and deeply loving relationship with the mother-in-law he was only beginning to get to know:

To start life as a beauty on a picture postcard and end it as a Dame of the British Empire . . . the whole story of her success, from her first appearance in 1905 in *Bluebell in Fairyland*, has an element of fairyland make-believe . . . but she never discussed past triumphs or disasters, and, if you ever asked her about acting, all she would say was that she had learnt it from Charles Hawtrey . . . She could be very sharp at times, was no good at feeling sorry for people, perhaps because she had never felt sorry for herself. If you were in trouble, you got out of it, with her help of course, but in the end it was all up to you, just as her life had been all up to her. If you got ill, you got better. She was, in her way, something of a health fiend: she never ate much and always worshipped the sun. When we were with her, that first summer in California, she would come back from the studios at dusk and start cooking our dinner, and then, when everything was in hand on the barbecue which she seemed more or less to have invented, in the open air beneath her beloved orange trees, she would disappear for her evening swim. Ten minutes later she would be back, and five minutes later after that she would reappear in the sort of shift dress she always wore, gold bangles on her arms, her hair and make-up immaculate, to mix a final round of daiquiries and take the lamb off the spit. How is it done, I used to ask myself, how can she be so elegant? If she was vain about anything, it was her cooking. Two things you were never allowed to criticise with Gladys were her driving and her marmalade, both of which I felt privately left a good deal to chance. But about everything else, she was always eminently reasonable. How good an actress she thought herself to be, how seriously she took her profession, I was never sure. She acted, like she did everything else, utterly naturally. But of one thing I am sure: she was immensely proud of the affection and gratitude of her public. She answered every letter, acknowledged every compliment, and, when she came home to Henley, no day was ever too wet or cold for her to pause wherever she was and have a chat with some faithful patron who wished to compliment her on some past performance on stage or screen, or just on being Gladys Cooper.

By this time Robert had fallen so totally under Gladys's spell that he and playwright Ronald Gow had started to think of writing a play which might tempt her back to London.

By no means everyone can write a play for his mother-in-law and, even if they could, it wouldn't do them any good. You cannot get rid of a mother-in-law simply by writing her a play and telling her to go away and act it. The average mother-in-law can't act, and what's more, won't . . . Better by far give her something to eat this Christmas, not something to act. My case is, however, rather different: my mother-in-law acts to eat, that is when she remembers to do either . . . You might think, therefore, that Gladys will be impatiently awaiting my script when it comes back from the typist in its smart, stiff cover with the little starry dots around the title; but you would, of course, be wrong. Gladys will read it, or some of it, as soon as it arrives, and then probably put it aside for a month or two, and go back to her garden. But one morning, sooner or later, she will come indoors from those impossible flower beds and, putting on her huge horn-rimmed glasses, she will sit down on her porch overlooking the Santa Monica golf course and start reading a play. Something, perhaps a dragonfly, or the scent of a flower, or even the bark of a dog, has reminded her that it's time to be off. This is the time when I trust my play will be on top of her pile (surely nepotism must count for something), for Gladys is apt to choose a play as she chooses a plane – casually, and for the same reason: a desire to go places. It may be to New York to see her son, or London to see her daughter, or Hawaii just to see Hawaii. On these occasions, she travels on the first available flight with the first available play. As a rule, the plane proves the more reliable vehicle.

13

*Edward Goes
on the Road*

1948–1949

*We used to drive for miles, always expecting that just around the next corner there
would be something fascinating to look at, and of course there never was; that is the
whole charm of Australia.*

After that magic Hollywood summer with Gladys, when Garbo once came
to tea and Dietrich for a drink, and both seemed obsessed with the wash-
ing-up, it was time to head back East to the comparative reality of New York
and Robert's return to Broadway for the first (and, as it turned out, only)
time since his debut there in *Oscar Wilde* a decade earlier. As well as Peggy
Ashcroft, Leueen MacGrath had come over from London to rejoin the
production, but, apart from them, there was a large new cast for Peter
Ashmore to rehearse and, for Robert, the resumption of amicable hostilities
with his two gargantuan managers, Gilbert Miller and Henry Sherek, who, at
close quarters for the first time, seemed to cancel each other out like evenly
matched Sumo wrestlers, leaving Robert unharmed in their midst to score
most of the points he needed.

Robert was still immensely proud of *Edward*: of having written it, acted in
it and turned it into a huge success. It had worked beyond his wildest dreams
in London and somehow, as he approached his forties, he knew, not with
regret, that as a dramatist and perhaps also as an actor he was unlikely to do
anything better. But even that did not guarantee him a Broadway success;
many were the long-running London hits which had already come to rapid
grief in New York and, of course, *vice versa*. Indeed both theatrical capitals

seemed then, as now, to delight in establishing their differences as well as their similarities of taste, and a rocky try-out in New Haven, as the new and old casts learned to adapt to each other, did not fill anyone with much confidence.

The first night at the Martin Beck Theatre on Broadway on 30 September 1948 went like magic, however, Brooks Atkinson in the following morning's *New York Times* declared:

As a writer, Morley thinks like an actor: he gives you the surface of characters, but what the play lacks in depth and substance he supplies out of the magnificence of his acting ... He is an actor in the grand manner: imposing and deliberate, with a broad sweep to his style of expression. But on the big surfaces he can give you some exquisitely neat details, for he is also witty and droll, a master of satiric inflections. There is something warm and informal about his grandiloquence: without the constant glitter of intelligence, this style of acting might become intolerable; but with the discipline of intelligence, it is downright superb.

Other critics were not far behind, with Wolcott Gibbs for the *New Yorker* hailing 'a matchless villain' and only George Jean Nathan noting irritably that 'such shameless box-office hokum has not been seen hereabouts since they fastened a plastic tail to an out-of-work chorus girl and sold her to the Atlantic City boardwalk yokels as a mermaid at fifty cents admission'.

Others were, though, more impressed, and so Robert, my mother, my sister and I settled gladly enough for the fruits of his victory: winter in a Park Avenue apartment, where for Christmas I was given an electric train set so enormous that it could run from room to room. My sister still being too young for school, I was sent to the Central, about which all I can recall is befriending another actor's eight-year-old son, who also grew up to be a drama critic and is now happily employed as such by the *New Yorker*, John Lahr. In remarkably parallel lives across half a century, we also managed to publish our first biographies (mine a life of Noël Coward, his a marvellous account of his 'Cowardly Lion' father, Bert) in this country and America on the same day in 1969.

During this New York season Robert also began performing several live Sunday night radio dramas for such sponsors as Lux, whose custom it was to hire current Broadway performers and drop them into roles, and frequently entire plays, of remarkable unsuitability, which they would then read into the microphone, often as if they had never seen the words before in their lives, largely because rehearsals were usually confined to the afternoon of the actual transmission.

Robert also began to write articles for the *New York Times* on a variety of topics from restaurants to travel, a habit he would continue for the rest of his life for whichever publication would commission him. Privately, though, he was already admitting that, for him, some of the magical lustre he had found in New York on his first visit with *Oscar Wilde* was wearing off:

> I suppose I should have been more prepared for the changes I found there after the war: the glittering white walls of the skyscrapers had dulled a little, and their confidence seemed, like ours, to have somewhat evaporated . . . It wasn't only the skyscrapers; I missed enormously the radio voice of Roosevelt, and the friendliness he engendered . . . Advertisements that had once amused me in *Time* and the *New Yorker* no longer did so, because too many young Americans seemed to be taking them seriously. I heard now, for the first time, the full horror of the singing commercial: I, who had never stopped railing at home about the old-fashioned nature of the BBC, realised that as usual I was wrong, and by the time we got to Easter I was eager to move on.

Specifically to Australia, where Robert, Gilbert and Henry had decided *Edward* would be given his third childhood, still unseen.

George Sanders, it was announced, would take over in the Broadway run, though in the event it was Dennis King who stepped into Robert's ample shoes, playing opposite Adrianne Allen, who in turn had replaced Peggy Ashcroft. George had been called away unexpectedly to marry Zsa Zsa Gabor, a still more dramatic role.

Robert's plan was to nip back to England for a month or so around Easter, mainly to see how his elderly mother had settled into her final home, a flat in a manor house in Wargrave, a mile or two from Fairmans. She was coping well enough, he discovered, especially as his sister Margaret and her two daughters had, after a rather tricky divorce, taken up residence in Fairmans so as to be near Daisy and also to supervise the extension which was at last being built on to the cottage.

The rest of us went back to Gladys in California as soon as the spring term was over in New York. Robert soon joined us there, having declined an offer from John Huston to go to Rome to play Nero in *Quo Vadis*, an aborted film project which was finally made three years later with Peter Ustinov in the role. While he was still in London, however, safely away from Joan's potential disapproval, Robert did something which was to condition his spare time for the rest of his life: he bought his first race horse, a temperamental colt which he insisted on calling The Gloomy Sentry after the private detective sent by Lady Holt to shadow him and his mistress in *Edward, My Son*: 'There he stands, getting very wet. The gloomy sentry: but I suppose in a way he's the winner. Let's give him three cheers.'

The Gloomy Sentry, like most of the other half-dozen horses Robert was to buy and train near Newbury in the course of four decades as an owner, rarely came home a winner, and some of them never did. But the delight he always found on a race course was second to none and, when Robert died, his devoted daughter-in-law Margaret arranged for his first proper memorial: a plaque on a bench beneath a tree at Windsor race course, which had been his spiritual home. Just as I always think of Pa first of all backstage in a theatre, Margaret and our children – his grandchildren – all recall him best at the races, leading them on to victory or often defeat at the Tote following a very good lunch.

On the way back to join us in California, Robert stopped over in New York for what was to have been his first television appearance, a live telecast of *Edward, My Son*, which was extensively and expensively rehearsed, but then abruptly abandoned when MGM threatened to slap in a writ on the grounds that it could damage the box-office takings of their recently released Spencer Tracy film. Not entirely regretfully, Robert pocketed the money and hurried on to California in time for my sister's third birthday party and another summer beside Gladys's pool.

Despite his original success for MGM with *Marie Antoinette*, the studio seemed remarkably uninterested in his postwar return and made no offers of any kind, although his mother-in-law was a firm fixture of their payroll and they can hardly have failed to notice him popping into the studio with her for the occasional lunch. But Robert was unperturbed; he had Australia and *Edward* again to look forward to, and was still gravely doubtful about whether he wanted a career in films. Nevertheless he did fancy California and seriously thought of trying to stay there to make his living as a writer by the pool. Then he thought better of it, and took us all off to Sydney.

In those days, to get there from California, one took a flying-boat first to Hawaii. These were amazing devices, complete with full-length beds along the sides of the passenger cabin in which you tucked yourself for the night before awaking in time to see the flying-boat land on the water off Waikiki Beach. Gladys came with us that far for a brief holiday, and we had an idyllic time splashing about in the surf off the pink Royal Hawaiian Hotel; there was some kind of shipping strike at the time and so we seemed to have the sands almost entirely to ourselves. My father and I even ventured out in a catamaran, to the considerable hilarity of the local Hawaiians; we came back to find Annabel in floods of tears and had to reassure her that we had been in no real danger of disappearing beneath the waves. 'No, no,' she said, 'I was crying because they were all laughing at you.' One of the strongest divisions in our family has always been between those of us, like Gladys, my father and myself, who would always gladly settle for any kind of public attention, even gentle mockery, rather than none at all, and the others who have managed to get by without the terrible fear of anonymity which besets the more overtly theatrical among us.

Then it was on to Australia and to a love-hate relationship with that country which was to form a strong part of Robert's professional and private life for the next four decades. In time his daughter would marry and settle out there, his younger son would become an Australian theatrical manager, and he and my mother would pay annual new-year visits to Sydney, where Robert would either be doing a play or a regular series of Heinz television commercials. There were times during the 1980s when Robert had as many children and grandchildren in Australia as in England, and both he and my mother came to love the life out there.

All that started on this first trip down under in the summer of 1949; by then the original London and New York companies of *Edward, My Son* had long since gone their several ways, and the casting director Daphne Rye was on loan from H. M. Tennent in London to put together an Australian cast led by Ellis Irving as the doctor; his wife, Sophie Stewart, would be playing the Peggy Ashcroft role, with Robert the sole survivor of previous productions.

For a nation which has always taken history very slowly indeed, these were still the early postwar years, and Robert got into considerable press difficulties for good-natured mockery of what seemed to him early Victorian social habits in New South Wales: the way the entire nation would close at weekends, for instance, or restaurants shut regularly at 9 pm or bars at about 7. On the other hand, there was the climate, the racing and the beach, and an undoubted warmth in his reception. Starved of any kind of visiting theatre all throughout the war, Sydney was still only just recovering in 1949 from an epic tour by the Oliviers at the head of the Old Vic company. Internally, that tour had proved pretty disastrous, leading to Vivien Leigh's affair with Peter Finch and the first serious breakdown in her mental health; but outwardly it had been a public relations triumph of considerable brilliance, with Olivier giving his Richard III and the whole venture being solemnly and seriously billed as 'a reward' to Australia for its immaculate behaviour as one of the Allies during the Second World War. Britain had not as yet got around to sending out any actual postwar royalty, but it had at least sent them the Oliviers.

So it was on this tide of showbusiness goodwill that Robert arrived with a rather different kind of theatrical treat, one which non-classical Australian theatregoers already knew from his generally avuncular and comical press conferences they were going to enjoy more than the classical heights up which they had been dragged by the Oliviers. His management was to be J. C. Williamson, an organisation then in total charge of the Australian theatre and its touring circuits, and run by a formidable family of Tait brothers, irreverently known in the business there as Hesitate, Cogitate and Agitate. 'Gentlemen', said Robert, when they came to meet him at the harbour after the long voyage from Hawaii, 'I am told it is customary for English actors on tour out here to leave you in floods of tears. When I leave here, I promise it is you who will be in tears.'

And with that he set off on his usual round of battles over sets, costumes and budgets. The tour was to take in Sydney and Melbourne, before going on to Auckland, Wellington and Christchurch, in New Zealand; it was to last almost a year. In that time Robert also managed to make regular live Sunday night radio drama appearances, even reviving his prewar Old Vic *Pygmalion* opposite Diana Wynyard, who fortuitously happened to be on an Australian tour with Anthony Quayle and the contemporary Stratford company. But it was as a roving public figure that Robert began to make his greatest impression on the Australians: whereas other actors, out from England, would limit themselves to gracious public comments on their work or how thrilled they were to be on tour, Robert began cheerfully haranguing the Australians on their food, social habits, educational system, lack of a national theatre – more or less anything and everything that came into his head. In a grey, conformist time, he stood out like a beacon of overweight eccentricity and the Australians loved him for it from then onwards, welcoming him back to their shores time after time, apparently in the hope that he would soon say something to insult them, which of course he always did. It was an odd, cantankerous, but mutually loving relationship, and I always thought that, if my father were ever to die happy anywhere away from Fairmans, it would have to be in Las Vegas or somewhere in Australia, preferably near a good restaurant on the beach or at the races.

Relishing the battles with the Tait fraternity, Robert effectively became his own management. Gilbert Miller and Henry Sherek had been left far behind on the other side of the world, Sherek first of all presenting Robert with *Edward*'s Australian rights 'for the good of the Empire' and then denouncing his departure from the Broadway production as 'deeply unpatriotic'. Miller, on the other hand, had left Robert with one great parting gift: a young publicist called Morton Gottlieb, who had worked with Gertrude Lawrence and her husband, Richard Aldrich, at their summer theatre on Cape Cod, had graduated to Broadway and was later to make his name there several years later as the producer of Brian Friel's early plays and the hugely triumphant thriller *Sleuth* (one of many gold-mines which Robert peered briefly and then failed to clamber into quickly enough to prevent it falling into other hands).

At this time Robert, sensing that he was likely to need allies for fighting the Australians on their own territory, persuaded Mort to leave America and join him on the voyage and the tour as business manager.

Soon after their arrival, the Morley team was strengthened by the addition of the young, stage-struck son of a local doctor whom Robert was eventually to encourage to go to London, where he became one of the most distinguished directors in both the National and the commercial theatres. At this time Michael Blakemore was still in his early twenties; in a superb as yet unpublished memoir, he writes of the first appearance of Robert in his life:

> Morley had already declared war on all aspects of Australian sloth. He fought first with the stage staff, who had refused to do overtime at the dress rehearsal. They responded by sabotaging the first night: pieces of scenery arrived in place late, and standard lamps went on and off mysteriously in the course of the action. Morley, not in the least perturbed, ad-libbed where appropriate and on waves of applause the play sailed through to its final ovation. The reviews were excellent, but the business, especially in the light of the standing-room-only conditions he had just left behind him in New York, left much to be desired and for this he blamed an ossified and complacent management. His differences with them had begun in America, where they had asked him to sign their standard contract, of which not the least impertinent clause was one that forbade actors to keep drink in their dressing-rooms. He had taken a pen, crossed most of this out, and was now campaigning against their lackadaisical method of selling seats, which were not on sale at the theatre itself, but could only be obtained at a ticket agency some streets away. However, his most indignant complaint was about their lack of interest in any form of publicity.

Eager to escape the medical career to which his father had committed him, Blakemore offered himself as Robert's personal publicist and he was thus able to witness my father at close quarters for the rest of the tour; he was also kind enough to complete my elementary education in reading and writing, and on those few occasions in subsequent years when I have had occasion to review his productions unfavourably, Michael has been tolerant enough never to remind me that, had he not taught me how to write, I would not be in a position to attack him.

A dozen or so years older than me, Michael's observations on Robert at this time are considerably more acute than any other I have come across, and I am grateful to be allowed by him to continue quoting them here for the first time in print:

> Each evening before the show I had to report to Robert in his dressing-room. 'What's new?' he would invariably announce, barely looking up from the small magnifying mirror in which he did his make-up, and I would trot out something already prepared which I hoped would amuse him. Like all actors at that time, he believed in the full slap: sticks of Leichner blended together until the face came up a burnished tangerine, followed by rouge on the cheeks, blue on the eyelids, and the whole lot swamped with powder, which would then be reduced by scrubbing the face with a very soft brush. A cloud of talcum would sink to the floor like stage smoke. The effect was as startling as a totem pole, but highly effective from the front, where you could see those penetrating blue eyes from the very back of the theatre. During these preparations anyone who came into his dressing-room, and most would, was expected to be amusing. Robert had no time for shyness, which he considered a product of laziness and pride. If you didn't put up a fight on behalf of your own personality, he tormented you until you did, or worse, he just dropped you to the side like a dull magazine.
>
> The most alarming thing about him was his low boredom threshold, and few things were as discouraging as seeing those eyes glaze over in the middle of your sentence and that lively mind go wandering elsewhere ... but this was only one aspect of an abundant and recklessly generous personality, whom it amused to enlarge the pleasure in life of those who collected around him. He was then in his early forties, at the height of his fame as a performer and playwright, a prodigious earner and blessed in his private life. Resolve and talent accounted for part of this, but, as he often insisted, so did luck. Like a big winner at the race track, he wanted to spread some of that good fortune around, and did so by the handful ... Throughout the tour Morley was an indefatigable performer, and whatever the house or his own frame of mind, I never saw him give a slack or inconsistent showing. This professionalism was at odds with a provocative flippancy about the theatre in general. He liked to give the impression that

there were other and always more important things to do. In Sydney, for instance, he changed the day of the mid-week matinée so that he could enjoy the races. While approving of comedy, because it gave him and his audiences a good time, he pretended to baulk at dramatic scenes. 'Couldn't we get Freddie Valk in to do this bit?' he would ask in rehearsal, referring to the distinguished German-born actor who had just had a big success in London as Othello. Yet, in a radio broadcast before a studio audience, I once saw him give a performance as Crocker-Harris in Rattigan's *The Browning Version* which it would be hard to improve on. Because he was an actor through sheer force of personality, with only one voice and one shape at his disposal, his moments of emotional exposure had a kind of autobiographical authority about them. Areas of pain and longing, left behind somewhere in his youth, were unexpectedly on show, and the effect could be extraordinarily touching.

14

Brookery Nook

1949–1950

Rehearsals of The Little Hut under the direction of Peter Brook were not especially enjoyable; he had an exaggerated idea of the importance of the director, whose function was once accurately described by my friend Willy Hyde-White as to fetch one's script if one happened to have left it in the car.

As the *Edward* bandwagon started to roll across Australia and New Zealand, we settled contentedly into the touring life. In Sydney ('You might as well call a city Bert,' was one of Robert's more public utterances on that subject) my parents rented an enchanting house on the harbour at Point Piper, and gave a large firework party to celebrate the opening of *Edward* at His Majesty's. Wandering down to the harbour's edge during the festivities, Robert encountered an irate neighbour uncertain where the noise or indeed the pyrotechnics were coming from. 'Disgraceful disturbance of the peace,' roared the neighbour; Robert agreed with him courteously and promised to telephone the police, before returning hastily to his own party.

'Nobody really prepared me for Australia,' wrote Robert of this first mutually tentative encounter, 'and, what was worse, nobody had really prepared Australia for me.' He decorated both Mort Gottlieb and Michael Blakemore for gallantry after several encounters with the Tait brothers, who had taken to regarding Robert as some terrible English disease which could prove catching to their local backstage staff unless quarantined whenever possible. At one point, stung by his announcement that Sydney was 'just like Manchester with a harbour' and that its pubs and bars were 'Hogarthian in their squalor', the Williamson management thought it prudent to send an early warning announcement to their farther-flung theatres of his imminent arrival there; in the words of John Tait's memo:

> Morley is a very difficult man who finds fault with almost everyone in our organisation. He can even be rude to the man in the street. He is an outstanding actor and it is an equally outstanding play, but Morley has been so antagonistic to the stage manager that he has begged to be relieved from the New Zealand part of the tour; we are replacing him with his assistant, who can cope with temperamental artists and who doesn't get on Morley's nerves.

As for me, I spent a couple of reasonably enjoyable terms at Cranbrook, a boys' school in Sydney, where they tried without success to make me into a boxer or capable of swimming across one of the narrower bits of Sydney Harbour. I wish now that, like my almost exact contemporaries Clive James and Barry Humphries, I could claim to have been aware then of the greater lunacies of Australian suburban and educational life, but the truth was that for a nine-year-old out from England the miracle, as in California, was an apparently total absence of any rainfall. Almost all the snapshots taken of us at the time show my father and me up to our necks in the harbour like two generations of a hugely contented family of water buffalo.

Melbourne I vaguely recall being rather less fun; if Sydney was Manchester with a harbour, Melbourne in early 1950 was like Tunbridge Wells without the pulsating night life. Nothing much appeared to have happened there since the arrival of a few dozen British convicts some 200 years previously, and the same amazing lack of activity seemed to have overtaken the whole of New Zealand, which Robert proclaimed officially closed throughout his visit.

The locals there turned out to be sheep farmers rather than theatregoers, and by the time we reached Auckland an awful truth had to be faced: for the first time since his 'birth' in Leeds exactly three years earlier, *Edward* had started to lose money at the box-office. The time had come to call a halt and head for home and the new decade of the 1950s, but there was one great treat left, and it was for me. At the end of the play, of which Robert had given considerably more than 1,000 performances, there was a moment when, though the unseen Edward of the title has been killed in the war, the audience is made to believe they are about to catch a glimpse of his son, Arnold Holt's grandson, also christened Edward. At that moment, just before the final curtain, a large red balloon would come instead bouncing down the stairs, but for the farewell performance in Auckland I was allowed to come down with it.

Apart from the occasional charity matinée and television chat show, this was the only time I ever appeared on a stage with Pa, and I remember enjoying it immensely, especially the half-crown he solemnly paid me for the performance, my first professional earnings and also my last for about a decade.

Then it really was time to go home. Robert and Joan bade a fond farewell to the company and, of course, to Mort, who was returning to Broadway to resume his managerial career. Robert wrote a note to Michael Blakemore's father, encouraging him to let his son seek his fortune in the London theatre and promising, if so, 'to keep an eye on him – probably my blind one'.

We all set off for home, Annabel clutching her 'aspiring bottle', in which she had managed to collect a little gold dust while prospecting in the Australian hills. Our boat was the P & O liner *Stratheden*, which moved so slowly through the water that the Captain told Robert he fell into a deep depression whenever he looked over the side. By the time we reached Bombay, about half-way home, my parents decided they deserved a childless holiday by themselves, so, leaving us on board in the faithful care of Nancy Stubbs, who had accompanied us all through America, Australia and New Zealand, they set off overland through India, Egypt and Italy, before rejoining us back at Fairmans in the mid-summer of 1950.

Now forty-two, Robert's life was, in fact, precisely half spent and it was as though he sensed that this was a kind of mid-term break: *Edward* and the war were over, the century had also just reached its half and somehow, however incoherently, he recognised that it was time to make a fresh start back home after all his travels. First, though, there was India to see, and Egypt, and then Rome, where he and Graham Greene met up for the first time since the crossing to America two years earlier.

Rather flatteringly, the young Peter Brook, then only twenty-five, but already a Stratford and Covent Garden director of considerable reputation, flew out to Rome to show Robert the script of a long-running Parisian boulevard hit by André Roussin called *La Petite Hutte*, which Brook hoped he might agree to star in under his direction for the West End. Robert read a rough translation and found, to his amazement, that it would work for London without any need of his usual rewriting. 'What do you do,' he asked Felix Aylmer, who happened to be staying in the same Rome hotel shooting a film, 'when you get a script which doesn't need any rewriting?' Aylmer puffed thoughtfully on his pipe for a moment. 'Usually then', he said, 'I find it sufficient just to act it.'

This first Roman holiday was also the occasion of Robert's legendary (at least in our family) audience with His Holiness Pope Pius XII. Then, as now, it was not difficult to catch a glimpse of *Il Papa* if you hung around the Vatican on a Sunday morning in the tourist season, but it was possible to secure brief, semi-private audiences, and this both Brook and Aylmer had managed, kindly offering to take my parents along with them. All that happened, in the event, was that the Pope passed briefly through the room, pausing in distinctly royal fashion to have a momentary chat with each of the VIP guests. When he reached Robert, he asked, in immaculate English, where he had come from. Robert answered, 'Australia', and then, terrified lest His Holiness should take him for an Australian, hurried on to explain that he was, in fact, an actor from England, who had only been touring Australia with a play. 'I don't think it is possible to confuse a Pope', wrote Robert later, 'but on this occasion I did feel I had distinctly bored one.'

When my parents returned to the hotel, there was Graham Greene, who for some reason had been denied one of these semi-private VIP audiences and was, therefore, desperate to know what had happened. Robert took the swift decision that reality would on this occasion prove insufficient, especially as Greene, like all new Catholic converts, was, despite characteristic cynicism in most other matters, curiously susceptible to total belief where Catholicism was concerned. So Robert bought him a drink and told him the whole story: how His Holiness had immediately asked him to stay behind at the Vatican for a private lunch, at which he had displayed a wide knowledge of the British film industry and a particular interest in the career of Anna Neagle, after witnessing her stunning portrayal of Queen Victoria. With none of this did Greene appear to have the slightest crisis of faith or belief, and Robert stretched out the story to encompass His Holiness's good wishes for all future film projects, including those especially of Morley and Greene. Then, of course, he went too far. 'When the meal was over,' he continued, 'it did occur to me that perhaps we were outstaying our welcome, though I hesitated to suggest it, in case the custom was for His Holiness's guests to await some formal kind of dismissal. At last, however, I plucked up my courage to say that I felt we had already taken up too much of our host's valuable time, and that we should really be taking our leave, but he would have none of it. 'I was so much hoping', he said, 'that you'd be able to stay for tea, because my wife will be joining us then and she was very much looking forward to meeting you.'

Greene left the hotel bar without a word and would probably never have spoken to Robert again had it not been that several years later he gave a very classy performance in the first film version of Graham's *Loser Take All*.

Back in London from his Vatican rag, Robert had to think rather urgently about the future, especially as he was already in considerable trouble with the Inland Revenue. For the rest of what might, in many other ways, be considered to have been a reasonably charmed life, Robert was to be haunted by tax problems and they all started at this point with a major, damaging disagreement with the Inland Revenue which, though eventually resolved in his favour, was one the taxation authorities never forgot or forgave.

Briefly, it hinged upon an interpretation of what Robert had decided to do when going to American with *Edward, My Son* in 1947. He maintained, with absolute truth, that for a while he had decided to emigrate; England in the immediate aftermath of the war did not seem an especially attractive place to stay, he had the promise of a long Broadway run in *Edward* and the distinct possibility then of resuming his Hollywood career, and it might well have been that America was the place to make his family home, especially as Gladys was by then a widow firmly settled in California.

Soon after he arrived in New York, however, Robert had changed his mind; no matter how attractive America had seemed in the short term, he and Joan had rapidly reached the conclusion that it was not where they wished to spend the rest of their lives, nor bring up their family. Fairmans, which had briefly been put in the hands of estate agents, was taken off the market again and plans went ahead for the rebuilding under Aunt Margaret's supervision.

And that was the end of that, until Robert returned to England in the summer of 1950, whereupon the Inland Revenue slapped in a massive taxation bill for all the *Edward* money he had earned abroad, despite the fact that tax had already been paid on it in America and Australia. From Robert's point of view, there was no way he could pay the extra tax bills; from the Inland Revenue's point of view, if they allowed Robert's claim that he was, however briefly, an exile and therefore not liable to local tax, then every British actor with a job in America would claim similar dispensation by pretending to start an exile which they had every intention of rescinding once the job was over and they had dodged British tax. The only way the Inland Revenue could win would be to prove Robert a liar and to claim that he had never intended to take up residence in America. This he was not prepared to allow, either economically or morally, and an unholy war was declared between the two sides, which was to drag on for nearly five years and affect forever afterwards the unyielding severity with which the Revenue treated Robert's annual tax returns.

This was not the warmest of welcomes home, but at least we were back at the newly enlarged Fairmans and Robert already had his eyes firmly set on a return to the West End: soon it would be time to go into rehearsal with Peter Brook under the management of Robert's prewar *Staff Dance* impresario, Hugh Beaumont of H. M. Tennent, for *The Little Hut*.

Binkie had by then sent the French original of the play to Nancy Mitford, an inspired choice of translator since she was living in Paris and had already displayed in her novels a particular affinity for this type of elegant boulevard comedy. The plot, fragile as it was, concerned a triangular affair between wife, husband and lover, all of them marooned on a desert island and uncertain how best to determine sleeping arrangements within the two available huts. In the Roussin original the tale had been told through the eyes of the husband; for London, Nancy (who first called her version *Island Fling*) switched the focus to that of the wife, for which role the American actress Joan Tetzel was hired.

The actor chosen for the part of the lover was an even happier casting idea: David Tomlinson was then in his mid-thirties and had already established himself on stage and screen as a light comedian of considerable off-hand talent, in some ways akin to that of Ralph Lynn in the Aldwych farces. In certain respects David, like Wilfrid Hyde-White with whom Robert starred in his next Shaftesbury Avenue comedy *Hippo Dancing*, was a Laurel to my father's Hardy, but there was rather more to it than that. Though sadly all three men never appeared together as a trio, as had been achieved in earlier Ben Travers times by Tom Walls, Ralph Lynn and Robertson Hare, they too had a tremendous amount in common both on stage and off. Morley, Tomlinson and Hyde-White were actors of immaculate, underplayed comic timing who shared a deep distrust of directors and an absolute belief in the theatre as a form of postprandial entertainment. All were also far better and more versatile players than they were usually given credit for, and if I write of their only survivor, David Tomlinson, in the past tense it is simply because he has taken a far too early retirement.

All were gamblers of one kind or another, and all shared an instinctive, intuitive understanding of their audiences and the changing mood of the stage moment. This had surprisingly little to do with what had happened on the printed page of the script or even in rehearsal; within certain agreed limits, all were first-class improvisers and all could sense and take the temperature of an audience within seconds of reaching the stage. To watch them in action was an education for any incipient drama critic, for what they taught was the volatile craft of the performer on the wing and on the hoof, staying always just that crucial split-second ahead of their audience and sometimes indeed of their play.

The only other characters in *The Little Hut* were a native chieftain, played by Geoffrey Toone and understudied by a young Roger Moore, and a monkey, in which guise could generally be found either the choreographer Billy Chappell or, when he was unavailable, the production's assistant stage manager, Rosalind Chatto. Ros also took to cooking sensational meals in Robert's dressing-room between the shows on Saturday for the entire company, a Shaftesbury Avenue tradition she was to continue for the next decade before becoming Robert's loving agent and manager. Once the rehearsal period was over, these were some of the happiest times Robert ever spent in a theatre.

15

On the Avenue

1950–1951

It was during the run of The Little Hut *that our third child arrived, precisely on time and extremely composed. He was the only baby I ever saw who, on his very first morning, looked as if he had expected to be born. We called him Wilton, after my father.*

For Nancy Mitford, in one of her rare encounters with the theatre, there was a mixture of delight and bewilderment at *The Little Hut*; both Noël Coward and Emlyn Williams had been considered as possible translators, but, as Nancy wrote to her mother, she was the one who ended up with the prize assignment:

It's a terribly funny play about husband, wife and lover on a desert island . . . lover gets very low all alone in the little hut, while husband and wife sleep in the big one, so they insist on taking turns . . . then a handsome young negro appears, ties up both husband and lover by a trick, and indicates that he will only let them go if the wife will go into the hut with him, which she is only too pleased to do as he is very good-looking . . . 'Disgusting' I hear you say, but actually it's terribly funny and has run over three years here in Paris . . . I've skated over the worst indecencies, and Roussin, the author, is an utter love, but doesn't speak a word of English, so I've got away with altering it a great deal.

As for Robert, Nancy wrote to her sister Jessica in California: 'He's made for you. He is the only actor I have ever met who is a human being.'

Oliver Messel, a highly fashionable designer of the time and uncle to Lord Snowdon, had been hired by Binkie to create a desert island of unusual glamour and elegance, and Pierre Balmain had been hired to create Joan Tetzel's island rags, which he did to Robert's lasting admiration simply by dressing her in one of his most exquisite and expensive ballgowns and then going at it with a razor.

From the very outset, Robert and David got along wonderfully, not least because they discovered on the first day of rehearsal that both had been brought up in Folkestone, albeit ten years apart, and could therefore share fond memories of Canon Elliott in the pulpit and the massed bands along the Leas. Joan Tetzel, too, fitted in amiably enough and in later years Robert was prepared even grudgingly to admit that Peter Brook was the right director, with a strong Parisian sense (around this time he was also to direct Anouilh's *Ring Round the Moon* and, later, *Irma la Douce*). 'We didn't always get on', Robert recalled, 'but then sometimes it's a very good thing for a play not to have a mutual admiration society backstage.'

For his part, Brook found my father undisciplined and unprepared to take too many notes, but there was a wary admiration there too, as if both men recognised the other's usefulness to the project. They opened on the road in Edinburgh early in August 1950 and in Pa's usual pre-Shaftesbury Avenue trouble. A certain amount of this was caused by the set, which Messel had conceived as a baroque confection of butterflies, palm trees, breadfruit and huge exotic plants, around which the company had started to give huge exotic performances. The first night, again traditionally for Robert, ran about three hours in Edinburgh and there was the usual post-mortem in my parents' hotel bedroom at midnight, during which my mother managed to reduce an already distraught Peter Brook to tears by remarking that he had not even managed to get the stage floor cleaned, with the result that Robert's feet were making ghastly marks all over the sheets of their bed.

Things improved on the journey south, however, and *The Little Hut* opened successfully at the Lyric, Shaftesbury Avenue, on 23 August with even Nancy Mitford more or less reconciled to what she regarded with some justification as the lunatic ways of her actors. Having suffered through a long Edinburgh dress rehearsal, she failed to show up for the first performance there. When Robert rang her hotel room next morning to enquire what had happened to keep her away, she replied, 'Good Lord, I never thought you'd all be doing that thing two nights running – anyway I had a very important dinner engagement.'

With Joan Tetzel, David Tomlinson and (in monkey suit) William Chappell on Oliver Messel's set for *The Little Hut*, 1950.

The best of his stage partners: (above) David Tomlinson, and (below) with Wilfrid Hyde-White in *Hippo Dancing*, 1954.

The two Bogart/Huston movies: (above) with Katharine Hepburn in *The African Queen*, 1951, and (below) with Peter Lorre in *Beat the Devil*, 1953.

'The art of character acting is not to look like other people, but to assume other people look curiously like me.' As W. S. Gilbert in *The Story of Gilbert and Sullivan*, 1953; Mr Asano, *A Majority of One*, 1960; the Emperor of China, *Genghis Khan*, 1964; and as Hilary in Alan Bennett's *The Old Country*, in Australia, 1980.

Musical moments: rehearsing Harold Rome's *Fanny* at Drury Lane, 1956; and in the all-singing, all-dancing finale to Cliff Richard's first screen musical *The Young Ones*, 1961.

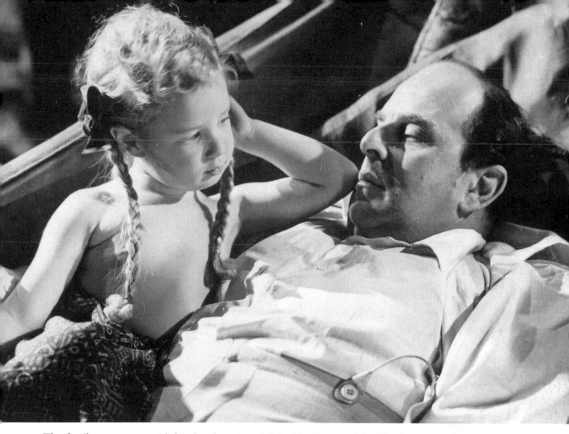

The family on screen: with his daughter Annabel in *The Outcast of the Islands*, 1951; and with his son Wilton in *Oscar Wilde*, 1960.

At home with his eldest grandchild, Hugo; a rare owner's victory on the racecourse; and by the pool with the *Sporting Life*.

Reviews in London were somewhat mixed, with the *News Chronicle* in high dudgeon: 'In the third act immorality is capped by snobbishness, and the curtain falls on downright vulgarity; I was embarrassed and so were many people around me; maybe the Censor needs a new pair of glasses.'

Even in these matters Robert's premières were acquiring traditions of their own: a rough time on the pre-London tour, severe cutting and rewriting on the way in, followed by mixed overnight notices, but then very much better Sundays, and a queue outside the box-office by about Monday morning formed as much by word of mouth as by anything in print. For the *Sunday Times* Jack Lambert saluted 'Morley's constant volcanic astonishment, palsied in dismay, and then copious in rediscovered joy; here is brimming abundance, quick with mischief and delight.' Moss Hart, on a Shaftesbury Avenue summer tour for the *New York Times*, thought Robert 'an astoundingly good *farceur*, though the part of the cuckolded husband is certainly one he could play in his sleep, which he did seem to be doing the night we attended'.

Nevertheless *The Little Hut* rapidly became a standing-room-only hit, much helped by an early royal visit from Queen Mary and her granddaughter Princess Margaret, followed by one from the ailing George VI. All in all Robert was to remain at the Lyric with that play for nearly three years, during which time David Tomlinson, who also managed to stay the course, fitted in a total of eight film performances during the daytime, and Robert managed to make both *Outcast of the Islands* and *The African Queen*.

By now, with the Inland Revenue hot on his heels, Robert had realised the urgent need to reawaken his movie career, which had lain dormant since the end of the war unless one counts (as he very seldom did) a fleeting appearance as a pompous civil servant in *The Small Back Room* and a quirky low-budget comedy in which he and Felix Aylmer played *The Ghosts of Berkeley Square*, from a minor comic novel by Caryl Brahms and S. J. Simon.

For his return to films early in 1951, Robert was greatly helped by the arrival of a charismatic new agent. Hayes Hunter had died of a heart attack during an air-raid in 1944 and, since then, through *The First Gentleman* and *Edward* years, Robert had largely looked after himself. But it was clearly time to get his career back on to a firmer and more professionally managed footing, so he signed up with the man who (along with Ros Chatto's actor husband Tom) was to become the last great personal friend of his life.

In 1950 Robin Fox was just thirty-seven; educated at Harrow and originally a solicitor, he had fought an immensely courageous war, for which he had won the MC, and had married Frederick Lonsdale's illegitimate daughter Angela; their three sons were to be the actors Edward and James (William)

Fox, and the producer Robert Fox. Robin was much more than an agent, though in this role his client list included at various times such disparate talents as those of Vanessa Redgrave, Paul Scofield and the film director Joseph Losey. Because of his legal training, Robin was also adept at sorting out corporate as well as contractual difficulties: the Royal Court Theatre would never have survived its Osborne and Devine years without Robin's business acumen, and he performed a similar legal and managerial role in setting up the Grade Organisation for the brothers Lew and Leslie, under whose vast and complex umbrella Robin's own agency (formed with Ros and Robert as the Robin Fox Partnership) was, for a while later, to be found.

On the surface Robert and Robin initially had little in common beyond their theatrical relationship as actor and agent. Robin was a man of infinite elegance, a meticulous dresser and a chronically unfaithful sexual charmer, whose wife only discovered that he was having an affair with the then Duchess of Kent, Marina, when she saw them side by side in the Royal Box at Wimbledon on live television. And yet, perhaps because they were such an odd couple, Robert and Robin became devoted to each other, and often inseparable on casino holidays.

Robin set about reviving Robert's film career with the obvious limitation that he would be playing *The Little Hut* eight times a week for many months to come and was, therefore, only able to take part in movies being shot close to London. Fortunately a good many still were in those days, and the first one Robin managed to land for Robert was something of a dream: an Alexander Korda-London Films production of Joseph Conrad's *The Outcast of the Islands*, for which his co-stars would be Ralph Richardson, Wendy Hiller and Trevor Howard, and the director would be Carol Reed.

Robert was cast as the greedy, jealous, pompous and grasping Almayer, a performance hailed by Milton Shulman in the *Evening Standard* as 'apparently unfettered by script restrictions', but in truth very close to Conrad's original. The film also carried an 'and introducing' credit for Kerima, an intriguing Algerian actress who later married the *James Bond* director Guy Hamilton. 'The great thing about her', said Reed by way of explanation of her casting in a pivotal role, 'is that, if you wet her hair and then photograph her looking through a Venetian blind, you can later cut her into any part of the picture you like.'

There was another role to be filled in *Outcast*: that of a four-year-old girl, daughter in the script of Wendy Hiller and Robert, who has the unhappy experience of seeing her father roasted by natives above an open fire. As my sister Annabel was then just about the right age and (not surprisingly) bore a remarkable resemblance to Robert, she was the logical casting and did about three days' work on the set in a pair of angelic false plaits. Curiously enough it was with her, rather than my father, that Robin had his first great Morley contractual victory. Several months after shooting was completed, both on problematic Ceylon locations and at Shepperton, where all the Almayer scenes were shot, Korda was thrilled to learn that his *Outcast* had been chosen for the prestigious Royal Command Film Performance of 1951. A few nights before the gala, Robin presented himself in Korda's office at 140 Piccadilly to congratulate the great Hungarian producer. 'Oh, but by the way, Sir Alex,' said Robin as he was leaving, 'there is just one little problem. One of my clients, appearing in your splendid film, seems not to have signed any form of contract. Without such a contract you are, of course, aware that the film cannot be screened even to their Majesties?'

'What you mean?' barked Korda; 'Your Morley signed his contract months ago.' 'Robert certainly did', agreed Robin silkily 'the client I am now referring to, however, is Miss Annabel Morley.' 'A mere child', snapped Korda, 'we give her bicycle as usual.' 'At this late stage', ventured Robin, 'I do not think, Sir Alex, that my client will be entirely satisfied with a bicycle. The Royal performance is only two days away. Have you anything else to suggest?'

Korda, unable to believe that he was being blackmailed over a non-existent contract with a child who would at the time have had extreme difficulty signing it, finally under Robin's pressure upped his offer to £1,000, but on one condition. 'There is', said Korda, who knew a thing or two about paintings, 'a very small Pissarro on sale in the window of a gallery in the Burlington Arcade. You will take my money and buy the child that.'

Robin did as he was told; twenty-five years later, my sister sold the Pissarro and bought a small house in Fulham on the proceeds. Those were the days when we really did have a British film industry, and its name was Korda.

1951 brought other adventures including the birth of my brother Wilton in August. Money still being something of a problem, since even ten per cent of the proceeds of *The Little Hut* was not going to assuage the Inland Revenue and there was now a family of five to feed, Robin and Robert also decided in this year that he should make his first serious venture into the comparatively new medium of television, specifically children's television.

Always eager to start something new, especially in untravelled locations, Robert wrote himself a six-part serial called *Parent Craft*, in its way a primitive family sitcom about domestic strife in a large household. Whether or not it could be considered a success is, at this distance, hard to gauge because there was almost no television reviewing at the time and no system of audience measurement. Indeed, immediately after the programme, at about 6 pm, the

BBC television service went off the air for a couple of hours so that children could be put to bed in relative peace before the transmission resumed with a news broadcast in sound only.

All that does survive of the experience is the memory of Robert at Lime Grove studio en route to his theatre and another evening of *The Little Hut* insisting that the BBC should supply a full high tea to all participants, and a somewhat acid memo from the Controller of Children's Television, the redoubtable Freda Lingstrom, noting to her superiors that 'working with Mr Morley is not an experience I would care to repeat.' Robert decided that, on balance, given the minimal money and considerable scripting and acting effort involved, neither would he. In a way he was always too big for the small screen, only taking happily to it in later life as the star of countless British Airways commercials and late-night chat shows, on which he was to be a pioneering and perfect conversational guest.

Soon enough it was time to turn his attention back to the wide screen, for Robin had managed to land him another very attractive offer: *The African Queen*. Before that contract could be signed, however, there was a problem to resolve: my education. Home from American and Australia with a random grasp of any scholastic subject. I had gone back to the local day school in Henley, but was now approaching ten and growing rather old for it. Unable to find anywhere else suitable in the vicinity, my father placed his advertisement in the Personal Column of *The Times*: 'Actor, apprehensive parent with gruesome recollections of own schooling would be grateful to hear of school for son where the latter would be really happy and the former hopeful that his son might be learning to think for himself.'

The advertisement was almost immediately reprinted by the *New Statesman*, where it was set as a competition: replies were invited from Plato, Wackforth Squeers, Mr Chips, Dr Arnold and other celebrated masters of fiction. Surprisingly, some genuine headmasters also wrote in, among them Harry Tuyn, who had just opened a wonderfully eccentric co-educational boarding school for children of all ages on the Suffolk coast at a place called Sizewell, now sadly the site of a nuclear power station.

Harry and Robert at once recognised themselves in each other; two bearlike extroverts with a passion for good food and lengthy conversation, one might have taken them for brothers had Harry not been unmistakably Dutch. Within weeks I was despatched to his school and I remained a pupil of his at the various educational colleges he later established at home and abroad until I went to Geneva and then Oxford University almost ten years later.

Like Robert, Harry was a passionate advocate of the pleasure principle and concentrated largely upon teaching his students the subjects he himself liked best: English Literature with special reference to Shakespeare, French, and a little Latin. As a result, to the amazement of more orthodox local educational establishments, we all passed GCE O-levels at about thirteen, while remaining totally (in my case to this day) ignorant of geography, the sciences, maths or virtually anything else taught in more conventional schools. In the summer terms we swam a lot in the freezing North Sea, which ran almost up to the school terrace, and in winter terms we ate vast Indonesian curries which Harry himself cooked from his childhood memories of the Far East. It was an idyllic education.

I might, I think, have felt torn between Robert and Harry, between home and school, had the two men not been so utterly alike in so many ways. Harry regarded us as his audience and his headmaster's desk as his stage, and it was perfectly possible to begin a conversation with Robert at Fairmans and finish it with Harry at Sizewell without being too aware of the 200-mile transition to be made between them at the beginning and end of every term.

Meanwhile, for Robert, *The African Queen* was getting under way.

16

Beating Bogart's Devils
1952–1953

There are only really three questions to ask about a film: how much, where, and when do we start?

It was John Huston who got there first, at the beginning of his filming of C. S. Forester's *The African Queen*. By the time Robert joined the unit at Shepperton to play the opening scenes as Katharine Hepburn's doomed missionary brother, she and Humphrey Bogart and Huston had already been with the unit on location in the Belgian Congo for two months. It had not been an altogether easy or happy experience. Several of the crew had gone down with malaria, Hepburn herself had caught a bad case of dysentery, spartan conditions sorely strained the long-established relationship between Bogart (who loathed Africa) and Huston (who loved it) and, worst of all, Hepburn seemed at first to have been totally miscast as Rose Sayer, the skinny churchmarm spinster who is taken by Bogart as Charlie Allnutt on board his ramshackle *African Queen* for a First World War journey down a dangerous river.

Several books have already been written about the African location filming, not least by Hepburn herself, Bogart's wife Lauren Bacall and Peter Viertel (*White Hunter, Black Heart*), but few dwell on the very real resentment between Bogie, who found Hepburn unbearably pretentious and affected, and Hepburn who constantly regretted the fact that he was not her own iron-jawed superstar Spencer Tracy. She was also having considerable trouble with the part of Rose, until Huston gave her the clue which was to condition not merely this one role but the whole of the rest of her movie career: 'Play her', he said simply, 'just like Eleanor Roosevelt.'

From then on conditions on the location improved, but relations remained strained through temperament and illness, and by the time they got back to shoot the interiors at Shepperton the atmosphere was not exactly convivial. Robert was to play, in effect, the only other role in the film, unless one counts the arresting Germans at the fade out, and for once in his life he was extremely nervous. He knew enough about the nature of cinema by now to recognise that his role was one of the smallest, but also one of the most important he would ever play, if only because he was up against two Hollywood superstars at the height of their fame and powers.

His first day on the set was a nightmare. Still playing *The Little Hut* six nights a week, he had, he thought, managed to learn his missionary role, only to find that, as he arrived on the set, the lines deserted him. Huston, Bogart and Hepburn all treated him with a polite, if distant, tolerance, and he was relieved when it was time to escape to the theatre that evening. After the show, to cheer himself, Robert went to some kind of theatrical party and there, to his horror, found Huston; as he approached his director, somebody asked Huston what it had been like to have Robert join them that morning on the set. 'I am told', said John with his familiar drawl, 'that the real Mr Morley starts with us tomorrow'; and sure enough he did, giving one of the great, albeit brief, performances of his film career.

He also began to forge a firm friendship with Huston, who was to employ him on two future films, seeing in my father a latterday version of Sydney Greenstreet, of whom John had become fond at the time of *Maltese Falcon* ten years earlier.

As Robert later recalled:

Huston was a strange, rather magical man, who always told everyone that they were going to be 'just fine' whatever the perilous indignity to which he had just subjected them on the location. Once we bought a race horse together at Newmarket after a selling-plate: 'He'll be just fine', said John reassuringly and, as he said so, the horse fell dead at our feet. Another time John was on Fifth Avenue and suddenly noticed a corpse on the sidewalk; the rest of his party climbed over it and hurried on, but John knelt to feel the lifeless pulse and reassure the surprised ambulance men that, 'He'll be fine, just fine.'

The African Queen was, as it turned out, just fine, acclaimed by the critics on both sides of the Atlantic. Robert collected some glowing reviews, though not the Best Supporting Actor Oscar nomination that some critics had promised him. He went contentedly on with the Shaftesbury Avenue run of *The Little Hut* – or at least fairly contentedly, for there were suggestions that he might perhaps like to take it to Broadway, or else leave the cast entirely and take part in a possible film of *Les Miserables* in Hollywood, a project for which he was being sought to reprise the Charles Laughton performance.

The truth was, however, that Robert could not afford to leave the regular income of *The Little Hut*, even for a return to Hollywood. By the reckoning of the Inland Revenue, he now owed them an impossible £80,000. When he went home one night in dejection to break this news to Joan, her only comment was, 'Yes, dear, and the Hoover's broken,' her reasonable theory being that there was nothing they could possibly do about the tax, but they might manage to do something about the vacuum cleaner.

With both *Outcast of the Islands* and *The African Queen* having been successfully made and released during the run of *The Little Hut*, Robert decided it might be feasible to get a third film finished before the run ended. This was to be *Curtain Up*, a low-budget backstage comedy which brought him into contact with Margaret Rutherford for the first time since *Short Story*. Together they would later go on to another film and a long-running West End comedy in a partnership which was made in heaven, as they shook their chins at each other across stage and screen.

Curtain Up was a forerunner of *Noises Off* and was derived from a stage hit, *On Monday Next*, about a provincial repertory company not a million miles removed from Perranporth. Later Rutherford was to echo the format in a rather more successful comedy about a derelict cinema called *The Smallest Show on Earth*, but in *Curtain Up* it was the trials and tribulations of live actors which formed the essence of the plot. Robert was wonderfully cast as the director impervious to the playwright's horror as he casually tears up the first thirty pages of a new script, impervious also to the cast's boredom at his theatrical reminiscences and to the stage manager's fury as he reads the racing form instead of hurrying to take yet another rehearsal. Officially the script was by Jack Davies and Michael Pertwee from Philip King's farce; unofficially there is a lot of Robert in there somewhere, and a touch of Kay Kendall, to whom it gave an early chance.

Then, with *The Little Hut* nearing the end of its long Shaftesbury Avenue life, Robert left the cast and focused instead on a play he had originally written for his mother-in-law with Ronald Gow entitled *The Full Treatment*. Gladys, however, had never much cared for it and was, in any case, still blissfully contented in the warmth of California and an ongoing MGM studio contract. Instead they decided to try it out at one of London's pioneer fringe theatres, the Q, with a cast headed by the ever-faithful Ambrosine Phillpotts and George Coulouris; Gladys's younger daughter, Sally, herself starting out as an actress, was also in the cast. There was unusual press interest in the play's club-theatre staging, largely because it was officially Robert's first play since *Edward, My Son* (always allowing for the retouching he had done to *The Little Hut* as the run wore on) but the critics were disappointed by the slight plot involving a trendy interior decorator virtually destroying the home and family of a conventional solicitor by demanding extensive remodelling indoors and out. All the play really left behind, after its short run at Kew, was a set of exotic animal-shaped cane garden furniture which was to last my father in his own Fairmans garden for the rest of his life, a constant reminder of a rare theatrical flop.

Disenchanted with the stage and not having a strong enough idea for a new script, Robert turned eagerly to the offers which were coming ever more rapidly from a suddenly burgeoning local postwar film industry. The next picture he made was *The Final Test*, a comparatively classy venture written as an original screenplay by Terence Rattigan and directed by his long-time collaborator Anthony Asquith.

This was a curious hybrid, inspired by the two men's lifelong passion for cricket, and featured members of the current Test Eleven including Len Hutton, Denis Compton and Alec Bedser. Originally the script had been written by Rattigan, for the magnificent sum of £300, as a BBC television play to celebrate the Festival of Britain; for the wide-screen version Robert was cast as an eccentric poet and playwright, a larger than life character Rattigan had vaguely borrowed from Sheridan Whiteside in *The Man Who Came to Dinner*, a debt he equally vaguely acknowledged by calling the man Alexander Whitehead, so that those 'in the know' would catch the reference to Woollcott as well.

The plot concerned a small boy, the son of a celebrated cricketer, who chooses to seek out the poet instead of his own father on the day of his final test and Robert, tightly bulwarked inside a Churchillian boiler-suit, managed a rather touching performance even if one critic did think he 'swallows role and film on an easy wicket with a malice worthy of Thurber and the look of a debauched panda'. Prime Minister Harold Wilson later saw the film five times, on one occasion travelling thirty miles through a Cornish snowstorm to view it again; the rest of us simply catch it on television, where it turns up regularly in the cricket season as a reminder of its small-screen origins.

From there, in quick succession, Robert appeared in two semi-operatic pictures, both biopics: the first of these was *Melba*, a doomed attempt to tell the life story of the great Australian *diva* who gave her name to peaches with ice-cream. A stodgy Patrice Munsel was cast in the title role, with Robert as Oscar Hammerstein I in an unconvincing American accent: the sole genuine surprise about the film was that it was made by Lewis Milestone, veteran director of *All Quiet on the Western Front*. Eagerly I remember asking my father if he had made the connection; 'I did,' replied Pa, 'but I'm not sure that Milestone still could.'

Robert then went straight on to a better part in a vastly better musical biography. This was *The Story of Gilbert and Sullivan*, made as a twenty-first anniversary offering by Alexander Korda's London Films and with a suitably starry cast: Maurice Evans played Sullivan with Peter Finch as D'Oyly Carte and Robert as a perfect reincarnation of the braggadocio W. S. Gilbert. The script by the Gilbert and Sullivan archivist Leslie Baily and Sidney Gilliat, who also directed, was not hugely distinguished, and there were some uneasy transitions from comic-opera highlights with the D'Oyly Carte Savoyards to backstage scenes of professional and domestic strife. None the less Dilys Powell thought Robert had a 'majestic absurdity' as Gilbert, while C. A. Lejeune reckoned that he and Maurice Evans 'break through the ampersand in the combination of Gilbert & Sullivan, establishing the one as an eccentric, petulant fusspot and the other as an oily social fawner'.

By the time shooting on *Gilbert and Sullivan* ended, Robert having turned in a very touching last scene as, newly knighted by Queen Victoria, Gilbert goes to thank the statue of his deceased collaborator, there was a much more intriguing film on offer on an Italian location. John Huston and Humphrey Bogart – friends and colleagues since *The Maltese Falcon* a dozen years earlier, in which time they had together also made *Treasure of the Sierra Madre*, *Key Largo* and *The African Queen* – had jointly purchased the rights in a little-known Claud Cockburn novel written under the pseudonym James Helvick and entitled *Beat the Devil*.

At this point, early in 1953, both Bogie and Huston were keen to establish themselves as European independents: the great exodus from the Hollywood studio system had already started, production costs were infinitely lower in Europe and the appeal of a sunny Italian spring was too strong to resist. True, there was a problem with the script, which such experienced old hands as Peter Viertel had already declared unworkable and overly complex for a movie. Matters were not made easier by Huston's feeling that he would somehow like the picture, although totally unrelated in origin, to be a companion piece or maybe even a parody of *The Maltese Falcon*, echoing several of its villainous themes and preferably with at least some of its original cast of heavies. This, too, was problematic however; in those pre-video, pre-television rerun days, very few people had seen *The Maltese Falcon* in over a decade and they therefore had only the haziest recollections of its storyline.

Undeterred, Huston drafted in Jennifer Jones for the Mary Astor role, and then he hoped to recreate the most memorable of the *Falcon's* double acts, Peter Lorre and Sydney Greenstreet as the Laurel and Hardy of the sinister screen. Sadly, Greenstreet was already mortally ill, but it did not take long for Huston to recall Robert's performance in *The African Queen* and realise that he would be a suitable replacement.

Others in a starry cast included Gina Lollobrigida, making her first English-language picture and known to Bogart as Lollfrigidaire because of a certain coolness towards him on location high in the hills south of Naples, in the picturesque village of Ravello, where Gore Vidal later went to live. Huston once said that his film career was the story of a man either too early or too late with an idea, and this time he seems to have been rather too early. *Beat the Devil* was later to become a high-camp classic, largely because of the unfathomable script by a young Truman Capote, who had been drafted in to make sense of a baroque tale about a gang of latterday pirates trying to get to a uranium deal in East Africa, but delayed along the way by all manner of alarms and excursions.

'There are', said my father once, 'only really three questions to ask about a film: how much, where, and when do we start?' In this case the money was a generous $80,000, the timing would allow him a gentle drive through Italy with Robin and Angela Fox, and the location was utterly enchanting, if already slightly chaotic by the time they arrived. Capote was still in Rome, unable to complete the script because of the illness of a pet raven in his hotel bedroom which was refusing to speak to him. The screenplay was thus arriving a page or two at a time, much to the consternation of Jennifer Jones's new husband, the *Gone With The Wind* producer, David O. Selznick, who was sending Huston memos about her costumes several thousand words longer than the script itself, such as it was.

Then again there was a young camera assistant called Stephen Sondheim, and just down the road in a neighbouring village were Ingrid Bergman and her lover Roberto Rossellini, whose elopement from Hollywood and other marriages had been the international movie scandal of the last few months. All in all, what was happening behind the cameras on *Beat the Devil* was vastly more dramatic and entertaining than anything Capote was managing to dream up in his raven-infested Rome bedroom.

My memories of that location, confined as they are to a school holiday when I was twelve, would be considerably hazier by now had it not been for Steve Sondheim, who made a miraculous home movie on the set: what it shows is a Bogart already prematurely aged and careworn, not least perhaps because he was for once bearing most of the negative costs himself, an ebullient Huston, a characteristically sinister, lurking Lorre, and a withdrawn, infinitely nervous Jennifer Jones with the shadow of Selznick forever looming over her on the set.

We were not to know that Bogart was already dying of cancer, nor yet that this was to be his last Huston picture and therefore an epitaph to their work together. Almost everybody seemed to be in some kind of emotional or physical pain except, of course, Robert, who was enjoying himself under the Italian sun and, encouraged by Huston, touching up Capote's script with some dialogue of his own. Bogart at this point was not saying a lot either on camera or off, as on the drive from Rome his chauffeur had been unable to decide whether to turn left or right and driven him straight into a brick wall, thereby causing him to break several teeth, for which he was eagerly awaiting a new bridge.

Robert found Bogart distant and Lorre unfriendly, but one of Huston's great, if backhanded, achievements in the film was to let them be themselves as often as possible, with the result that they gave three of the most characteristic performances of their long careers. Others were not so fortunate: Jones and Lollobrigida looked confused throughout, as well they might given the twists and turns of the plot.

One night the cameraman Ossie Morris and assistant director Jack Clayton returned to their hotel to find Huston's bedroom door ablaze. Staggering to bed in an unusually drunken stupor, Huston had kicked over a heater, which had duly ignited the door. 'Ah,' he said, as they dragged him to safety in the nick of time, 'sure and it's wonderful, that smell of burning pine,' and fell back into a sound sleep.

When Capote did eventually arrive on the set to distribute missing pages of his script, he was immediately dubbed 'Caposy' by the homophobic Bogart, at least until Truman challenged him to several arm-wrestling contests and to general amazement won them all, after which Bogart was duly more respectful. On another occasion a vintage Rolls-Royce had to be sent over a cliff with Bogart apparently at the wheel. The plan was for a very small Italian mechanic to be secreted on the floor of the car to put on the brakes in the nick of time. As the car was about to leave the road, however, Bogey glanced down and saw that the mechanic had failed to put in an appearance: he leapt out with only seconds to spare and screamed at Huston, 'I might have been killed.' 'Yes,' said Huston thoughtfully, 'but you weren't, were you, kid? So now you're fine, just fine.'

On yet another occasion, a cargo steamer was hired and all put to sea to shoot off the coast of Salerno. Ordered to climb a perilous mast, Jennifer Jones understandably refused and several hours were lost. When the sun went down, Huston ordered the captain to make for home and was then genuinely amazed to find that the journey took all night, it having never for a moment occurred to him that time taken going out to sea must equal the time taken for the return journey on the identical route.

When filming was finally completed, the cast and crew returned to London, where Robert sent a telegram to the co-producer of *Beat the Devil*, John Woolf: 'We have now returned to our capital', it read, 'and I hope that yours will eventually be returned to you. But I rather doubt it.'

Later, recalled Robert, 'I became a firm fan of Truman Capote's, reading everything he ever wrote except, of course, the script of *Beat the Devil*.'

17

Hippo Dances

1953–1955

I am the sort of writer who only really gets down to a play when the bailiffs are already on their way; luckily they were never able to find Fairmans, as it is rather tucked away. Perhaps, if they had, I'd have written a few more plays.

Robert's doubts about the commercial fortunes of *Beat the Devil* were well founded. *The Times* thought it was 'a comedy which makes itself up as it goes along' and Dilys Powell reckoned its plot 'desperately lacks the impetus to carry it over some very awkward joins'. However, back in London in the Coronation summer of 1953, Robert's thoughts had turned once more to the theatre: the Old Vic offered him *Henry VIII*, but he saw no great joy or profit in that and was understandably chary of yet more comparisons with Charles Laughton. Besides, as he was later to tell Peter Hall in response to the offer of Falstaff at Stratford upon Avon, he had never been able to take any pleasure in Shakespeare.

Instead, his thoughts returned to the boulevard comedies of André Roussin in Paris: if *The Little Hut* had given him two enjoyable years in the West End, perhaps lightning could be made to strike twice from that direction? Moreover, Robert had learnt a thing or two; this time there would be no Nancy Mitford to take an adaptor's royalties; he would do that himself.

A play of Roussin's had been running in Paris for the past three years; called *Les Oeufs de l'autruche*, (The Ostrich Eggs), it was effectively *La Cage aux folles* years ahead of its time, since the plot concerned a conventional father's appalled discovery that his son was homosexual. This was fine for Paris in the mid-1950s, but Robert realised that he would never get it past the Lord Chamberlain, who then censored all West End scripts, and so the play would have to be very drastically adapted. Working alone, in the wooden chalet he had built at the edge of the woods in Fairmans' garden, the adaptation of Roussin's play into what he was to call *Hippo Dancing* took him most of the rest of 1953. He paused for a family holiday in Cornwall near Fowey, where Robin and Angela Fox had a summer home, and where Joan was reunited with her childhood friend Daphne du Maurier. He also paused for a few Sunday-night charity concerts associated with the Coronation and then, towards Christmas, he discovered a whole new career in television panel games.

Gilbert Harding, one of the earliest and biggest stars of the genre, had been suddenly taken ill, and Robert sat in for him on the BBC's *What's My Line*, immediately establishing a talent for impromptu tele-chatting which was to carry him through countless live appearances on both sides of the Atlantic over the next thirty years. He once invented a short-lived television game of his own and was a frequent panellist on those of others; the epitome of this particular branch of his career was the three opening years of *Call My Bluff* for BBC2, on which he led a team (comprised largely of close relatives) against that of Frank Muir, until eventually Robert handed over to Patrick Campbell.

But his major energies were directed towards *Hippo Dancing*, due to go into rehearsal early in 1954. David Tomlinson being unavailable, Robert turned to one of the few other actors on their precise, cavalier and often impromptu wavelength, Wilfrid Hyde-White, who over the following two years on Shaftesbury Avenue was to make him an equally suitable and beloved partner.

First, though, there were a couple more films to make. In one of these, *The Good Die Young*, Robert had but a couple of scenes as the baronet father to Laurence Harvey's corrupt gangster son. The other, however, was a distinctly classier and more enjoyable affair: *The Rainbow Jacket* was an Ealing Studios drama scripted by T. E. B. Clarke and produced and directed by Michael Relph and Basil Dearden; set almost entirely on several race courses, it allowed Robert, Willy Hyde-White and Michael Trubshawe to give characteristically quirky performances as owner-stewards and spend many hours on location watching the sport they all relished.

By the time those races were safely photo-finished, it was time to think about the *Hippo* production. Having decided never again to work with a 'star' director like Peter Brook, Robert managed to persuade his old *Edward* friend Peter Ashmore to keep an eye on him in rehearsal, and Binkie Beaumont of H. M. Tennent was once more to be the producer. Robert had switched the location of the play to Golder's Green, but decided nevertheless to give himself a French wife, so he and Robin spent a few delightful days in Paris interviewing suitable actresses. Unfortunately the one they chose, Colette Proust, proved to have an impenetrable French accent and had to be sent back across the Channel after a couple of days' rehearsal. 'Don't give her a fortune,' said Binkie Beaumont, gloomily surveying her signed contract, 'give her a fiver.'

Brenda de Banzie was brought in to take her place. The usual long road tour Robert had planned to get the comedy into shape duly commenced in Dublin and then Blackpool, where Willy Hyde-White's current mistress announced that his part was not good enough and she would therefore be withdrawing his labour on the Saturday night. A new scene hastily written by Robert on his portable typewriter in a Blackpool hotel bedroom rapidly resolved that dilemma, and *Hippo* danced into the Lyric Theatre early in April 1954, where it was to stay for almost two years, praised by no less an expert on the Parisian stage than Harold Hobson of the *Sunday Times*: 'Morley's performance is rich in its exuberance, engaging in its periodic confidences with the audience, and true and exact in its pathos.' Others were not so sure: *The Times* thought it 'a comedy which triumphs over having no spinal column and no recognisable nationality', while Alan Dent and John Barber both took the view that a single line in the programme acknowledging 'the author's debt to André Roussin' was less than adequate gratitude for the original source, especially as André had also given Robert *The Little Hut*, his last successful run at the same theatre.

Robert, never one to accept criticism lying down and always taking a journalist's delight in the quick riposte, was rapidly in print explaining that Roussin himself had insisted on this being his only credit, so different was the original from *Hippo Dancing*. 'I am neither as ungenerous nor as dishonest as your critics suggest', Robert asserted, 'and, if they are either generous or honest, they will admit their mistake.' Both did.

With *Hippo* settled into the Lyric, guaranteeing Robert £300 a week plus a share of the profits as author and star, the Inland Revenue could at last be temporarily eased off his back. The middle years of the 1950s were turning out to be lucrative ones, especially as the British division of MGM came back to him with the offer of a couple more Technicolor kings. The first of these was to be George III in *Beau Brummel*, for which Peter Ustinov had already been cast in Robert's *First Gentleman* role of George IV. What was left was his father, on this occasion conceived not as the sensitive victim of Alan

Hippo Dancing: as Harry ('Hippo') Osborne

Bennett's later play, but rather as a barking-mad killer of footmen in the fine old knockabout tradition of MGM royalty. With Robert and Peter Ustinov as the two Hanoverian Royals, *Beau Brummel* also boasted Stewart Granger, Elizabeth Taylor, and a script derived (apparently on the backs of envelopes) from an old American play by Clyde Fitch.

The Ustinov-Morley double act, which climaxed in the former being half-strangled by the latter, was applauded by *Time* magazine: 'These two amiable monsters, as shapelessly alike as two corpulent snails, seem to be engaging in a contest as to who can stick his long-stemmed eyeballs farthest out of his head. Morley, as the mad monarch who talks to trees and mixes paint with his feet, is the winner by a cornea.' Others were rather less delighted, notably the descendants of the monarchs concerned. For some unfathomable reason, *Beau Brummel* had been selected for the Royal Command Film Performance of 1954; apparently it had never occurred to anyone that Her Majesty might not be best pleased to witness one of her recent ancestors attempting to strangle another of them in close-up on a wide screen in full colour. It was to be several years before the Queen attended another Royal Command Film Performance. Robert and Peter were, however, to proceed amicably to such other joint ventures as *Topkapi* and *Halfway Up a Tree*, while maintaining a tactful distance from each other on the kind of television chat shows where they were apt to give similar performances.

During the early weeks of the *Hippo* run, Robert also consented to introduce Marlene Dietrich at the Café de Paris, a tradition which had recently been inaugurated in verse by Noël Coward and was being followed on a rota basis by several other contemporary West End stars. Delighted by his first glimpse of the Café, where a few years later he was himself to play an eccentric cabaret season, Robert launched into an overlong paean of praise to Marlene, who was soon to be heard from her dressing-room upstairs muttering, 'Who this Morley and why he not shut up and let me get on?'

Forever in search of other diversions with which to entertain himself during a long run, Robert signed up at this time for a regular column, the first of many, with the *Sunday Express*, for whose feature pages he would hold forth on such diverse topics as why the French were already making better films than the British and why it was always the amateurs who were best on television. He began to write frequent restaurant and hotel reviews in his columns in the vain lifelong hope that he could then offset the bills against tax, while also regularly sounding off about the evils of education and sport.

In addition, he became involved, albeit tangentially, in a memorable row which broke out in the West End that summer of 1954, when, in the House of Commons, Woodrow Wyatt queried the non-profit status of a theatrical production company set up by Binkie Beaumont as a subsidiary of H. M. Tennent. With the wisdom of forty years' hindsight, it is clear that Wyatt was making a fair point: Beaumont was bending, if not actually breaking, tax laws, but so powerful was he at the time and so total was the West End monopoly by Tennent's that few dared side with Wyatt outside the privilege of the House of Commons.

In later and more radical years, when he was in any case thoroughly disenchanted with Binkie, Robert might well have supported Woodrow but he decided that this was not the moment to do so, especially as he was the star of Tennents' most successful Shaftesbury Avenue hit. Instead he gave a tongue-in-cheek interview about 'the terrors of Binkie' and thus neatly avoided the fray, for which Binkie rewarded him by moving the Lyric matinées from Wednesdays to Thursdays, thereby allowing Robert and Willy Hyde-White to take in the Derby and several other hitherto unattainable race meetings.

Quite soon, however, Robert was to revert to his usual pattern of filming all day at Shepperton or Pinewood and then playing *Hippo* at night. MGM wanted him for another period epic monarch, Louis XI of France in *Quentin Durward*, a costume swashbuckler starring Elizabeth Taylor with Robert

Taylor and the usual assortment of stalwart British character actors from Willy Hyde-White through Marius Goring and Alec Clunes to Ernest Thesiger and Harcourt Williams.

History students of the period may have wondered why it was that most kings called George or Louis in Hollywood films from the mid-1930s to the mid-1950s bore a quite remarkable resemblance to Robert Morley, and all seemed to wear more or less the same clothes while speaking variations of the same dialogue. Such was the American cinema of the time, when it was believed that audiences would be reassured by familiarity, particularly if the films themselves were set in unfamiliar historical periods.

Hippo danced on right through 1955 at the Lyric, by which time Robert had managed to complete the construction of a swimming-pool at Fairmans and was mourning the death of his mother, poor Daisy, who, after long tranquil years in Wargrave, had died peacefully at eighty-two. 'Your life', she used to tell her only son, 'has been one long holiday,' and in a way, of course, she was right. Though temperamentally and in character much closer to his father, Robert had been very fond of his mother and was to miss his daily walks down the road from Fairmans to see her in the village. At the age of forty-seven, he was now an orphan.

18

Love is a Very Light Thing

1955–1956

Once I had got over my disappointment that Fanny *was not a Drury Lane success, I loved every performance of that stupendous flop; I never cared how few people were in front, so long as I could be on the stage pretending to sing and dance for them. After a while the conductor gave up all hope of my being willing or able to follow the orchestra, and they would follow me instead; all he demanded was that we should start and finish each song at roughly the same time.*

As he approached his half-century, Robert's life seemed to have settled into a series of comfortable routines. He was working hard on stage and screen, usually leaving home at six in the morning for the studios and not getting back until around midnight from the theatre, but he had acquired a wonderfully faithful dresser and driver in John Jonas, and Joan's careful, loving organisation of Fairmans meant that, even by the standards of most of the men in our family, he had to do remarkably little around the house.

In London he was surrounded by Ros Chatto and Robin Fox and Ros's actor husband Tom, for whom whenever possible Robert would find work with him so that the two of them could share racing tips and backstage gossip. On stage he also had Willy Hyde-White to fulfil the old Tomlinson function of querulous but affectionate sidekick, and at weekends Peter Bull and Sewell Stokes were still regular guests, helping in summertime around the pool to fulfil Robert's lasting fantasy that he was living in some elegant cognac commercial set deep in the French vineyards.

But there was, somewhere deep within him, a restlessness which he had inherited from his father and was to pass on, if not to all of us, then certainly to his younger son; a change in the weather, a slight quarrel, the end of a show or film, the unexpected discovery of some spare cash in the bank or just a good tip for the Arc de Triomphe would have him hot-footing it to the airport or railway station. In truth he loved the journey as much as the arrival; a compulsive picker-up of unconsidered travellers, he would gleefully roam around airports, ports or stations for hours, chatting to anyone who vaguely recognised him or might have an interesting story to tell.

Later in life, as we children gradually moved off his hands and the bank balance eased, he would spend more and more of his time gently and often aimlessly pottering around the world. Until that time came, however, these were momentary interludes to be cherished in an otherwise busy schedule. When *Hippo* eventually began to subside at the box-office early in the autumn of 1955, Robert went back to New York for the first time in five years to make his American television debut in the broadcast of *Edward, My Son*, long postponed because of the contractual objections arising from the MGM movie.

Ann Todd joined him as Lady Holt, with Gladys's daughter Sally Cooper playing the part of the mistress made famous by Leueen McGrath. None of them much enjoyed the experience of getting a complex stage play in front of the cameras and cut to a running time of only one hour, but they survived and were all afterwards invited to a party given by Leueen and her husband George S. Kaufman. The latter was not one to be gracious about the success of a rival playwright and had always been fairly jealous of Robert's on-stage relationship with his wife. 'Damn lucky to get away with that one,' was his only comment on Robert's masterpiece.

Back in England early in 1956 he picked up another film, this one Graham Greene's own adaptation of his novella *Loser Takes All*; Ken Annakin was the director of a light-hearted tale about a shadowy tycoon and the young couple he inadvertently introduces to a casino fortune. The character of Dreuther, the tycoon, was loosely based by Graham on that of his old producer and nemesis Alexander Korda, and they wanted Alec Guinness for the role. But he was then under contract to Korda and Alex, recognising the parody of himself all too clearly, took his revenge by refusing to release Alec. The role therefore went to Robert, who, as Greene noted somewhat acidly, 'played the role rather differently from the way we had originally envisaged. The trouble with Morley is that he only really ever plays Morley.' Reviews were, however, rather better for Robert than the film.

Time then for another crack at a long-running West End comedy. Robert had been sent a new script by Gerald Savory, the author of *George and Margaret* and a distinguished television producer, which intrigued him by offering the chance to play two roles on stage simultaneously. By using an agile double and with some dextrous stage management, *A Likely Tale* would star Robert as a man of sixty-five and as his own forty-year-old son.

Robert and Gerald had a good deal in common, not least the lifelong friendship of Sewell Stokes and the fact that both had made their names as playwrights with dramas in which the title characters never appear on the stage. In this play the plot was distinctly fragile, yet it did offer Robert not only the double role but also the opportunity once again to appear opposite his beloved Margaret Rutherford. She had just come through a severe nervous breakdown, so severe in fact that my parents took her to live with them at Fairmans while she recuperated and sallied forth into the winter landscape of Berkshire for bursts of chill fresh air, which she felt essential to her recovery.

When Gerald had first written *A Likely Tale*, there was no thought of the same actor playing two of the leading roles and in determining to pull off the double, Robert had considerably weakened the central structure of the plot, but Savory was reasonably amenable on the issue. Peter Ashmore was brought in to direct the stage traffic and they opened a long tour rather surprisingly at the Memorial Theatre in Stratford upon Avon, where Robert had last appeared with Benson a good twenty years earlier.

They then journeyed on through Glasgow and Blackpool before opening in London for Tennent's at the Globe Theatre and falling into the hands of Kenneth Tynan. This was his only real chance to get at Robert in the genre of theatre for which he stood, and which Tynan stood to destroy:

> A pseudo-Chekhovian study of two relict sisters and their brother, a fussy poetaster, wanly awaiting the death of their bedridden father. A vagrant spiv who is the brother's son sets the household wondering where the inheritance will fall; hearing that the housemaid may be the beneficiary, he blithely woos her, but his hopes are shattered and the play ends, as it began, in a mood of dim yearning ... Mr Morley has doubly miscast himself as the brother and the son, thereby wrenching the play out of joint and transmuting a half-hearted Chekhovian comedy into a half-hearted Morley farce ... This is neither good theatre nor bad, it is simply irrelevant.

Six weeks later, on 8 May 1956, *Look Back in Anger* opened at the Royal Court and Ken Tynan had the revolution to relevance for which he had waited so long and written so hard. As for Robert, 'I have been thinking in my bath', he wrote a few days later to his old friend Peter Bull, 'about many things, including your recent and considerable triumph as Pozzo in *Waiting for Godot* by Samuel Beckett. In my view, it represents the end of the British theatre as we have known it.'

None the less he still had a living to make and fortunately the other reviews for *A Likely Tale* had been considerably more enthusiastic than Tynan's, guaranteeing them a decent run at the Globe, during which Robert went off to play the Governor of the Bank of England in Mike Todd's all-star *Around the World in Eighty Days*, the man who sends Phineas Fogg off at the start of his journey and is there to time his return to the steps of the Reform Club.

Theatrically the times were now a-changing very fast indeed, and Robert had some serious thinking to do about his stage future. Like Formosa (to borrow Tynan's famous analogy, written about Terence Rattigan at this time, but equally applicable here), Robert was geographically occupied by the old guard, but strategically inclined towards the progressives. The fact that he had very little time for the Royal Court and Stratford ('I have the highest regard for those members of my profession who continue to act in Shakespeare, but I have reached an age where I can no longer bear to watch them doing so') did not mean that he believed in a return to drawing-room comedy, for in a curious way he was not that kind of actor either. Physically unsuited to the silk dressing-gown or the cigarette-holder, he was as alien to Coward or Lonsdale as he was to Pinter or Brecht.

His frequent cross-Channel sorties to raid the boulevard comedies of Paris and André Roussin were not, therefore, prompted by any special passion for the French theatre, merely a recognition that nobody in Britain was writing the type of vehicle he needed, except from time to time himself. Only at the very end of his stage career, when he got together with Ben Travers, who was then emerging from a long hibernation, did Robert find a major comic dramatist perfectly suited to his theatrical talents, and by then it was almost too late. In the meantime he was forever casting around for suitable material. Always both ahead of and behind his times, Robert was a constant pro-fessional and private contradiction in terms: an apparently bluff conservative with deeply, if idealistically, socialist beliefs; a stage technician of consum-mate skill who spent his life pretending that it all came naturally; a deeply loving father and husband who treated his family and close friends as if they were welcome guests at some country-house hotel he had mysteriously inherited and was now struggling to keep open against all the odds.

Sometimes he would be taken with the notion that he really ought to act a bit more on stage, try a bit harder to be less himself; hence the decision in *A Likely Tale* to play both father and son: 'As the father I had grey hair, and as the son I wore a red wig and a patch over one eye, but few people ever remarked on any other differences in my performances there.' Acting became for him rather like dieting – something one really should do more of at some time, but preferably not right now.

It was at this point that he found something new which he really wanted to try: a stage musical. In New York for the television production of *Edward, My Son* a few months earlier, he had seen and fallen totally in love with a musical by Harold Rome called *Fanny* and based on the three Marseilles waterfront movies of the 1930s by Marcel Pagnol (*Marius, Fanny* and *César*). For Broadway, Joshua Logan had put together a production with Ezio Pinza from his earlier *South Pacific* and Walter Slezak in the leading roles. Although it had proved something less than a smash hit, Robert was utterly enchanted by both book and score, and he was determined to try to get it for London, regardless of the fact that his musicality was, to put it politely, minimal.

During the run of *A Likely Tale* the breakthrough had occurred. Word had come from Broadway that Rex Harrison had decided to sing Professor Higgins in *My Fair Lady*, while in London Paul Scofield was about to undertake *Expresso Bongo*. The hour of the non-singing musical star had arrived, and Robert determined to take advantage of it. He therefore persuaded Binkie Beaumont to close *A Likely Tale* after an unusually short six-month stay at the Globe, somewhat to the indignation of Margaret Rutherford and the distinguished supporting cast led by Richard Pearson and Judy Parfitt, who were playing to almost full houses. Robert went straight over to the Theatre Royal, Drury Lane, to start rehearsals of *Fanny* for Oscar Hammerstein's director son William.

Robert was to play the Walter Slezak role of Panisse, with the opera singer Ian Wallace taking on the Pinza role of César; wisely, Hammerstein had surrounded them with some of the most distinctive character players in town to people the Marseilles waterfront: Michael Gough played the Admiral, with Mona Washbourne as the mother and a fine, eccentric comedian called Julian Orchard lurking around the harbour. Rehearsals got off to a tricky start: 'Not only can I not dance,' Robert told the astonished Broadway choreographer Onna White on the first day, 'but I have always regarded those who can with the gravest suspicion, especially if they happen to be men.' Then there was the problem of his singing: 'I am totally tone deaf,' Robert told the equally astonished conductor, 'so perhaps if you'd just count up to ten and then point at me from the pit, using a little torch so I can see you, then we could begin the songs roughly together?' To those with a strong sense of music, this was not going to be an easy one; Billy Hammerstein, who had read several of Robert's articles on the uselessness of directors,

Fanny: as Panisse

decided simply to wait it out in the stalls, knowing that sooner or later he would need some advice.

One afternoon the company manager brought great news: 'Several parties have booked tickets.' 'I suppose,' said Robert gloomily, 'they are too frightened to come on their own.' The Suez Crisis and the advent of petrol rationing did not make this the best of autumns to be opening a big new musical, but once he had made his peace with the choreographer and the conductor, or at least reduced them to uneasy silence, Robert became convinced they were about to have a smash hit of such gigantic proportions that when his old enemy Harrison wanted the theatre for the London staging of *My Fair Lady* a year later, it would still be totally occupied by *Fanny*.

Sadly, it did not work out like that: they opened to a fairly terrible press and one apparent mystery. In those days of hot-metal printing along Fleet Street, it was possible to acquire the early edition reviews of the papers well before midnight, especially if the cast party happened to be around the corner in Drury Lane. Accordingly the cast and crew of *Fanny* were immensely cheered during their first-night celebrations to obtain a *Daily Express* review by John Barber headlined 'The Most Glamorous Show I Know' and Robert went to bed convinced they had a hit.

The next morning he awoke to the rest of the press, which was, though not bad for him or Ian, distinctly muted about the show and its chances of a long London life. Oh, well, thought Robert, thank God for the *Daily Express* and picked up a later edition, only to read that the show had fallen 'like a sack of wet sand on the stage'.

Barber, it appeared, had filed his early review after a preview and a headline writer at the *Express* had added an unjustifiably enthusiastic headline, which was then naturally altered once the full text of Barber's objections became clear.

But, when I think back now on all the nights I spent throughout my first quarter-century or so, standing in the wings watching Robert act, I find that I often think of him in *Fanny* first. To be sure, he could neither sing nor dance and this was indeed a musical; yet in the character of Panisse, the wealthy Marseilles shopkeeper who falls in love with a young wife only to find himself saddled with her child by another man, Robert reached an extraordinary depth of emotion and pathos which I do not believe even Slezak ever found in the Broadway original. His death scene, played with Ian Wallace as the grieving César, and before that his affirmation that 'love is a very light thing', a song he spoke to orchestral accompaniment rather than sang, were among the most touching moments Robert achieved on a stage, and characteristically he achieved them in the relatively unfriendly surroundings of a half-empty theatre. It was almost as though he were determined, every night for nine months, to reward the small audiences who did turn up by showing them precisely why he had fallen in love with a musical which was then sadly to vanish forever from this side of the Atlantic. In those days Broadway scores were seldom re-recorded during their West End runs, and it is one of my lasting regrets that there is now no trace of what Robert sounded like in *Fanny*: he was just wonderful.

19

Journey to Vienna
1956–1958

The luncheons of my theatrical management were widely recognised as the most lavish since the days of Charles Cochran; indeed our offices had no desks, only sofas and a dining-table . . . after a while I came to realise that I had none of the qualities necessary to become a successful theatrical manager, but I was immensely fortunate to have learnt the lesson under delightful circumstances and in amusing company.

Once he had settled into Drury Lane and become accustomed to nightly life in a long-running flop – a rare experience, but inevitable because nothing was ready to take the place of *Fanny* until the following autumn – Robert as usual began to look around for fresh diversions to keep himself amused. The brief depression he had experienced after the reviews was rapidly dispelled by a letter from Buckingham Palace announcing that Her Majesty 'had it in mind' to make him a CBE in the New Years Honours of 1957, and by a more eccentric, but equally welcome, suggestion that he might like to play a late-night cabaret season of his own at the Café de Paris in the wake of Noël Coward and Marlene Dietrich.

The Café towards the end of its life (it has long since become a Leicester Square disco) was finding it hard to attract vintage prewar cabaret stars, and was thus casting around a bit for other West End possibilities. Robert, ever eager to take up a bizarre challenge, sat down and wrote himself a series of comic monologues and persuaded Julian Orchard from the *Fanny* cast to play his stooge, a butler named Tulloch after the legendary real-life hall porter at

Buck's Club, then being triumphantly run in Clifford Street by my maternal grandfather.

To his monologues Robert also added a haunting early narrative poem by Kingsley Amis about a commercial traveller down on his luck, and he solemnly offered up this bizarre late-night confection to Café habitués who, accustomed to Sophie Tucker or possibly Josephine Baker, sat watching him over their coffee cups with the kind of stunned, open-mouthed amazement captured several years later by Mel Brooks among the audience for his *Springtime for Hitler*. 'You have', Sophie Tucker told Robert one night, 'a great beginning and a great ending. All you really lack is something in the middle.'

To say that the fortnight's season was not a success is to underestimate it: Robert's act was so far outside normal Café de Paris procedures that even he used to have regular nose-bleeds before descending the staircase at the start of an act which made up in sheer manic courage what it lacked in coherence. Quite soon after that, the Café closed its doors for the last time.

Backstage at *Fanny*, life continued to be comparatively normal: Ian Wallace once had what he himself described as a '*crise de nerfs*', inspiring Robert to ask if he could manage to collapse on stage during the first half, thereby guaranteeing some much-needed coverage in the morning, rather than the evening, papers next day. Ros Chatto continued to provide epic meals between the shows on Saturday nights, alternating Indian, Chinese and Italian cuisine on menus which became so famous and so envied around the West End that other companies would beg to be invited to share them; Michael Flanders and Donald Swann were regular visitors from their long-running *At the Drop of a Hat* across the road at the Fortune Theatre.

Ros, Robert and Robin were now considering a yet more ambitious venture than the Chatto catering. Into the dressing-room one night early in 1957 came the Broadway producer Philip Langner of the Theatre Guild, bearing the script of a comedy called *The Tunnel of Love*, which had recently enjoyed considerable success in New York. His idea was a novel one: not that Robert should play in it, but that he might for a change like to produce and direct it himself. Ros had long since graduated from stage management, and Robin was eager to move on from simply acting as an actors' agent; Robert, too, felt that a change might be in order, given his awareness that the days of his particular branch of the theatre could well be numbered. Thus, quite quickly, was born the idea of the Robin Fox Partnership, a management company which would also at various times in its short existence embrace the talents of Peter Ustinov and John Clements, and be dedicated to finding and putting on new plays.

Glamorous offices were taken on the corner of Old Burlington Street, conveniently opposite Buck's Club, where Robin also maintained a flat frequently occupied at this time by me and his two elder sons, Edward and William (James), all in our teens and eager to escape to the bright lights of the city from the rigours of school or college. I also remember the flat being graced by a tall, leggy actress called Tracy Reed, the step-daughter of Sir Carol and then at drama school with Edward who, to the intense envy of William and myself, in due course married her.

The entire Fox family, then as now, were creatures of infinite style and considerable dress-sense; we Morleys used to crash around in their wake, ill-kempt and untidy, but infinitely happy to be among people who seemed to speak so naturally a body-language of thin elegance, which remained as alien to Robert and myself as if it had been Hindustani.

But the Robin Fox Partnership did not solely exist to provide its relative teenagers with a London base and a glimpse of the good life: *A Tunnel of Love* was to be its first production, and Robert duly started to assemble a cast. He sought the type of young, stylish light comedians with an understated sense of timing who were becoming rarer as the theatre turned towards angrier young men, but Robert managed to enlist Ian Carmichael and William Franklyn, and set a rehearsal date for later in the year. In the meantime, the Partnership decided it would launch with one of Robert's own plays written in collaboration with the stockbroker Dundas Hamilton.

Six Months Grace was a slight board-room comedy, somewhat in the style of *Born Yesterday* and conceived for Yvonne Arnaud, one of those actresses who, like Marie Tempest and Margaret Rutherford, Robert had always admired for their high comedy as much as for their robust determination not to have much truck with dramatists or directors who did not drive their vehicles in precisely the direction they had chosen to travel across the stage. In truth, of course, Robert was one of their number from the masculine side of the tracks, but this play for Arnaud failed to catch fire, perhaps because Robert, still engaged at Drury Lane in *Fanny*, had to put Michael Shepley into the character he half-wrote for himself. Shepley was an engaging comic actor, but lacked Arnaud's fire power, and as a result they were unevenly matched. The play limped along at the Phoenix for a few months with bargain-price tickets; it was not the greatest of starts for the Partnership. 'Arnaud was a splendid clown,' reflected Robert later, 'renowned for helping lame plays over the footlights; alas ours proved too much of a cripple even for her.'

One afternoon, after a matinée of *Fanny*, when I happened to be backstage hiding from the tutorial college where I was supposed to be trying to clutch at a Maths GCE O-level on my way to Oxford, my father became suddenly unusually depressed about his career, which seemed to him to be sinking into the doldrums; neither the musical, nor the play for Arnaud, nor indeed the Café de Paris cabaret could have been considered successes, and he was not accustomed to failure. To cheer him up, I suggested we walk down the Strand to Charing Cross; if, along the way, I said, none of his fans came up to ask him for an autograph, then I would agree that he was indeed a failure. It was a curious experience and a sharp lesson in the general absent-mindedness of autograph collectors. The first woman who stopped him congratulated him on being Charles Laughton; two others thought he might be James Robertson Justice, and another settled for Orson Welles.

By the time we reached Charing Cross, however, Robert was a lot better, having discovered to his relief that other people were as bad about names and faces as he was; he had recently spent forty minutes in the bar of the Garrick with its only other occupant, an actor of remarkable tedium. He then went downstairs to the dining-room, there to greet a late arrival at the central table. 'My dear fellow,' said Robert, 'how good to see you after so long and how are you?' 'Much the same as when you left me in the bar upstairs,' said the other actor irritably.

But by far the best of these brief encounters occurred one evening when Robert and his father-in-law, Buck, took the train to Wargrave; the other occupant of their carriage soon shook my father's hand and announced what a pleasure it was to be travelling with him. 'Your speeches in the war', said the stranger, 'were the only ones that really made any sense; they should have made you Prime Minister. But I do so admire the way you still take the Cresta Run ... '

'I suppose at my age I really shouldn't,' said Robert. 'I'm a fool to myself.'

'But such courage,' continued the stranger, 'and to pioneer flying in the way that you did.'

'One just went up,' said Robert reflectively, 'and then one came down.'

By now the train had reached Wargrave and, as they bade farewell to the stranger, Buck was apoplectic with rage. 'Why', he asked Robert, 'didn't you tell the poor man you were not Lord Brabazon?'

'Oh, but I was,' said Robert, 'all the way from Paddington.'

That summer, as *Fanny* at last limped to a halt in Drury Lane, we had another of our family holidays on the Lido; these were miraculous annual affairs all through the mid-1950s, paid for by the Venice Film Festival which, in those long-lamented days, actually had a budget for actors to come and spend a week or two on the sands with their families in return for several personal appearances at the screenings of whatever movies they happened to have around at the time. We managed several summers on the beach there before we discovered the rest of Venice over the waters of the lagoon, and most of us have been going back there with our own families whenever possible ever since. My father was the perfect guide to Venice, if you were only interested in its restaurants and the Lido casino; occasionally, feeling deeply guilty about a general lack of culture, we would venture inside a church or two, but never for very long.

The highlights of Lido life in 1957 included a state visit along the sands by the Duke and Duchess of Windsor, who arrived rather surprisingly by bus from the port, and glimpses from a nearby beach hut of the future Marchioness of Tavistock exposing her already extremely glamorous limbs to the sun. Heady days.

Back in London, as autumn approached, Robert went into rehearsal with *The Tunnel of Love*, which luckily opened to spectacularly good reviews and retrieved the Robin Fox Partnership from its shaky start with *Six Months Grace*. Within the next month, they had opened another, rather more classical venture, Benn Levy's *The Rape of the Belt* with John Clements, Kay Hammond and Richard Attenborough, and were soon to add an intimate revue, *For Adults Only*, as well as a talented first play by the drama critic of *The Times* Jeremy Kingston, *No Concern of Mine*, to an impressively varied repertoire of opening productions. If it were not yet a rival to H. M. Tennent, the Robin Fox Partnership was certainly in business on a wide range of theatrical fronts, and some of them were even profitable.

In addition Robert found himself something new for the beginning of 1958: an offer from Lew Grade and Val Parnell to host *Sunday Night at the London Palladium*, then the highest-rated variety show on British television, and more than a little unnerving. The job, already made famous by Bruce Forsyth, who was then on some kind of sabbatical, involved not only introducing the various acts but also stage-managing and scoring a series of intricate games in the *Beat the Clock* sequence, alive with props and other technical hazards for someone as wayward and forgetful as my father. On the other hand, it was very good money, around £1,000 a week, and it provided maximum exposure, though Robert took it on with misgivings. 'Everyone knows, when one does this kind of thing at charity matinées, that one isn't being paid. This time I shall have to get my dinner-jacket pressed and try not to confuse the sea lions with the lion-tamer or the adagio dancer. If I make a success of it, I shall almost certainly go into politics and become Prime Minister, a vastly easier undertaking than *Beat the Clock*.' Critics were undecided: several welcomed Robert's air of 'avuncular uncertainty, as he tries to work out which of his star guests might be Buddy Holly and which

Tommy Steele', but the *Observer* thought he resembled 'a performing elephant, albeit of genius, participating with the utmost reluctance in a cabaret staged by a house of ill repute'.

Matters did not improve later in the month, when Robert managed to set fire to the Fairmans chimney and crash his car on ice all within twenty-four hours, experiences which left him determined never again to drive a car and to light the fire in the sitting-room only with the utmost caution. The adventures did, however, give him a couple of good columns for the *Sunday Express*, and soon he was off on his travels to Vienna.

The reason for this was a film called *The Journey*, with which the director Anatole Litvak intended to commemorate the Hungarian Uprising only a few miles and a few months from the reality of 1956. Litvak, never a man restrained by too much good taste, had seen in the uprising the perfect Hollywood strangers-on-a-bus movie, and cast it accordingly. Yul Brynner was to give his evil Russian army officer, Deborah Kerr her British matron in distress, Jason Robards was to be her American hero and saviour, Anne Jackson and E. G. Marshall were to be the American parents of the lovable little boys on the bus (one of whom grew up to be a successful Hollywood director called Ron Howard), and Anouk Aimée was to be the brave leader of the Hungarian resistance.

The fact that this could have been any aeroplane or ship disaster movie of the last forty years was reasonably clear to all, but Robert decided that the role of a portly British war correspondent was well within his range and that there were worse things in life than spring in Vienna. Besides, he was not now in the habit of turning down movies. The filming was causing a certain amount of press interest by the time he arrived there, largely because it was reuniting Brynner with Deborah Kerr immediately after their making of *The King and I*, and there were suspicions of a romance. The true story, which did not emerge until several weeks later, was that Kerr was in the process of leaving her war-hero British husband Tony Bartley for the American screenwriter and novelist Peter Viertel who, with the columnist Art Buchwald (then also on assignment in Vienna) and Robert, would spend several days gallantly trying to divert attention to themselves, always a pleasurable occupation.

Buchwald wrote one or two of his *Herald-Tribune* columns about Robert in Vienna, picking up on my father's better after-dinner observations: 'We British', he told Buchwald, 'are only really happy abroad when the natives are also the waiters. We don't altogether enjoy them being at the same table or in the same sea with us: we prefer them a foot or two behind our chairs, holding the bottle of wine.'

Filming dragged on for several weeks around the hills outside Vienna, so many weeks in fact that Anne Jackson, expecting a child by her husband Eli Wallach, was convinced she would have to give birth to it on the location bus. Reviews, when they finally arrived, were less than wonderful, though Robert did manage to lend some dignity and gravitas to such Hollywood hokum historical lines as 'Those Hungarians ... we always thought them a bunch of gypsy fiddlers, and now they've taught the world a lesson in courage it will never forget.'

Whether the Hungarian rebels ever managed to forget or forgive *The Journey*, or whether they even noticed it, is another question; one critic took the view that 'despite its elaborate contemporary-documentary trappings, Litvak has here contrived the usual Ruritanian romance, complete with joky Hungarian hotel proprietors, massed peasants appearing on cue to sing their national songs and the Red Army forever marching around ... One day it is possible that the Hungarian revolt of October 1956 will be appropriately commemorated on celluloid. Meanwhile *The Journey* will stand as an awful warning to anyone approaching the subject.'

But as the shooting came to an end, there was one memorable afternoon when Deborah was to escape from Brynner's clutches over the Austrian border and race down a hill into the open arms of Jason Robards in his first film. Jason, as was then his habit, had taken a rather long lunch; back at the bottom of the hill to start the afternoon shooting, he looked up and saw Deborah, not a small lady, hurtling down towards him. Very slowly, as I watched, he fell over backwards into the snow while she was still several hundred yards away. Alas, the moment is not immortalised in the final cut as seen these days on late-night television.

20

More Wilde Times

1958–1959

On the steps of the Grand Hotel in Rome, I asked the splendidly uniformed doorman to hail me a cab; 'That, sir,' he said, 'will not be possible for two reasons. Firstly there are none, and secondly, even if there were, I am the Papal Nuncio to the Holy See of the Vatican.

Home from *The Journey*, Robert filmed for a couple of days on a curious Anglo-Western, *The Sheriff of Fractured Jaw*, which starred Kenneth More, an actor whose stage appearances principally in the comedies of William Douglas-Home were coming to bear certain resemblances to Robert's. Growing up around More there was, in fact, an entire generation of accomplished light comedians, from Gerald Harper and William Franklyn to James Villiers and Jonathan Cecil, who would carry through from the 1960s into the 1980s something of Robert's boulevard traditions. Their problem, like his, was a general lack of dramatists either willing or able to work in this convention, and increasingly, as Robert took to the movies, they took to television sitcoms and serials.

On the film front there came a couple of more noteworthy pictures: first *Law and Disorder*, a Charlie Crichton comedy in the full Ealing tradition, which pitched Robert as a judge up against Michael Redgrave's gentleman smuggler, and then, from Anthony Asquith, an offer to star in his second Shavian screening, this one of the play which had made him want to become an actor almost fifty years earlier.

The Doctor's Dilemma starred Dirk Bogarde and Leslie Caron at the head of

an immensely strong team: Robert was to be Sir Ralph Bloomfield-Bon-
nington with Alastair Sim, John Robinson and Felix Aylmer among his
fellow doctors, Cecil Beaton designing the sets and costumes, and no expense
spared. But something went oddly adrift: what should have been a return to
the great prewar films of Bernard Shaw as screened by Gabriel Pascal became
a desperately wooden museum piece, with Asquith so determined to remain
true to the Shavian original that he ended up effectively photographing the
play from the front row of the stalls. Bogarde, the consummate film actor of
his generation, seemed ill at ease among so many theatricals and was haunted
by the fear that his fans might mistake this classic for another in his long series
of *Doctor in the House* comedies. In the event they stayed away altogether, and
the reviews were lukewarm, though rather better in America.

Theatrically Robert was in search of another moneymaker for himself and
his partners in the Robin Fox Partnership, and the logical place to start that
search would seem to have been Paris and André Roussin. After two
long-running Roussin hits with *The Little Hut* and *Hippo Dancing*, why not
go back to the well for a third?

This one, like its predecessors, had already scored a couple of years on the
Paris boulevards: originally called *Le Mari, la Femme et la Mort*, it was a
reasonably classic Roussin farce about a wife trying to murder her elderly
husband for a fortune which turns out to be mythical. Once he had achieved
his own adaptation, Robert had something of a brainwave. Since it was
already clear that the London theatre was dividing into two camps, the
revolutionaries of the Royal Court and the old guard of the West End, why
not raid the enemy for a co-star? Robert had seen Joan Plowright in a
dazzling double bill of *The Chairs and The Lesson* at the Royal Court in Sloane
Square and was urged by the astute Robin Fox to take her into the new farce,
in the hope that critics might therefore treat it rather more gently than if
it were cast entirely from Robert's usual pre-1956 stable. Joan, for her part,
had never starred in the West End and was eager to try her wings away from
the Royal Court. Already at the start of her relationship with Laurence
Olivier, this was not the easiest of emotional times for her, and Robert was
offering an escape, first of all to France, where he had decided they should
spend ten days at Juan les Pins, ostensibly rehearsing and soaking up local
atmosphere, but in fact having themselves a splendid holiday on the production expenses before returning to the chillier reality of a Manchester first
night.

After the usual weeks of try-out and error on the road, *Hook, Line and
Sinker* (as the play had come to be called) opened at the Piccadilly Theatre in
November 1958. Joan did not, alas, prove much of an insurance against the

critics, splendidly funny though she was in the role of the scheming wife. Most critics were after Robert's blood as star and author, with Doris Lessing, sitting in for Tynan at the *Observer*, leading the pack: 'Robert Morley plays the lead as Robert Morley, supposedly a uxurious Frenchman, but radiating the aroma of roast beef and two veg.' Milton Shulman for the *Evening Standard* thought he looked like 'a dinosaur slowly discovering that he is sitting on a bonfire', but it was T. C. Worsley for the *New Statesman* who really put the knife in:

> Potentially Mr Morley is a fine comic actor, when he bothers to do it, which is for about twenty minutes in the last act. The rest of the time he Morleys about and is apparently satisfied with his laughs . . . It is sad when a talented person is so complacent, so self-indulgent, so content to fob audiences off with the third rate when he is capable of the first rate . . . How long can he get away with it? Probably forever, more's the pity, certainly for as long as there is this indulgent middle-class audience willing to pay too much for too little . . . This is the public which has ruined all its spoiled darlings, from Yvonne Arnaud through Margaret Rutherford to Wilfrid Hyde-White . . . I don't just want to see Mr Morley show off, I want to see him act; the waste of his talent is his own affair; but he is cheating me of my pleasure, and that's what makes me cross.

Worsley's case, though more brutally expressed than in any other review Robert received, was not a new one, nor was it confined entirely to his critics. A number of his close friends, notably Sewell Stokes and Frith Banbury from Perranporth days, had been trying for years to persuade Robert to take himself more seriously as an actor, to venture towards some of the lighter classics if he were ever to win back the laurels of *Oscar Wilde*.

The problem was essentially how to do it. Already his choices were all too clear: he could either stay in a rapidly declining West End, hoping that enough boulevard comedies would come down the Avenue to see him through, given that most of his income was now derived from films; or he could try the plunge that Olivier and, with rather less success, Rex Harrison had taken and join the Royal Court; or he could grit his teeth and try for Stratford or the Old Vic. But, when he seriously thought about it, both the last two routes filled him with uneasiness: the Royal Court was unquestionably a writer's and director's rather than an actor's theatre, and his lifelong boredom with Shakespeare was not exactly going to stand him in good stead by the Avon. Though he would, I think, have been a magnificent Falstaff and an interesting Henry VIII or Toby Belch, the truth was that he felt about

classical acting much as he had felt about ballroom dancing since, at the age of
ten, the legendary Madame Vacani had taken him in hand. 'Master Morley,'
she had said then, after he had spent about fifteen minutes on the dance floor
clenched in her tutorial embrace, 'we at this school have one absolutely
golden rule, which is that we never, ever admit defeat. On this occasion,
however . . . '

There might, of course, have been another alternative: if Robert had been
fractionally younger or they fractionally older, a whole new generation of
dramatists from Alan Bennett through Michael Frayn to Ronald Harwood
might have suited him very well, and he them; but the generations were too
far apart and Robert was left waving, if not drowning, from the further shores
of Shaftesbury Avenue.

All the same, the company got about six months out of *Hook, Line and
Sinker* and, since Gladys was playing, albeit briefly, at a nearby theatre with
Kay Kendall in Judy Campbell's *The Bright One*, there were some cheerful
family dressing-room suppers between the Saturday shows, catered as exquisitely as ever by Ros Chatto.

When that run came to a close, Robert went to Edinburgh to film *The
Catbird Seat*, James Thurber's office comedy, which had been turned into a
Peter Sellers vehicle called *The Battle of the Sexes*, and then he returned to
work with Asquith and Dirk Bogarde as one of the Queen's Counsels in
Libel, donning the courtroom robes and wig in which Robert was in-
creasingly to be found on film.

Wary of going into yet another Shaftesbury Avenue romp at a time when
critics seemed decidedly hostile towards him, if not the genre itself, he turned
instead to directing and put two young classical players he hugely admired,
Dorothy Tutin and John Neville, into their first West End comedy. This was
an already established Broadway hit by Harry Kurnitz called *Once More, With
Feeling* and was soon to be made into a movie by Yul Brynner and Kay
Kendall. It told the story of a classical conductor in romantic and marital
troubles, and Bernard Levin was among many London critics who did not
care for a moment of it.

The problems now facing both the Robin Fox Partnership and its principal actor were considerable: both had somehow got themselves on the wrong
side of theatrical fashion in the late 1950s and they were never quite able to
find a path back. For Robert, however, this was not the catastrophe it might
have been for many other actors. His own expectations of himself as an actor
were never tremendous: he had, as he always said, fallen happily into a career
he much enjoyed, but his sights were never set very far above his own
particular parapet. That he always left as a vision for the rest of us.

Then again, although he was in perpetual trouble with the Inland Revenue, finally settling his debts only on death, the money troubles did not prevent him and his family living comfortably both at home and on annual Italian or French holidays. He was a constantly generous host and a wonderful provider, and, like all the best hosts, he also took the trouble to see that he himself was excellently provided with cigars, brandy, and the occasional race horse in the days when he could afford the Newbury training fees.

He was rarely out of work, but, unlike many of the Hollywood exiles of his generation, he seldom, if ever, made the kind of 'real' money which would allow for tax clearance, investment in real estate or contributing to an adequate pension scheme. He was a working British actor at a time when both stage and studio salaries were less than stratospheric, and if his career from this point on was to lose focus, apart from one or two exceptional performances, it was partly due to its variety and intensity. Robert would take whatever came down the phone, sometimes to stave off the boredom he began to feel when not working, but mainly because he usually needed the money and enjoyed the exposure.

I asked him once, around this time, if he ever regretted not having been a more disciplined or classical actor, whether indeed he ever envied such actors as Olivier, Gielgud or Redgrave. Never, he said, though he did sometimes find himself lying in the bath wishing he had been Ralph Richardson. Why Ralph? 'Because, unlike all the others, he remains so totally unexpected and unpredictable and touching.'

If 1959 had not started as the best of his few short years in management, it was soon to grow worse: the Partnership followed *Once More, With Feeling* with another flop, Wynyard Browne's *The Ring of Truth*, which brought together a couple of old friends of Robert's, David Tomlinson and Frith Banbury as director, for a rather limited run. Then the Partnership went full steam ahead into a seriously expensive fiasco: a musical of Molière's *Le Malade imaginaire*, retitled *The Love Doctor* and with a score by the *Kismet* composers, George Forrest and Robert Wright. By the time they reached Manchester, where the reviews were already the worst since Pearl Harbor, it was clear that some drastic script doctoring was required. Robert duly arrived at the scene of the accident, as did a young American librettist, Michael Stewart, later to make his name as the author of *Hello, Dolly!* This was not such an auspicious occasion: an already mortally ill musical died in the Manchester operating theatre, and by the time the corpse reached London (for sixteen performances only) Bernard Levin was able to announce that, among the lucky ones, he had managed to sleep soundly through most of the second half.

This was the moment when Robert, not altogether surprisingly, decided the time might well have come to try his fortunes on the other side of the Atlantic once again. What he had there was an offer from Alfred Hitchcock, not alas of a movie, but to star in one of the half-hour horrors he was then making for American television. Building on this, Robin Fox also managed to get Robert two live television appearances for *Playhouse 90*, first in a rather undistinguished *Oliver Twist*, but then in an all-star production of Shaw's *Misalliance* (Claire Bloom, Siobhan McKenna, Kenneth Haigh, Patrick Mac-Nee), which collected the best reviews of the season.

The American visit also allowed Robert to spend some time with Gladys at the Pacific Palisades home she was packing up for the last time, and to make the first of several joyous pilgrimages to Las Vegas, Robert's Mecca whenever he could afford the airfare and the gambling losses. Some of these he recouped on this trip by appearing on David Susskind's arts programmes as a pundit ('Britain's fieriest gift to the USA since they burnt the White House', thought *Variety*) and by sending back to the *Sunday Express* travel columns about Californian television life. 'I met Mr Jack Benny in the lobby of Television City on the day I arrived here,' he wrote from Los Angeles in November 1959,

a city with several studios and rehearsal rooms, but alas no restaurant, which seems unusual. Mr Benny asked politely after my co-stars and I asked after his: 'Who do you have on the show this week?' 'Just Harry Truman,' was the reply; I watched the show, during which Truman passed Benny the seal of office he had used in the White House. 'Pure gold?' he asked. 'Pure gold,' said Truman. It was some time before Benny could bear to hand it back; at such moments, though there are very few, American television itself is pure gold. Elsewhere its dramas are gloomy, full of problems and no servants; the best dramas in my day always had servants and no problems . . . A recent edict there at CBS in the wake of the 64,000 Dollar Quiz scandals has it that no programme may now include canned laughter, recorded applause or 'anything tending to mislead the public'. What is to be done about actors who persist in wearing toupées has yet to be decided.

After the television work was safely completed, Robert and Gladys decided to head for Mexico for a holiday on which he was to find himself in perpetual, terrified awe of her blind courage:

Whether pushing a wild bear into the sunshine so that she could take a better photograph of it (I wound up the window of the car and locked the door so as to delay the moment when I would have to wrestle with the creature over her lifeless body), or hurtling up to a sniper on a Mexican beach to tell him to put his guns away (I had already run into the sea), she was forever undaunted. Once, dressed inadvertently in shorts, we were refused admission to the hotel dining-room in Acapulco. 'The trouble is', said the head waiter, 'that we are holding a large party for General Motors and so tonight is formal.' 'That will be quite all right,' said Gladys, sweeping past him to our table, 'I know the General very well and I am sure he will be delighted to have us join him.'

Home for Christmas, Robert's thoughts turned to a play he had seen in New York which might enable him to win back the critics and escape the pigeon-holing of the French boulevard pieces, which had clearly reached the end of the line; in Paris, even André Roussin was thinking of retirement. The Broadway play was an eccentric comedy by Leonard Spigelglass called *A Majority of One*, about a late-life romance between a successful Japanese businessman and a Jewish widow from Brooklyn. True, Robert was not the most Japanese-looking of actors, but in America the role had proved a considerable success on stage and screen for Cedric Hardwicke, also not one of nature's most plausible orientals, and the feeling was that, with a little Sellotape around the eyes, a token Tokyo effect could be achieved in those distant, unrace-conscious days. What the objectors to Jonathan Pryce in *Miss Saigon* would have made of Robert in *Majority of One* is the stuff of nightmares, but Wendy Toye's deft steering of the comedy on to Shaftesbury Avenue did indeed win back the critics, though rehearsals had not been easy.

Wendy had decided that, in an attempt at authenticity, Robert and Molly Picon (a redoubtable and splendid doyenne of the New York Yiddish Theatre) should be introduced to the rituals of the tea ceremony and raw fish dinners at a house in Golder's Green, where the director knew of an orthodox Japanese family. Robert and Molly survived the tea and some of the raw fish, whereupon their kimono-clad hostess unwisely asked what they would like to follow. 'For me', said Molly, already half way to the door, 'just the doctor.'

Reviews were as good as Robert had hoped. 'Mr Morley', wrote Harold Hobson, 'may be an improbable Japanese tycoon, but he plays here with a dignity, a calmness and a stillness that are extremely moving.'

During the run of *A Majority of One*, which occupied him for most of 1959, Robert at last had the chance to make the film he had longed to do for twenty years: *Oscar Wilde*.

Oscar Wilde: in the title role of the film, with Ralph Richardson as Edward Carson

He was now slightly too old for the role, but the idea of getting back to the story which had originally made his name, bringing it to a vastly wider audience and still within the original Leslie and Sewell Stokes script, was far too good to resist. For years the problem had been one of cash and censorship; but with the moral climate at last turning more liberal on screen, a splendidly piratical Russian actor and director called Gregory Ratoff, in the best flamboyant tradition of Korda and Pascal, decided that the money could be raised for a quick, cheap, black-and-white film.

There was only one snag: an infinitely better-financed production company called Warwick Films had already commissioned a rival *Oscar Wilde* script from Ken Hughes, based on the classic Montgomery Hyde biography, and they too were about to go before the cameras. In the event, both companies ended up before the judge in an unusual case, during which each side tried to injunct the other on the grounds that they had thought of it first. But thought of what, the judge enquired wearily – of Oscar Wilde? After a short hearing, he told them all to go away and get on with it, if that was what they wished to do, but not to imagine that anyone could ever have exclusive copyright in a life of Oscar Wilde in any medium.

A marathon shooting race then ensued.

For the Warwick version, Peter Finch was to play Wilde with John Fraser as Lord Alfred Douglas, Lionel Jeffries as the mad Marquess of Queensberry,

Yvonne Mitchell as Mrs Wilde and James Mason as the prosecuting counsel, Carson. This version was to be wide-screen, Technicolor and eventually entitled *The Trials of Oscar Wilde*.

Robert and Ratoff's version of *Oscar Wilde* was, by contrast, black-and-white and so low budget as never to leave the studio; it looked like a television drama, which ironically is why it nowadays seems so much better than *The Trials* when repeated on the small screen.

Despite financial limitations, Robert and Ratoff managed to recruit an equally distinguished cast: Ralph Richardson would play Carson with John Neville as Lord Alfred Douglas, Edward Chapman as Queensberry and Phyllis Calvert as Constance. They had one other advantage: working quickly in the studio, even though shooting had started later than the opposition and even though Robert had to disappear every evening to *Majority of One*, they managed to bring the film in on budget and in a much shorter time, which meant that they were first into the cinemas, thus stealing an all-important lead of a few days, which the glossier version was never quite able to make up.

General critical feeling was that, though production values were undoubtedly higher on *The Trials*, Finch and Mason were a poor match for Robert and Ralph in the crucial courtroom duelling: 'It is here that they are at their most impressive,' opined *The Times*, 'with Mr Morley wilting and seeming to change shape physically when Sir Ralph, as Carson, presses him to the point where he makes his fatal slip about a certain boy being "unattractive" to him.'

What critics could not have known was how close this *Wilde* came to never being completed. By the end of the trial scenes Ratoff's money had run out, as had his studio time. All he had left was Robert and about a day to come up with an ending. Undeterred and remembering the original stage play, Robert told him to borrow a café table and a couple of chairs, and shoot him in close up as he delivered the closing speech – and that indeed is how the film ends. It may not be great cinema, but it is, thank God, a photographic record of the greatest stage performance Robert ever gave.

As the film shooting and the run of *Majority of One* came more or less simultaneously to an end, so too did the 1950s. Robert himself was just over fifty and would live another thirty-three years to make another fifty films, some of them highly successful and some so unmemorable that even while shooting them he could not recall what they were. But with *Wilde* safely in the can, his last truly important performance bar one was already given, and that one was to turn up unexpectedly on a stage in Australia two decades later. In the meantime, he went back to America to pioneer some late-night chat shows, and then to Rome to play Potiphar in a terrible biblical movie of *Joseph and his Brethren* without benefit even of a Lloyd Webber score. That was where and when he accused the Papal Nuncio to the Holy See of being an unsuccessful hotel doorman.

21

No Time to Laugh

1960–1965

I accepted the invitation to ride in what is called a motorcade to one of Kennedy's rallies. Always one to believe what I see on the newsreels, I visualised myself standing up and waving triumphantly to the natives while tickertape floated down on me from the windows of skyscrapers and people fought with the police to shake my hand as we sped up Broadway. What nobody had told me was that it would be raining, which not only put a damper on the proceedings but also a cover on the car.

By now Robert's family back home at Fairmans was fast growing up. I was eighteen and on my way up to Oxford, spending the year teaching or rather shouting at very small, deeply bored choirboys at a cathedral school in Chichester. My sister Annabel was thirteen and just starting her own scholastic battles, which mainly involved refusing to board at whatever boarding school was attempting to educate her at the time. My brother Wilton was eight and had just made a brief, but very touching, appearance as one of the sons of Oscar Wilde in Robert's film, for which, to his indignation, he received nothing more than a new bicycle.

As America prepared to greet a new president in 1960 and the coming of Camelot, rather to his surprise Robert became one of that country's newest television stars, though, as so often, he was cast as himself.

What Robert had discovered, by way of Jack Paar, was the miracle of the late-night chat show. Paar was a considerable and rather lovely eccentric, one of the few people I met for the first time at my own wedding; he had a thing about going to weddings, rather like a collector or inspector of them, and he used to ask to be invited to those of virtual strangers to check out the catering. But he was a rare talent who had practically invented the art of late-night chatting on live network television, long before it became the province of Johnny Carson or any of their lesser British imitators. He was also extremely touchy; when accused by one of his sponsors of having uttered the unforgivable words 'water closet' on live television, he took himself off suddenly to Japan for several days, thereby leaving an unexpected hole in the schedules.

Paar, described by Robert as 'America's number one tranquillizer', had realised that by and large the British made the best pundits, and he was therefore cheerfully paying $2,000 a show plus airfare and New York hotel accommodation not only to Robert but also to such other regulars from Britain as Malcolm Muggeridge and Peter Ustinov. At a time in the early 1960s when British television had nothing like a chat show, Paar had managed to invent the equivalent of a salon, or at the very least a saloon bar, to which twenty million or so Americans would drop in every night to overhear a conversation in which they could not participate. Even John F. Kennedy told Robert that Jackie had enjoyed him on the show; 'His rival', said Robert indignantly, 'never even suggested that Pat Nixon had heard of me at all. No wonder Kennedy won.'

Since television seemed to be the medium of the moment, back at Fairmans Robert began to think about writing himself a comedy series, one which might manage to reunite the old team. The idea he eventually came up with was a Ruritanian situation comedy entitled *If The Crown Fits*, in which he would star as King Rupert x of Grabnia, a mythical monarchy with no ruins, museums or monuments and where the sole local custom was fleecing the tourists. This was the first of three attempts Robert was to make over the next quarter-century to crack a curiously difficult market: the situation-comedy routines which ought to have come naturally to him after years in Anglicised French farce proved forever elusive. The truth, I suspect, was that precisely those qualities which made him the perfect chat show guest, a certain unpredictability and the talent for making something out of nothing, were not those best suited to the rigid mechanical disciplines of the twenty-eight minute sitcom.

Nevertheless, he managed to assemble a wonderful cast, mainly of relatives: Gladys Cooper guest-starred in one episode, Robin Fox's daughter-in-law, Tracy Reed, had a regular role, as did Peter Bull, and another of the guest stars was the actor Robert Hardy, who had just married Gladys's daughter Sally. Although *If The Crown Fits* was to be a disaster as a series (ITV failed to repeat it even during a technicians' strike a few months later), Robert had at least kept it within the family and a few million viewers.

Moving on swiftly from the ruins of Grabnia, Robert turned his attention to Cliff Richard's first musical. For *The Young Ones* he was cast as Cliff's father and was required to do a soft-shoe shuffle with him at the close, which is still reckoned in our family something of a collector's piece, if only for the look of eager embarrassment on both their faces at the final fade-out. Robert, however, enjoyed the experience, finding in Cliff, as he had in Tommy Steele during their Palladium television shows, an unspoilt energy and innocence which he thought for a while might be the saving of the British musical on stage or screen.

A couple of minor comedies followed, one of which (*Go to Blazes*) introduced Maggie Smith to the screen and the other (*Road to Hong Kong*) saw at long, long last the end of the Bob Hope and Bing Crosby screen partnership in the seventh of a tired series. 'What were they like?' I asked Robert curiously. 'Who?' 'Crosby and Hope.' 'Two rather crotchety old men who couldn't wait to get back to the golf course in California.' So much for Hollywood Greats.

Robert was already thinking of a return to the stage, in this instance to that of his local Windsor Theatre Royal, in a play sent him by Ronald Gow about the founding father of Rhodesia. *Mr Rhodes* was a faithful historical recreation with leading roles for both Robert and Gow's wife, Wendy Hiller, but it nearly proved the end of their lifelong friendship. As was his wont in rehearsal, Robert could not resist the urge to rewrite, and Ronald was not an author who cared to be rewritten. Wendy barely managed to hold the ring between them, and the play did not travel beyond Windsor.

Robert did, however: he had been summoned to Bombay to play a wily Indian politician in *Nine Hours to Rama*, the first and worst of the screen attempts to tell the life of Mahatma Gandhi. Long before Sir Richard Attenborough came on this scene, a Gandhi movie had been the cherished project of both David Lean and Otto Preminger, neither of whom had managed to raise the money for it. Mark Robson, the director of *Peyton Place* and *Inn of the Sixth Happiness*, put together a remarkable team of unlikely Indians (not only Robert but also José Ferrer, Horst Bucholz, Harry Andrews and Diane Baker), none of whom attempted to rise very far above dialogue like 'You Brahmins were always too proud for my taste.'

The actor playing Gandhi was a friend of the Mahatma, a former schoolmaster called J. S. Casshyap, who had been persuaded that the film was a holy mission and he should not, therefore, expect too much in the way of material gain; only when the rest of the cast took to telling him precisely how much they were being paid by the day did his air of saintly martyrdom show signs of strain. It was to be several years before Sir Richard Attenborough could persuade the Indian authorities to consider another movie on the same sacred subject, especially as José Ferrer had been caught spitting on holy ground during the shooting (of Gandhi in the film) and Robert was seen to be wearing by mistake the robes of a holy prophet. All in all, it was not one of the most cordial chapters in the history of American-Indian filming. 'The curious thing', reflected Robert, 'is that Indians make wonderful films when we leave them alone to do so.'

Back in England, Robert, Robin and Ros had to face the fact that their Partnership days were numbered: *The Love Doctor* had been a costly flop, Robin was much involved with such other projects as the Grade Organisation and the Royal Court, and Ros had joined him in the agency business. Still, time perhaps for one last try at a production all their own? This was to be a real curiosity: a first stage play by an American television dramatist, Robert Crean, called *A Time to Laugh* and concerned with a terminally eccentric papal countess and the worldly bishop who arrives to try to make sense of her household. What everyone seems to have seen here, if not much of a play, was a marvellous role for Robert and also for Ruth Gordon, who was duly imported from Broadway to play the Countess. An eclectic supporting cast was to include Cleo Laine, in a rare non-singing appearance, and Michael Blakemore, then about to give up his life as an actor for a rather more congenial one as a director. Best of all, Tyrone Guthrie had agreed to renew his old partnership with Robert and direct, so rehearsals began in a haze of optimism only to disintegrate as the problems with the play became evident. Ruth Gordon threatened to leave it on the road, Robert began to do his usual drastic on-tour rewriting, and devout Catholics who believed they were being blasphemed began noisily leaving the theatre during the first act. Robert, who had his own money invested in it, took to instructing the front-of-house manager and box-office staff to disappear rapidly as soon as the curtain went up, so that at least the aggrieved could not demand refunds.

Situated oddly half way between *The Garden of Allah* and a Tennessee Williams play, *A Time to Laugh* limped into the West End a few weeks later to face a barrage of critical hostility. Kenneth Tynan subtitled it '20,000 Leagues Beneath the Holy See', and Godfrey Winn saw it as another nail in the coffin of Christianity; most other people did not bother to see it at all and, after barely three weeks at the Piccadilly Theatre, *A Time to Laugh* closed, taking the Robin Fox Partnership down with it.

Robert went speedily back to the cinema, first of all to give his usual, Bullish courtroom performance as a QC in a motorbike gang-warfare saga called *The Boys* and then to renew one of his favourite partnerships, with Margaret Rutherford, for the first of her Miss Marple series, *Murder at the Gallop*. By now his enthusiasm for the theatre had started to diminish; over the next five years he was to average five movies a year, rejecting almost nothing unless dates clashed, but finding his interests increasingly in journalism and the travelling which movie locations in those days made possible on expenses. If a good play had come along, he would probably have taken it; none did, and he had learned to stop investing in his own.

After *Murder at the Gallop* came a Peggy Mount farce about criminal charwomen, *Ladies Who Do*, and then an unsatisfactory remake of the James Whale classic gothic thriller *The Old Dark House*. From there he returned to Hollywood to make a feature film for the first time in a quarter of a century, but nothing so distinguished as *Marie Antoinette*: a supporting role in *Take Her, She's Mine*, playing a few scenes with James Stewart.

Back in England, he did a couple of rather better pictures, *Hot Enough for June*, which was a James Bond parody of considerable style with Dirk Bogarde. Ironically Robert had not only rejected the original *Dr No* but had also advised his *Oscar Wilde* producer, Gregory Ratoff, to sell cheaply the Bond rights he then owned to Cubby Broccoli; it was not always wise to regard Robert as a fount of accurate advice. And then he did *Of Human Bondage*, in which he played Laurence Harvey's tutor.

All were minor roles, involving at most a few weeks on the set; it was not until 1965 that he got his next crack at a more involving and enjoyable project, one which had strong echoes of *Beat The Devil*.

Once again this was to be a crime caper organised by a flamboyant *auteur*-director, Jules Dassin. *Topkapi* was to feature his wife, Melina Mercouri, and a star-studded gang of gentlemen thieves (Robert, Ustinov, Maximilian Schell and Akim Tamiroff) in the heist of a priceless jewel from the eponymous Istanbul museum. Based on a thriller by Eric Ambler (*The Light of Day*), the film was to afford Robert many pleasurable weeks checking out the hotels and restaurants of Istanbul, and steaming up the Bosphorus on day-trip ferries when he was not called to a reasonably relaxed Dassin location. For a while Robin Fox went out to join him, and the two of them got caught up accidentally with a Turkish rug-seller who kept promising Robin exotic sexual encounters at a price. 'I should be a little careful there', advised Robert with all the wisdom of a few extra weeks in Istanbul, 'all that man has ever laid is a carpet.'

Topkapi came as a sharp reminder of just how good Robert could be on screen if anyone bothered to give him a character, a plot or some decent dialogue to work on; increasingly, however, few did. His casting came to be seen as an end in itself, with Robert the kind of actor who is sent for when a film is in trouble, knowing that his mere presence on screen will divert the audience for a minute or two from realising the shambles going on elsewhere.

Recognising this, Robert began to give armour-plated performances which varied solely on those scarce occasions when he came up against a director who wanted and knew that he could deliver more than a routine turn.

In a rare break from this avalanche of film roles, Robert diverted to American television for a show of his own, a one-man monologue, which over the next twenty years he would occasionally try out on audiences everywhere from Hong Kong to Brighton in the vague belief that he might discover the type of solo routine which was proving so successful for both Emlyn Williams and John Gielgud. They, however, had Dickens and Shakespeare; what Robert had was a random bunch of his own childhood memories, after-dinner anecdotes and occasional breathtaking insights into people or places, all of which somehow failed to add up to a coherent show. 'I always found', he noted sadly, 'that I was enjoying myself so much more than the audience, though they were always kind enough to pretend they were glad they had come.'

By this time all Robert really asked of a film was the chance to find a friend or two on the set ('Bad actors are so much more fun than good ones to lunch with') and the opportunity to get back to the race course, the Fairmans pool or one of London's new casinos as soon as possible, preferably with a little money to spare. Despite the fact that Robert was now catching films the way others catch planes or trains, a habit he had copied from his mother-in-law, he could hardly have expected the call to become Emperor of China.

22

Up Ustinov's Tree

1966–1968

Hell is a play by Brecht; Hamlet *with Nicol Williamson; a medical examination for an insurance policy; macaroni cheese. Hell is the Earl's Court Road, and a story I've told too often, and a letter from my accountant before I've opened it. Hell is knowing how much I have in the bank. Hell is the bathroom scales, and an unexplained spot on the end of my nose. Hell was my name on the games list at school.*

Of all the actors who might be considered likely casting for an Emperor of China, Robert does not come swiftly to mind; but Hollywood works in mysterious ways and, since Irving Allen had already collected in Belgrade a multinational cast (Omar Sharif, Stephen Boyd, Françoise Dorléac, Telly Savalas, Eli Wallach and James Mason) for his *Genghis Khan*, an emperor resembling someone out of a touring Gilbert and Sullivan operetta did not seem so very far out of the ordinary. It must be admitted that Robert did not help the cause by retaining his grey flannel trousers, which can clearly be seen beneath his robes in several shots, nor by insisting that, in order to save make-up time and thereby avoid having to arrive on the set too early each morning, his pigtail should be glued to the back of his hat.

It was an eccentric performance in an eccentric venture: for reasons which now escape me, the gala world première was held in Munich, and Pa and I went to it on tickets kindly provided by the film's releasing company. The audience sat in stunned silence throughout this epic to end all epics; 'Don't worry,' the director told us afterwards, 'it's just that they couldn't follow it in

English.' It later transpired that few English-speakers around the world could either.

Back then from Belgrade to California for one of those movies which promised much more than it delivered. The director Tony Richardson, having recently forsaken the British film industry he had almost single-handedly recreated in the early 1960s, had settled in California by 1965 and was eager to make a movie of *The Loved One*, Evelyn Waugh's classic satire on Hollywood burial practices. Like the story, the film opens with Sir Francis Hinsley and Ambrose Abercrombie, two great relics of the British Raj in Hollywood and lightly modelled on C. Aubrey Smith and Cedric Hard-wicke. For these roles Richardson brilliantly decided to cast Robert and John Gielgud in an unholy alliance.

The film itself had been through many hands before it reached those of Tony. 'It is a constant annoyance to me', wrote Waugh around this time, 'as I had hoped for Alec Guinness and now it has been sold to a mad Mexican, who has in turn sold it on to Hollywood, where they will doubtless produce an elaborate and tasteless travesty: no redress.' As usual, Waugh had got it in one: the 'mad Mexican' turned out to be Luis Buñuel, but, by the time it fell into Richardson's hands, he and Christopher Isherwood, another stalwart of the new Hollywood Raj, made the fatal error of trying to update it to the 1960s, complete with bodies flying around in outer space.

What might have been a brilliant period gem became instead a neurotic travesty, fatally miscast with Robert Morse in the central role and not much helped by some over-the-top supporting performances from Liberace, Rod Steiger, Margaret Leighton, James Coburn and Dana Andrews. Where restraint was needed, Richardson went into overdrive, trying to persuade Robert and Gielgud to take part in some transvestite bar sequences which both actors knew were totally out of keeping with the style of the original. Tony refused to heed their warnings, though, and the result was a fiasco: billed desperately as 'the motion picture with something to offend everyone', it ended up by boring most. 'A spineless farrago of collegiate gags,' thought Stanley Kauffman, while Pauline Kael for the *New Yorker* added: 'This sinking ship only makes it to port because everyone on board is too giddy and self-obsessed to panic.' Richardson's career as one of British cinema's greatest directors was never to recover fully from his move to California, and sadly the rot started here.

Disillusioned, but no longer surprised at the ways of a wayward Holly-wood industry which had declined beyond all belief in the thirty years since he had started out there at MGM, Robert returned home to a rash of minor but generally more successful parts. *Those Magnificent Men in Their Flying*

Machines had him as the jovial press baron sponsoring the first London-to-Paris air race; in *A Study in Terror* he was Mycroft Holmes, worldly-wise brother to John Neville's Sherlock; *The Alphabet Murders* saw him as a dim Scotland Yard detective deputed to help Tony Randall's Hercule Poirot; in *Life at the Top* he played Laurence Harvey's father yet again; *Hotel Paradiso* found him in Paris with Alec Guinness and Douglas Byng for a disappointing screen version of the Feydeau classic; *Way, Way Out* took him back to Hollywood to support Jerry Lewis in a dire space-age farce; *Tendre Voyou* took him to Tahiti in support of Jean-Paul Belmondo; and in *Finder's Keepers* he was back with Cliff Richard for the last in a series of British musicals which they had launched together five years earlier with *The Young Ones*.

By 1967 Robert was spending such time as he had away from the studios either writing columns for the *Sunday Express* or making fleeting television appearances, the best of which was in a documentary for the *One Pair of Eyes* series on BBC2, during which he managed to demolish almost every popular theory about British private education, largely by examining the effect that it had had on him and his immediate family. He was also not averse to brisk summaries of his co-stars, or such of them as he had enjoyed meeting on the set. Gielgud? 'A great Shakespearian, you know; when he had to play dead in *The Loved One*, I used to recite my Shylock over his corpse just to see how long it would take for him to wince. About ten seconds.' Ustinov? 'People always think we are very alike, but we're not, you know: he is a genius who happens to live like an actor, whereas I am an actor who happens to live like a genius.'

Robert then found a fresh lease of life on the small screen, chairing one of the original teams of contestants on *Call My Bluff* opposite Frank Muir, a jolly time which only came to an end when, slipping on some ice outside Television Centre, he broke his ankle. Fortunately another of the contestants that week was Jonathan Miller, who swiftly got him into hospital; he only left when he realised there might be some quick money to be made playing a patient with a broken ankle on the long-running ITV hospital series *Emergency Ward Ten*, on which he appeared for several episodes in real plaster.

By then, reckoning that he was in need of a holiday and some sunshine, he had also decided on a return to the stage, not in wintry England, but instead in Australia, which he had not revisited since the *Edward* triumph of seventeen years earlier. Robert had always remembered it fondly, not least the pleasures of the race track, the beach and the sunshine of Sydney. In the last two decades of his life Australia was to play an increasingly important part in his calendar, since both his daughter and his younger son were eventually to settle out there, and he was to return almost annually with my mother to escape the damp of a Berkshire January.

On this first return he took only Tom Chatto and his one-man show, which was still proving difficult to get right even though he now had a new title, *The Sound of Morley*. He did, however, enjoy several amusing afternoons at the race track or in the sea, and came home having rediscovered, after all of five years, a liking for live audiences, which was to lead him back at last into the West End.

This time he was in distinguished, even classical hands; he had been sent by his old manager, Binkie Beaumont, a new play by Peter Ustinov which John Gielgud had already been engaged to direct. Called *Halfway up the Tree*, this was a brittle, quirky comedy of modern manners chiefly concerned with General Sir Mallalieu FitzButtress, who returns from military duties in Malaysia to find that his beatnik son has been sent down from university and his daughter has become pregnant by an unknown lover.

The General's reaction is to retire to a walnut tree in his garden, from where he returns in full hippie gear himself, complete with beads and a voluminous kaftan, to hold forth to his amazed family on the state of a changing nation. This one really should have been the dream ticket: Robert coming together with both Ustinov and Gielgud, under the Tennent management, and with a wonderfully comic supporting cast led by Ambrosine Phillpotts as his wife, Mark Dignam as a visiting cleric and Jonathan Cecil as a manic scout master. But all did not go smoothly in rehearsals: 'Trying to direct your father', said Sir John to me later, 'was about as useful as trying to change the sequence on a set of traffic lights. He knew what he wanted to do and did it regardless of all other suggestions.'

One of the things he wanted to do was to rewrite some of Peter's dialogue; Ustinov, who was away filming until quite late in rehearsals, came back to whole tracts of unfamiliar speech and was indeed beginning to be quite relieved when he recognised a few lines of his own. But the world history of the play is instructive. It was staged both in Paris and New York (where Ustinov himself starred) quite soon after the London première, and in both cases it was played line for line as originally written. In Britain, however, where it was somewhat changed, it ran for twice as long as anywhere else. Robert still knew his audience and what they wanted, even if it was not precisely what the playwright had in mind.

On this occasion there were no major rows on the road; Gielgud had *Tartuffe* at the National Theatre to return to, Ustinov was otherwise engaged and Robert was left to steer the play triumphantly into the West End; three considerable egos had moved unusually tactfully around each other, and the result did them all a lot of good. Reviews were generally enthusiastic, though Hilary Spurling for the *Spectator* found it 'a floppy, sprawling, chumbling piece, expert only in its nicely calculated judgement of audience reaction'. Even so, she thought it was 'the ultimate in reassurance and should run for years', while Harold Hobson noted that 'Mr Morley is the last of our *monstres sacrés*, and we do right to worship him'. The worshipping lasted at the Queen's Theatre for a year, during which time Ustinov came to revisit his play and ask the director if one of its younger actresses could be made more assertive. 'You're right,' mused Gielgud, 'I should have allowed her to wear a hat after all.'

23

To Russia with Pa

1968

I have never been a keen student of church architecture or national galleries; what I have most enjoyed in a lifetime of travel is the people along the way. I have encountered Popes and Presidents, Greta Garbo and the Duchess of Windsor and Mrs Eleanor Roosevelt. It never occurred to me to ask any of them what they were doing on my path and, what was worse, I never even asked myself; I just enjoyed meeting them, in Samarra or on Blackpool Sands.

During the run of *Halfway up the Tree*, in May 1968, Robert celebrated his sixtieth birthday with a major outing: the plan was to charter two small aeroplanes from an airfield at White Waltham and fly a large assembly of family and friends across the channel to Le Touquet. Unfortunately France had chosen that month to hold a national strike, at the time of the student uprisings; undeterred, we flew into Le Touquet and had the entire town to ourselves for one magical Sunday, memorably preserved on some extremely scratched home movies.

This was the last great gathering of the clan around Robert, and of about four generations: Gladys was still much in evidence, aged almost eighty and for some unfathomable reason driving a Go-Kart at high speed through the deserted streets on the way to Florio's, which was open for lunch despite the national emergency. There, too, on the film are Aunt Margaret and all the Barham cousins from Kent; my mother, brother and sister, of course, and Margaret, whom I had married three years earlier, and our baby son Hugo, who was about six months old. There, as well, is Gladys's sister Gracie, deaf from birth, but already a redoubtable old lady, and Gladys's daughter Sally, her husband Robert Hardy and their two young daughters, and Ros and Tom Chatto with their sons James and Daniel, and my godfathers Sewell Stokes and Peter Bull, and Angela and Robin Fox – all of us lining up on an otherwise totally deserted French beach like characters in some obscure Truffaut film, small children being aimlessly pushed around the sands in prams, while the parents and grandparents who were not doing the pushing wandered off towards casino or restaurant.

It was a strange and miraculous day, and I am glad it never occurred to me at the time that we would be unable to repeat it; within only a couple more years two of the party were dead, and within a decade it would have been hard to assemble more than about half of us.

But around Fairmans little seemed to be changing; with Robert back for the first time in ten years with an established West End hit, life appeared to be carrying on much as it had in the 1950s. True, we were all somewhat older. I had left ITN, where I had started out as a newscaster after an eccentric year's teaching at the University of Hawaii, and had joined BBC2 for seven happy years as an interviewer on a nightly arts programme called *Late Night Line-Up*; I had also started to write the first biography of Noël Coward, and had the joy of bringing him and Robert together for a charity matinée to celebrate Noël's seventieth birthday. My sister was already in her early twenties and setting out on a London life, and my brother had recently left the American School in Switzerland and was considering a career backstage in the theatre.

At weekends, especially in summer, all of us would gather around my father, thereby creating a vast amount of cooking and cleaning for my mother, who remained wonderfully unopposed to these vast lunches and teas, at which Pa would preside. Around the pool on most Sunday afternoons could be found not only large numbers of Morleys, Coopers, Merivales, Barhams and Hardys but also many of our friends, including Christopher Matthew and Nigel Frith, whom I'd known since Oxford days and in whom Robert also took delight.

Like me, my son had managed (with considerable help from his mother) to be born on one of Robert's first nights, when *Halfway up the Tree* was on its pre-London tour the previous autumn; content though I have always been to be called after the leading character in *The Man Who Came to Dinner*, we figured Hugo might not be so happy with Mallalieu and thus he was named after one of my former Oxford tutors. Pa and Hugo formed an almost instant rapport; like Churchill, Robert not only always looked like a huge baby but also managed to get on with them spectacularly well. 'Slumped in our chairs', he wrote, 'my first grandchild and I spend many afternoons on the lawn. Time was when we would both have napped, but my grandson soon passed the age for sleeping in the afternoons, whereas with me the habit becomes more and more compelling.'

Out of the pool and away from the garden, he was still attending race meetings whenever possible and celebrating the occasional win by one his horses, an event which gave him perhaps the greatest pleasure of later life. He also continued writing food and travel columns for *Express* Newspapers and sounding off on his usual range of political and educational topics; any diary or features page editor stuck for a story would simply phone him at home and Robert would go straight into gleeful rentaquote, often getting better and better the less he actually knew of the subject in hand.

He was filming, too, whenever the opportunity arose and frequently agreeing to sit for portraits, notably those by Michael Noakes, Judy Cassab and, a few years later, one by David Poole, which was the subject of a television profile, during which both painter and sitter were quizzed about what each thought of the other.

When the run of the Ustinov play came to its close, my television programme *Late Night Line-Up* was taken off the air for a month to make way for some sporting extravaganza, possibly the Olympic Games, and with time suddenly on our hands, Pa and I accepted an unusual commission from the travel editor of the *Evening News* to set off on a father-and-son journey around the USSR, then newly opened up to foreign tourists.

This was one of the few periods in our lives when Robert and I were alone together, except that in Moscow in those days you were never really alone. We were forever watched by eager guides from Intourist. After filing a few rather desultory travel pieces about Red Square and Lenin's Tomb, Pa decided we should become more adventurous and travel south; he had formed a plan to join the Trans-Siberian railway and then cross by sea to Japan, a further voyage I would have to forego as *Late Night Line-Up* was due back on air. In order to sort out Pa's travel plans, we duly presented ourselves at the new Intourist office on the corner of Red Square. 'Us English,' we said hopefully to a large lady behind the counter with a small moustache, 'Us tourists. Us wish to go Samarkand, maybe Bukhara. Catch big boat. Go Japan,' and with that we pointed helpfully to a large blue area on the wall map behind her desk. The lady looked up and sighed; 'Mr Morley,' she said in perfect English, 'I think you will find that the large blue area to which you are pointing on my map is in fact China. Few travellers, in my experience, have ever managed to cross China by boat, big or small.'

Undaunted, we did get as far as Bukhara (where they were rather surprisingly holding the first Soviet Science Fiction Film Festival) and Samarkand, though not on the golden road. There I left Pa to make his way to Japan, a country he did not much care for, having a low tolerance threshold for raw fish and a language he could not begin to understand. 'I therefore confined my acquaintanceship to the Americans I found in the Hilton hotel bar. Most of them seemed to be gay, and were living with Japanese Monsieur Butterflies. I was asked to dinner with one or two, duly took my shoes off outside the front door, and almost always then fell straight into a small pit around the dining-room table. Sometimes I was mistaken rather curiously for Babe Ruth, so after a few days I got bored of that and went home.'

Robert returned in time to organise Gladys's eightieth birthday party, on 18 December 1968. Her first husband, Buck, having died a couple of years earlier well into his eighties, it fell to Robert to take charge of the proceedings, which were complicated by the fact that Gladys was then playing with Michael Denison and Dulcie Gray in a light-weight Broadway comedy at St Martin's Theatre called *Out of the Question*. After considerable family consultations with the Denisons and the theatre management, it was decided that for the Monday night of Gladys's eightieth we should buy out the theatre, fill the stalls with her friends and that early in act one Robert should appear on stage with a tray of champagne glasses. The play could then safely be abandoned and we would all take Gladys across the road to the Ivy for dinner.

Gladys, who had of course not been let in on the secret, was amazed and appalled by the sight of her son-in-law suddenly on stage, and it took several minutes to explain to her that all paying customers had been diverted to another night. Nevertheless the following night's *Evening Standard* carried an irate letter from James Roose-Evans of the Hampstead Theatre asking, 'Is the theatregoing public to be deflected at the last moment from seeing a production for which they have booked merely to indulge the wilful humour of Robert Morley, who wishes to play a private family joke on his mother-in-law? Can our theatre afford the precedent?'

Our theatre seems to have survived it and, indeed, the publicity did the play no harm. We had already offered paying customers their money back or seats for an alternative night on which to watch Gladys wandering in and out of a fragile text; Denison took to clapping his hands and calling 'Olé' like a particularly exorbitant Spanish dancer, at which she would finally come back to earth from some eccentric solo and return to the script.

As for Robert, he was in no financial state to consider any move towards retirement, even had he so wished:

What does an unemployed actor in his early sixties, already partially deaf and weighing eighteen stone, do when he discovers that he has £30,000 in the bank and owes £80,000 to the Inland Revenue? I shook hands all round, borrowed £25 from my agent and went to play roulette for an hour. It cheered me up, took me out of myself, cured my depression. It's not the end of the road, though it is a familiar milestone along it: bankruptcy figures in the index of a good many theatrical memoirs ... All I know is that I have paid the Revenue roughly a quarter of a million in Income Tax and Surtax during my lifetime, without ever being able to understand a tax form or even to which year it refers. For thirty years my accountant has struggled to keep my head above water, swimming tire-lessly by my side, turning me sometimes on my back and often gripping me in a vice-like frontal attack whilst striking me repeatedly on the chin, lest I should panic and drown ... I have always been out of my depth, but I have in a curious way enjoyed the bathe; indeed there have been moments when my feet seemed actually to touch bottom and I believed in my ability to wade to the shore ... If anyone from the Revenue had ever sat down across a table from me, found out how much I could afford to pay and then asked for the cheque, I would happily have given them one. But they never did: instead they bullied and frightened by demanding enormous, impossible amounts and each time they were beaten back, they simply waited and let the arrears pile up for a final kill. When I asked my accountant if anything could get me out of the financial mess I am now in, he thought for a long time and I didn't much care for his answer. Death, he said, might help.

Guided as ever by Robin and Ros, Robert chose to stave off bankruptcy by a less painful method: another batch of rapid movies. In this next collection he was to turn up with Stewart Granger in a bank-heist caper featuring bogus nuns (*The Trygon Factor*); with Shirley MacLaine and Peter Sellers in a dire sex-comedy anthology (*Woman Times Seven*); with Peter Ustinov and Maggie Smith in yet another financial-scam comedy (*Hot Millions*); with Richard Johnson in a Bulldog Drummond thriller, in which Robert played a camp cookery writer called Miss Mary (*Some Girls Do*); and as the Duke of Argyll in a deeply disappointing John Huston attempt to make his own Irish *Tom Jones* (*Sinful Davey*). Huston was the only director ever to employ Robert on three separate locations, and it was sad that, after *The African Queen* and *Beat the Devil*, this last film should have been such an anti-climax, though Huston was later to claim it had been destroyed by re-editing in Hollywood whilst he was otherwise engaged.

Between these films Robert found the time to write a new libretto for Mozart's *The Impresario* for Wendy Toye to direct at Bath Festival ('Next:

The Ring,' was his only comment on his operatic debut), and to have a final go at writing himself a television situation comedy. This was to be called *Charge* and was to feature Robert as Herbert Todhunter, an upper-class version of Alf Garnett, living on a Thames houseboat and tilting at the windmills of his local golf club. Writing with Jeremy Paul, Robert managed to create a memorable character out of step with the times, but alas not much of a situation for comedy. Peter Black thought the trouble was the difficulty in raising sustained laughs out of disgruntlement, while the *Sunday Times* thought that 'as the guest on chat shows Morley is always great fun, rattling on in his quirky way with scant respect for progressive sensibilities, but in this contrived show the jokes were feeble, the pace funereal and the punches not merely telegraphed but notified by semaphore.'

One of the guest stars on *Charge* was the actor Richard Wattis, with whom Robert had been a student at RADA:

I was eager to discover how life had treated him, this companion of my youth, and more importantly how he had treated life. 'What do you do', I asked him, 'about breakfast? Do you get it yourself? Do you go back to bed with coffee and *The Times*? What happens in the mornings? Do you go for walks? Have a dog? Are the children grown up? Tell me about lunch. Who cooks the lunch? What sort of thing do you eat? Curry? Liver? Sausages? And afterwards, do you take a nap? When do you write your letters, read a book, start watching the television? Do you watch the schools' programmes? Do you have colour? In the evenings, do you go out? Do your friends give parties? Do you dine in front of the box or round the dining-room table? What time do you go to bed?' Sensing some bewilderment at my inquisition, I hastened to explain that I was conducting a time-and-motion study among my contemporaries to try to discover how it was that we had all missed the bus . . . I later came to the conclusion that, except for the fact he played bridge and his wife owned a potter's wheel, my friend's life had been no whit different from my own. Forty years ago we had parted outside the stage door of the Pavilion, Weston-super-Mare, since when we had separately and feverishly pursued the bubble reputation, chosen the wrong plays and occasionally the right ones, rehearsed on innumerable empty stages, and performed sometimes in equally empty theatres. We had risen with the lark, and driven ourselves times without number to the film studios of Denham or Pinewood or Elstree or Shepherd's Bush, Ealing and even Welwyn Garden City. We had silently turned the pages of our scripts before countless microphones at Broadcasting House. We had mouthed advertisements for cornflakes and commentaries for cartoons. We had intoned for *son et lumière*, and what had we got out of it, my friend and I? What had we expected to get out of it? Ellen Terry once asked the same question of Irving. 'What is there to get?' The great actor had replied; 'A few friends, and a whisky and soda whenever I felt I need one.'

Thus reassured, Robert gave up the ghost of Todhunter and went on to be Pope Leo x in an impressive American tele-film of *Luther*. 'Undershaft in Overdrive,' as the *New Statesman* noted.

24

The Other Half

1969–1970

Stick your neck out on radio or television with any opinion of any kind and you will get an immediate response in the mail, a fair proportion of which is abusive and often anonymous. I am always immensely cheered up by letters which start 'You fat nit' or 'Come off it, Blubberbags'; I feel I have been of some use to the community. My unnamed correspondent in Bridlington will sleep more soundly for having got it off his chest; he may even decide not to murder his great-aunt after all. I assume that all abusive letters to me are penned by the incipient insane.

By the spring of 1969 Robert had decided to return to the theatre; the old gang had begun to disperse somewhat, with Willy Hyde-White already settled in California. 'Why did you have to go?' Robert asked him sadly. 'Two reasons, old fellah,' replied Willy, 'couldn't bear my current wife, and couldn't bear the Inland Revenue.' Then, with just the perfect pause, he continued, 'That was a very caddish thing I just said – about the Inland Revenue.'

But David Tomlinson was still around, indeed still flying light aircraft: he offered to take Robert to Paris, where someone had told them there was a new boulevard farce which might suit. They flew from Lydd in a light fog; after an hour or so, Robert asked David at the controls where they might be. 'Just circling Paris now,' said David, at which moment the fog lifted to reveal Lancing College beneath them as clear as day; 'They've moved that, I see,' remarked Robert. The play did not prove too strong either and they ended the day in the bar of the Garrick club with a sepulchral fellow drinker who had not cared for Robert's recent television series; 'That', said David, 'hardly singles him out from the crowd.'

Others were voicing rather more loudly their discontent with my father, most spectacularly Robert Maxwell. Pa had always had a sharp eye for a flamboyant villain, the result of years of work in movie studios for middle European directors, and about twenty years before most others he sensed that all was not well with Maxwell. Indeed, he said as much on a live BBC Radio 4 *Any Questions*: 'When you read, as I do, what goes on with Pergamon Press, you understand that there are many people in this country who are out to get everything they can for themselves, and these are the people with the power and the money.'

Maxwell issued a libel writ within twenty-four hours of the broadcast, and Robert discovered to his amazement that the BBC left panellists on *Any Questions* to fend for themselves if sued; he never appeared on the programme again. He did, however, face a massive libel suit from Maxwell and, realising he did not have the money to challenge it, had to publish a grovelling apology in the *Observer*. Maxwell demanded a full page; Robert retorted that he could not possibly manage the bill for that but he might be able to pay for a quarter page. Maxwell, still wanting a full-page apology and fully aware of the expense, paid the balance of its cost himself. Robert was left with an unpleasant taste in the mouth.

Summer came and with it another grandchild, his second. Our elder daughter, Alexis, had been born in April, after which we decided to leave London and move to a house in the village of Waltham St Lawrence, about four miles from Fairmans, thereby putting my parents in more or less constant touch with their grandchildren. Over the course of the next few years I left the BBC, when *Late Night Line-Up* closed, to join first of all *The Times* as a features editor and then *Punch* as its arts editor and drama critic throughout the later 1970s and 1980s; I was spending more and more of my time in London, but for Margaret and the children Berkshire was home. For Robert and Joan, as their other two children began to move away to their own lives, my wife and our children became their most regular visiting relatives, not merely around the pool. As soon as the children learned to walk, Robert would lead them all on regular outings to Windsor races and to the restaurants of the Thames Valley, where, claiming often accurately to be a food critic, he would run up yet another bill to be bickered over several months later with the Inland Revenue.

There were also occasional outings to Henley cinema, where they would be joined by Gladys, who had settled into life along the regatta towpath at

Barn Elms, the house she had bought in the early 1950s, but had only recently begun to regard as home. 'OAP?' enquired the box-office lady at the Henley Regal of Gladys on one celebrated outing; 'No, no,' she replied, 'I always sit in the stalls, thank you.' Old age was not, even then, anything Gladys had ever heard about.

At the moment when Robert was beginning to despair of ever finding another script, four more films came along. The first two of these were terrible beyond belief: *Twinky* was a Swinging Sixties relic with Charles Bronson and Susan George, while *Doctor in Trouble* was the death rattle of that long-running Richard Gordon series with Leslie Phillips by this stage standing in for Dirk Bogarde and Robert vaguely trying to recall how James Robertson Justice had dealt with Sir Lancelot Spratt.

However, there then came two much happier experiences: firstly a long location shoot on the Isle of Mull with Anthony Hopkins for an above-average Alistair Maclean thriller, *When Eight Bells Toll*, and secondly a return to period costume for the Earl of Manchester in the Richard Harris-Alec Guinness *Cromwell*. Much of the acting of this role had to take place on a horse, a position in which Robert was seldom at his best. A suitably large and docile animal was duly engaged, though, and all went well for an hour or two until the cameraman noticed a curious phenomenon. A sequence would start with Robert and Richard Harris on equal-sized horses, but, by the time it ended, Harris was always several feet higher in the saddle. Tactful enquiries were made as to whether he had taken to standing up in the stirrups or in some way padding his saddle? Not at all; but they were riding on soft ground, into which Robert's horse was very gently sinking under his weight. Later they took to filming Robert in a carriage; 'Marston Moor, I see,' he would say on alighting, thereby giving the audience some idea of where they were. 'I seem to have become a subtitle,' observed Robert.

Cromwell completed, Robert once again tried to find himself a play for the London winter, but the search was not made any easier on account of a serious falling-out with his usual management. For a year or two past Robert had been fund-raising very seriously on behalf of the National Society for Autistic Children. His old friend David Tomlinson has a son, William, who has had to fight autism all his life, and Robert was deeply involved with David in trying to raise the money for a new residential care home. In this endeavour he had been much helped by a couple of chance encounters: back stage at a television chat show John Lennon had given him a cheque for £5,000 on the basis of a single request, as had Lord Grade. But, when Robert approached Binkie Beaumont with a request for donation, Beaumont refused outright on the grounds that he never gave to charity. So stunned was

'I've not done too badly out of life, and life hasn't done too badly out of me. In that sense it has been a more or less even struggle.'

Left: With Sewell Stokes, one of his oldest friends, his first biographer and the co-author of *Oscar Wilde*.

Below: With Gina Lollobrigida, Alec Guinness and the cast of *Hotel Paradiso*, 1966.

With bagpipes in *Sinful Davey*, 1968; and with Vincent Price in *Theatre of Blood*, 1973.

Selling the flag for British Airways; in Red Square, Moscow, 1968, photographed by the author; back home at Fairmans.

Comedy tonight: on television with Morecambe and Wise; and in *The Great Muppet Caper*.

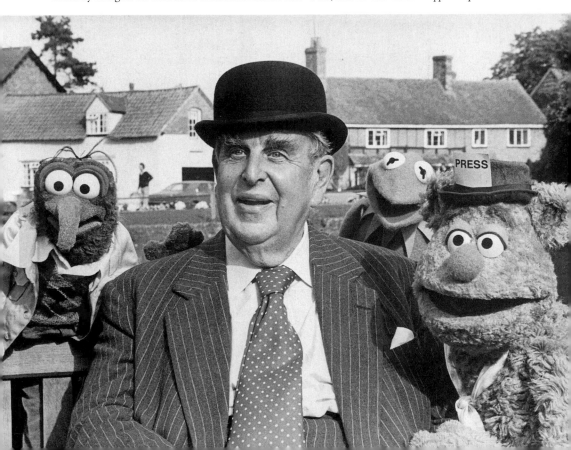

Family album: Robert and Joan and their five grandchildren. Above: Alexis, Hugo and Juliet; below left, with Daisy; and below right, with Jack.

Robert and the author at the *Punch* table, 1985.

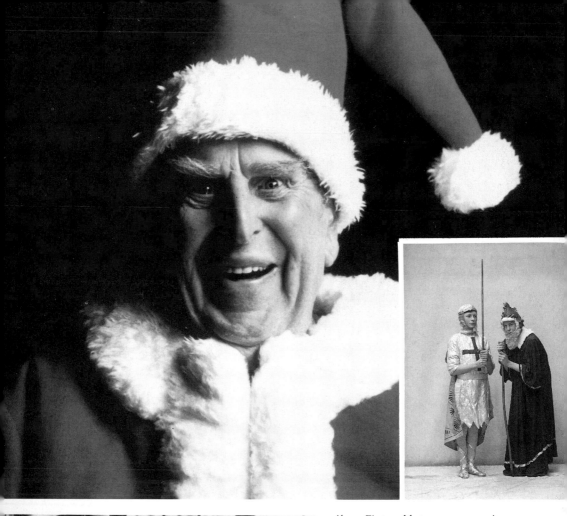

Above: First and last appearances. As Father Christmas (television commercial, 1991) and Folkestone parish play, 1913.

Left: Robert and Joan at the time of their golden wedding in 1990.

Robert by this refusal that he sat for the whole of one day in Binkie's outer office, unable to believe that the old impresario would not in the end relent in view of all the years they had worked together around the West End. Binkie never did, however, and at the end of the day Robert left his office; Beaumont was to live for another ten years, but the two men seldom spoke again.

Late in 1969 word reached Robert from Leicester that there was a new comedy trying out there which he might like to have a look at. In truth, had he not had a horse running at a nearby race course, he might well not have bothered; luckily for him, though the horse did not do any good, the play did. It was called *How the Other Half Loves* and was an early comedy by Alan Ayckbourn, who had already made something of a name for himself in the West End with *Relatively Speaking*.

The latter had been a critical rather than a vast commercial success, and Ayckbourn, then just thirty, was by no means nationally established. On the other hand, he came of a generation of dramatists who believed that actors were there to perform their plays as written. My father did not. Naturally this led to considerable acrimony once Robert had decided – largely on the basis of advice from his devoted and resourceful chauffeur-dresser John Jonas, who loved the play on first sight and was eager to get him back to the West End – to go ahead and take on the leading role.

How the Other Half Loves is a characteristically intricate Ayckbourn domestic comedy of appalling manners, built around the notion of two dinner parties taking place in separate households on separate nights, but seen and acted simultaneously on stage. It is not perhaps the very best of his plays, but it does have an absolutely mechanical precision which was to win it two years on Shaftesbury Avenue, one of the longest runs Alan has ever enjoyed there. Those of us on Robert's side of the battle which ensued tend to ascribe this to Pa's presence in the cast list; others, noting Alan's reluctance to use established stars from then onwards, are less certain. Alan himself once managed a reasonably neutral summary of what happened:

> Robert is an actor who rapidly gets very bored, and in order to refresh himself and engage himself, he always treats the theatre as one huge game organised by himself. The joy of the man is that he does have great enjoyment for what he does, an infectious, playful enthusiasm. Unfortunately, the people who suffer are the people on stage with him, or who are attempting to get on stage with him ... So you have a few working actors ploughing doggedly through their scripts, clutching on to characterisations which Robert delights in bombarding and trying to upset

– hiding their props, or locking doors, or jumping out at them from cupboards, which tends to make the play look a little ropey . . . In the case of *How the Other Half Loves*, because it was such a complex plot, he was unable to do as much with it as he would have liked . . . In the end I stopped going to see it, as it made me unnecessarily upset whenever he changed anything . . . The trouble with an actor-manager is that they want to manage everyone else as well as themselves; a lot of *How the Other Half Loves* is about people getting extremely angry with each other, but Robert wouldn't have any of that. I remember him quite vehemently in rehearsal saying, 'Look, nobody wants to come to the theatre to see people squabbling,' which I would have thought dismissed about three-quarters of all British drama. But he said, 'We don't want these nasty cross people shouting at each other,' and although he turned in a lovely performance himself, I always thought it could have been an even better one if he'd stuck more closely to the script. But I learnt one great maxim from Robert, which was that you can't argue with the system. Eighty per cent of that audience had paid to see Robert Morley, and I, as an unknown dramatist, had really no right to interfere with that process if I wanted to take the money. If I could have suffocated Robert to the extent of preventing him from doing his own thing, I would actually have offended many of the punters who, because of him, were coming to see my play.

It needs to be added in Robert's defence that nowhere in the world had *How the Other Half Loves* run anything like the two years on Shaftesbury Avenue that first time round. Rehearsals were also not easy for reasons which Ayckbourn could not have guessed at the time. True, there were the usual early confrontations about the script, with Robert narrowly being deterred from playing the dinner-party scene in full Japanese costume, but once the production got under way for the Peter Bridge-Eddie Kulukundis management, Robert was to suffer two sudden severe blows in his private life; the deaths of Robin Fox and of his mother-in-law.

Rehearsals for *How the Other Half Loves* started on his sixty-second birthday, 26 May 1970, a thoroughly merry occasion as he and the director Robin Midgley had managed to persuade his old co-star from *The Little Hut*, Joan Tetzel, to return to the stage after a long absence as his wife; this was reckoned to be a good omen since it was almost twenty years to the day since that earlier long-running hit had first gone into production. The press turned up for some champagne celebrations, as did Ros Chatto and Robin Fox, the latter looking unusually fragile as Robert later wrote:

How the Other Half Loves: with Heather Sears and Brian Miller

As always, I was reassured and happy to be in his company, and we managed the ritual *bonhomie* and drank the champagne, blissfully unaware of the impending catastrophe. Somehow, though, he didn't seem himself, and a few days later I was to learn that my trusted friend and manager had terminal cancer; the shadow of his approaching death made life suddenly so very much colder. In the evenings, after rehearsal, I would drive down to the King Edward Hospital at Midhurst for a picnic in his bedroom, bearing caviare and curious mousses from Fortnum's and drinking champagne by his bedside. It didn't really help very much, but in times of crisis I find extravagance sometimes helps me. Late one evening I left him and walked along the corridor to where a nurse sat at a table, writing reports on her patients. 'I'm off now,' I told her unnecessarily. 'I gather the news is rather good about Mr Fox; they haven't found anything sinister.' She didn't answer for a moment. I had caught her, I suppose, off guard. Into her eyes came a look of disbelief, instantly checked by professional caution. 'Oh, yes,' she said, 'Mr Fox is doing very well.' I never again had any hope at all.

Over the following six months in hospital, at the Issels Clinic in Switzerland and at home, Robin was to die a lingering and terrible death. For Robert and Ros and many others this drowned any of the joy they might otherwise have felt at the triumph of *How the Other Half Loves* on the road and in town. In any case, Robert felt oddly distanced from the show; unusually for him, he was not involved as writer, manager or director, but simply as an actor hired for a role in much the same way as he had always been on film. Through the 1970s he was to have two more long-running West End hits, but they were never again to involve him as immediately or as intimately as the hits or flops of his Shaftesbury Avenue past. For the rest of his acting life, success or failure was to be someone else's problem; this took away much of the worry when things went wrong backstage or on stage, but it also took away a lot of the joy when they went right.

The director of *How the Other Half Loves* was Robin Midgley, then in charge of Leicester's Haymarket Theatre and one of the few young directors of whom Robert whole-heartedly approved: 'Gets on with the job, not as talented as Guthrie perhaps, but not as gloomy as Jack Minster, who always used to tell his casts not to look at the floor while they were acting: "All you'll ever find down there is the play," he would say. Midgley remains more cheerful, holds the balance between those of the cast who wish to find the truth of the play and those of us who just wish to know where to stand or, more importantly, where others were planning to stand. Most of the rest is a matter of lighting: I like them full up all the time, though I will allow imaginative directors to keep them low until I burst into view, after which the rule, if I am allowed to make it, is light, light and still more light.'

How the Other Half Loves set off on a long regional tour before it approached the West End, causing Robert once again to reflect on the changes to England since he had first set out on the touring circuit forty years earlier:

Leicester appears to have been entirely replanned since my last visit, with multi-storey car parks everywhere to depress me with their cement understains, and crush barriers to keep back the non-existent crowds; the theatre is in a bus depot, but I suppose even that makes sense these days. The object is that you should always drive straight through cities without noticing that they once had centres where real people lived and worked; nowadays you hardly notice you have even travelled through them. Leeds also seems to be totally barricaded against some future riot, or just possibly a pageant. Business was not sensational, but about average; touring nowadays seems to break many more hearts than in my time. There was a note left for me at the stage door by Leonard Rossiter, who had been playing there the week before; all it said was 'Help'. After another week we moved on to Nottingham, where once two theatres stood side by side like elderly maiden aunts; one has now passed on, her grave a car park, though goodness knows what is planned as a headstone.

On 5 August they reached the Lyric on Shaftesbury Avenue:

We played that night much as we had been playing for the last six weeks on the road and the notices, when they appeared next day, were uniformly encouraging with one exception: only Harold Hobson in the *Sunday Times* was unwontedly abrasive. He reported that most of the cast gave performances which looked as if they had been recruited from the rejects of an annual pantomime in a backward village, or could he have meant backwoods village? We shall never know; by the time his notice appeared, we were home and dried.

25

Responsible Gentleman

1970–1972

We survive wars and peace, we survive childhood and middle age, and we very nearly survive death. We survive love and hate, inflicting appalling cruelties on ourselves and one another. We are gloomy, silent, sullen and lachrymose, but in Las Vegas we are often both noisy and drunk. We are as brave as lions. We shiver in our shoes, but we also occasionally dance in them. We are raucous, and boorish, and alive because we don't know what else to be, and I like to be reminded of all this. I don't want to be reminded of trees and mountains and pink-footed geese. I want to be reminded of what I am: a hopeless, horrible human being. That is why I go back every now and then to Las Vegas, and have a look at myself.

How the Other Half Loves was to stay for two years at the Lyric Theatre before Robert took it on to Canada and Australia; he was never one to let a good play die before its last gasp. In the meantime, he put in a brief appearance (along with such other unlikely Norwegians as Edward G. Robinson and Harry Secombe) in a musical movie life of Edvard Grieg called *Song of Norway*, which proved to be one of the more hilarious location experiences of his later films. It was to take place largely in Oslo, with the head of the Norwegian National Theatre playing Grieg: 'Kiddo,' said the American director memorably, 'when this film is released, you'll never again have to worry about those crummy little theatre jobs.'

This director was, in fact, Andrew Stone, a specialist in disaster movies, who believed whenever possible in shooting on location. On one occasion

Robert arrived in Stone's office to see him reach for a phone and dial the owner of a local Norwegian stately home.

'Mrs Eiler? You remember me, Andrew Stone? We met once at a dinner party in Buenos Aires or possibly Melbourne. I happen to be here in Norway, right on your doorstep, shooting a picture about your Edvard Grieg and you know you told me he used to come to your house to visit a sweetheart? Well, we've not got that scene written in so far, but you never know. Anyway, I'm just calling to ask if we might come to tea. When I say we, I have the great English actor Mr Robert Morley right here with me. Never mind, you'll know him when you see him. Anyway, we would just so like to come to tea and, although we've been told you don't like your house being photographed, I wonder, do you have a bed? It's just that we do need to get a couple of scenes in the can before nightfall and then, of course, a cup of tea would be wonderful. And you won't mind a few arc lights and about twelve of our technicians, will you? There will be hardly any marks on the carpet at all ...'

Song of Norway turned out to be another of Stone's disaster movies, although unfortunately in this instance not intentionally so.

Quite often, when his schedule permitted, Robert would return to see his beloved Robin at the Issels Clinic in Bavaria. There he also met other patients and their relatives with a last hope of curing their terminal cancer:

In the children's ward there is a huge picture window and the mothers take the children on their laps and sit watching the snow. It's a sort of Disneyland: 'Ever so pretty,' one of them says. The children are the only ones Issels doesn't tell ... There is a little girl here who may be allowed out of bed in three weeks if the x-rays prove satisfactory. Her father is confident she will walk again. She has a ring on her finger, and I notice that someone has attached a rubber band to the back. 'We had to do that,' says her father, 'otherwise it would fall off now.' The child produces a tape-recorder. 'Why don't you say something?' Idiotically, because I can think of nothing else, I start to recite *If*. When I get to the bit about 'If you can force the heart and nerve and sinew to serve their turn long after ...' I stop abruptly. 'I'm afraid I've dried up,' I tell her.

When I said goodbye to my old friend on my last visit, I asked if perhaps he felt like coming home, giving up the fight; not altogether, of course, but for a little breathing-spell. I thought perhaps he deserved a rest from this dreadful battle. He shook his head. 'I shall stay here', he told me, 'because here at least I have a chance. More important, perhaps, I'm giving Issels his chance. You know what I like about him best? He really hates cancer.' My friend's voice has got much softer lately, but these last three words were shouted in my ear.

But Robin did come home at the last, and died in Cuckfield the following January surrounded by his loved ones. Robert never quite got over his death, nor the loss of the best manager his career ever had. Theirs had been an odd-couple friendship, not as easily explained as the longer ones Robert cherished with more similar characters as Peter Bull or Sewell Stokes, but he loved Robin very deeply for all that. It was left to Ros Chatto to take over the reins of Robert's career, which she was to manage admirably on stage and screen for the following twenty years.

1971 was not a good year for Robert: it also brought, towards its close, the death of his beloved Gladys, characteristically still on the road in a revival of *The Chalk Garden*. 'On the last night of her life', wrote my father later,

my splendid and courageous mother-in-law rose from her bed and, making her way not without considerable effort to her dressing-table, proceeded to brush her hair and make up her celebrated face. Then, gazing into the mirror for what was to prove the very last time, she remarked to the nurse, 'If this is what viral pneumonia does to one, I really don't think I shall bother to have it again.' She got back into bed, and presently died in her sleep.

It was 16 November 1971 and Gladys was almost a month away from her eighty-third birthday; the next night they dimmed all the lights along Shaftesbury Avenue, starting at the Lyric with Robert's own.

As if aware suddenly of the passing of time and old friends, Robert began more and more to drift into anecdotage. An early and rather partial autobiography, *Responsible Gentleman* written with Sewell Stokes, had not been a total success, coached as it was in dialogue form between Robert and Sewell, but in his journalism he would frequently explore his past and how it had got him to his present. When the weekly columns on the *Sunday Express* came to their natural end, he moved across to the *Tatler*, writing for several years a monthly column there. Then, when I went to *Punch* in the mid-1970s, he moved his column there and, soon after me, became a member of the *Punch* table: we were the first father and son to carve our initials into that table in a century, and for the subsequent fifteen years, under the editorship of William Davis and then Alan Coren, as arts editor I had the joy of publishing Robert at least once a month on a vast range of food, travel, theatrical and sometimes even political matters.

In these latter he was a confirmed socialist, though of the idealist Fabian/Shavian variety, with a certain distrust of what had happened to the Labour Party since the death of Gaitskell. Indeed when, at around this time, Harold Wilson offered him a knighthood, Robert politely turned it down. He did so firstly because Joan had said she had no particular desire to be Lady Morley, especially if it was likely to increase the local tradesmen's bills, and secondly because he felt very strongly that knighthoods in the theatre ought to be reserved for Shakespearians or, at the very least, for general classicists. His audience, he felt, at a comedy would be made oddly uneasy by being asked to guffaw at Sir Robert Morley.

Wilson, unused to having his knighthoods declined, took several years to get over the shock and would regularly introduce Robert thereafter as 'the only man who ever turned me down'.

Robert, meanwhile, got on with the business of being a comic actor in a long West End run, the business he had always known best:

Audiences, like salad dressings, are never the same twice running, or if it comes to that 500 times running. I am often accused of playing the same role too often. My defence is that I play to each audience only once. Younger colleagues, and most of my colleagues are younger nowadays, hold that an audience is not there to be played with, that an actor's duty (however evocative the phrase) is to play with himself. The challenge for them lies totally within. Scofield, Guinness and Olivier are their high priests, ministering to the faithful, while my role is that of a potboy serving my customers with their gin and tonic. My patrons are a fun-loving bunch, seeking a night out. They seldom leave my premises with the hushed reverence and sober mien of theatregoers who have had an Experience. They walk into Shaftesbury Avenue wondering about supper, or a girl, or possibly both. Often an audience which begins by appreciating every nuance, and laughing at exactly the right moment for exactly the right length of time, will finish the evening in sullen lethargy and hostile silence. On the other hand, a house which begins by not laughing at all, and driving the actors to despair by coughing themselves silly in the early scenes, may end up as our pride and joy, laughing uproariously and applauding wildly. Our fault or theirs? I can never be sure. All I know is that every audience has to be watched every minute of every evening. Take your eyes off the customers, turn your back and the brute springs. I once asked a circus proprietor her opinion of lion tamers. 'Any fool can do it,' she told me, 'but only a fool does.'

With daytime heavy on his hands before the nightly trip up the M4 to Shaftesbury Avenue, a journey he and his driver John would frequently make by way of the nearest race course, Robert also started up a splendid West End dispute about the rights of audiences to arrive at and leave theatres when they, rather than the management, chose. His eye had lighted on an announcement from the Royal Court and Aldwych theatres that 'latecomers would no longer be admitted until a suitable break in the action' and this, he thought, was a disgrace:

'Sir,' he therefore wrote to *The Times*,

It is natural, I suppose, that the bullying and vituperation directed against theatre latecomers should emanate from the *boudoirs* of those establishments largely maintained by the Arts Council. In the commercial theatre, we have no such cushions against which to loll so pettishly. Patrons are late for a variety of reasons, some of which are beyond their control and range from the late arrival of baby-sitters to road accidents. They are disappointed as we should be that they have missed part of the fun, and we should certainly not stand them in the corner as a punishment. Many of them are visitors without whom there would be no West End. Visitors who have waited too long under their hotel porticoes for the non-existent taxi promised by the hall porter, visitors who get lost, misdirected, or just forget which theatre they have booked for. But they still pay: let us remember that the customer is always right; we above all cannot afford to forget it.

Debate was quickly joined, with Robert having the last word when someone complained that late arrivals tended to disturb an audience already seated: 'Not at all,' he boomed, 'keeps them awake – always a good idea not to let an audience get too comfortable in their seats.'

It was about half way into the run of *How the Other Half Loves*, sometime early in the spring of 1972, when a miracle occurred. Robert was home at Fairmans, worrying, as he and the faithful John always did as Easter approached, about the need to repaint the bottom of the swimming-pool, when Ros rang with an unusual offer. Would he like to go, that very afternoon, and stand outside the railings of Buckingham Palace with a union jack to advertise British Airways in a television commercial to be directed by Bryan Forbes?

Never one to refuse a quick £1,000, Robert went off to the Palace, said the few words about BOAC (as it then was) taking good care of you, and thought no more about it except vaguely to wonder who had dropped out at such short notice. In the event this proved to have been Laurence Olivier, who had agreed in principle to appear, but had suddenly had second thoughts about whether such an appearance was becoming for the director of Britain's National Theatre. Larry can have had no idea of the favour he was inadvertently doing Robert: that one commercial appearance grew into a ten-year relationship with British Airways, for whom Robert would film, all around the world, dozens and dozens of commercials. He would also appear on all their American posters and even for a while on their answering service: when callers dialled their ticket-office in New York at peak times, it was Robert's voice they heard apologising for the delay and asking them either to hold on or to call back later.

What this meant was that for the next ten years, as he aged gently into his seventies, Robert never really had to worry about where the work was coming from: when it came, he took it as usual, but, when it didn't, British Airways made up the deficit. He had the longest-running commercials contract with them that any British actor has ever achieved for an in-vision series, longer even than William Franklyn's with Schweppes, and the joy of it was that these commercials were only to be screened in America, so local audiences at home would never tire of seeing him on their screens virtually every night.

In the end the contract only expired during the 1980s because British Airways changed their advertising agency and somebody in the organisation felt that the commercials, triumphant though they had been (Robert took pride in writing many of them himself), were becoming more successful at advertising Robert than at advertising the airline.

It always seemed to me very typical of my father that, where most actors of his generation and background would have regarded these commercials at best as a lucky break and a useful moneyspinner, he took to them like a child with a new toy, genuinely fascinated by the techniques of their making and treating his appearances in them and the scripting of them as seriously as he would any full-length play or film. Once *How the Other Half Loves* had closed in London, there was also the fun of quick trips to travel-trade sales conferences. Several of these were held conveniently in or near Las Vegas, and on such all-expenses-paid outings Robert was able to visit Palm Springs for a reunion with Willy Hyde-White and Los Angeles, where he found David Tomlinson working for Walt Disney and Vanessa Redgrave leading a workers' revolution – all of which gave him useful copy for the *Punch* columns back home.

In the break between the closing of the Ayckbourn play on Shaftesbury Avenue and its reopening in Toronto at the end of the year, Robert also managed to get himself cast in one of the best of his later films. This was a splendidly gory, gothic horror called *Theatre of Blood*, which starred Vincent Price as an old actor-manager determined to wreak vengeance on the drama critics who have ruined his career by having each of them bloodily murdered in classically Shakespearian fashion, drawing on several of the plays in turn for precise reconstructions. Robert's death was to come from *Titus Andronicus*, and involved him being fed his favourite dogs in a meat pie. Others concerned in this vintage classic were Jack Hawkins, Arthur Lowe, Diana Rigg, Michael Hordern, Harry Andrews, Robert Coote and Dennis Price, in a rare assembly of thespian talent which also included Robert's old friend from *The Man Who Came to Dinner* thirty years earlier, Coral Browne.

During the shooting, Miss Browne fell in love with and married Vincent Price, having recently lost her own husband, an agent of considerable distinction who sometimes wanted to be an actor. 'Here,' said Coral once, looking up from a Shakespearian script, 'I've found the perfect part for you. Look, it says Act Two, A Camp near Dover.'

When she and Price decided to set up house together in London, they went to Heal's in search of a double bed. Seeing one they liked in the window, they sent for the manager. 'We would be delighted to sell you that particular model, Miss Browne,' said the manager, 'only unfortunately there will be a four-week delivery delay.' 'Four weeks,' echoed Coral, pointing at her already cadaverous fianceé, 'four weeks – have you seen Mr Price?'

Time then to take a somewhat recast *How the Other Half Loves* on to Toronto (an old Oxford actor-friend of mine, Ian McCulloch, had joined the company) and then to Australia and New Zealand, this time with another friend of the family, the Australian actor Charles Little, who not long afterwards married my sister Annabel. Safely away from the clutches of the playwright and original director, Robert was able to remould the comedy into something closer to one of his own, though still always constrained by the complexities of its twin-setting, time-travelling plot.

Robert had both his daughter and his younger son with him for the Australian summer, the first of many since both fell deeply in love – Wilton with the climate and Annabel with Charlie Little, who came from there and would one day move back with his new family. By the end of the decade Wilton had become a touring theatrical manager based in Sydney, and soon afterwards Ab and Charlie were to move out to Bondi Junction, where they have lived ever since. Our family was becoming decidedly Australian.

26

A Ghost on Tiptoe

1973–1975

I would say that what I look forward to most each Christmas is the brandy butter and getting my 200th Christmas card. I need 200 to fix to the beams in the sitting-room. Without them, seasonal decor is hopeless.

As we approach, albeit slowly, the last act, it occurs to me that something needs to be said about Robert and Christmases past. We were never a family to take Christmas lightly; indeed, my mother has been known to call in lists of what we would each like some time during the summer holidays, on the principle that the sooner she and Harrods get through with the shopping the sooner they can start on Easter.

The first Christmas I can clearly remember was 1945; I was four, the war was over, people were celebrating, and I was taken by Robert to a panto-mime. On the way home we were walking down the Strand and a very old gentleman patted me on the head. 'That', said Pa solemnly, 'was George Robey.'

Then there was the Christmas of the electric trains. By this time we were in New York, and there was a firm called Lionel which made trains about twice the dimensions of anything contemplated by our own Triang/Hornby lads at home. That particular Christmas – it must have been 1948, there was snow in Central Park and I gave Anna Massey whooping-cough (not as a present, you understand, it was just that I happened to have it when she came to tea) – was one of Robert's finest.

Although not a mechanical man – a failing inherited by me to the extent of having, as I write this, just broken my foot while changing a lightbulb – Pa managed to rig the Lionel train set so that it ran right the way around the living-room of our Park Avenue apartment, out into the dining-room and back, a distance of what seemed to our English eyes about two miles, since New York apartment living-rooms in those days were always huge.

If there were a prize for good Christmases then 1948 would probably win mine: being seven helped a lot, since at that age one is old enough to enjoy it but still young enough not to have to do much else. On the day itself Pa took us all (except my brother, not yet born) to see Ray Bolger in *Where's Charley?* and at the end of the show he waved to us, and I started a lifelong love affair with the Broadway musical.

Then there was a Christmas in Australia, when it was far too hot; we got sand in the mincepies and swam with a sharp eye out for the munchies, as local sharks were called, in Sydney Harbour in case they too fancied a leg or two.

When Gladys was still alive and all our relatives seemed to be living around Henley, it was possible at Christmas to progress through about five different family households all around the Thames Valley on a sort of gastronomic tour. At Gladys's, she would hand out the presents with the scones; as we, her grandchildren, grew older and progressively more tiresome to shop for, she would simply pass on to us a selection of the presents she had received for her own birthday a week earlier. One year she passed on to me a massive log basket, having failed to notice that its original donor had filled it with all kinds of other goodies like smoked salmon and Russian caviare, and for some days afterwards the rest of the family debated the ethics of whether or not the contents had been a legitimate present from her to me or merely an oversight on her part. I need hardly add that, by the time the family upheld the latter theory, I had eaten most of the salmon.

Then there was the Christmas I brought Margaret home as my fiancée from Boston, and decided to break it to my parents that they were about to lose their elder son, an event they had, I think, been eagerly awaiting for several years. My mother maintains I began the conversation with 'It's, um, about the girl upstairs,' but Margaret soon became deeply beloved of them both, in many respects taking on the role of another daughter when their own moved out to Australia and in later years working with Pa on many of his anthologies of Bricks and Worries. Even when we were divorced a year or two before Pa's death and I moved back to London, it was she who stayed in a nearby village, closer to him in his last years than anyone else except my mother and Ros, and a wonderful friend for lunch and the Windsor races.

Then again there was the Christmas of my sister and the powdered glass.

Told by Margaret one Christmas Eve to bring home some cranberry sauce, I drifted into a late-night supermarket and acquired a jar marked down to half price because it had a nasty crack down one side, where someone had evidently dropped it. Ever alert for a bargain, however, I took it home and decanted it into a dish. Come Christmas lunch, my sister is eating with us and from her we hear a crunching sound not wholly consistent with cranberries. Seldom one to look on the brighter side, she naturally assumed that she was the victim of a fraternal murder plot, and the rest of the holiday afternoon was spent in heated discussion as to whether Agatha Christie characters died from powdered or fractured glass. My sister has still not entirely forgiven me, but she is lucky to be alive to carry on complaining, or so I tell her.

Early in 1974 Robert decided to return to the boards and in a play of his own; this would, in fact, be his seventh. It was co-written with Rosemary Anne Sisson, entitled *A Ghost on Tiptoe* and, it has to be admitted, not very good. Robert had felt constricted by the recent works of Ayckbourn and Ustinov, and was eager to move back into a self-tailored number which would allow him vastly more freedom of movement within a loose plot of his own construction.

Rosemary Anne proved a perfect, uncomplaining ally in this, and together they ran up a curious comedy about a man who, thinking he is about to die, lives out his last few weeks accordingly and then finds that, after all, he has been spared. Following a brief tour, they came in to the Savoy Theatre and were to stay there for well over a year, no thanks to Irving Wardle of *The Times*:

> No professional egotist of our theatre can rival Mr Morley's displays of omnipotence: his explosions of outrage, that ascend from a bellow to a petulant squeak; his gobbling rages, and his tremendous sulks; the un-believing amazement that dawns on his face when other people's plans do not automatically fall in with his own. Unfortunately, this great theatrical monster seems unable to live within the confines of a good play. With each show, it seems that the character has overflowed from the stage and got at the script. Fantasies arise of terrible pre-production conferences in the tuck shop, with Mr Morley, cap pulled down over his eyes and guzzling pop by the gallon, killing off supporting roles, savaging the plot and extracting copious additions to his own part from all co-authors.

For the *Guardian* Michael Billington was rather more loving: 'Mr Morley is always a pleasure to watch; with his semaphoring eyebrows, accosting stomach, pontifical profile and look of wounded schoolboy innocence, he seems to colonise the whole stage instead of merely occupying its vacant spaces like other actors.'

Thinking (wrongly as it turned out) that *A Ghost* might need a little help at the box-office, I put together with Eamonn Andrews at Thames Television a *This Is Your Life* on Robert, which we managed to televise from the stage of the Savoy during the week the show opened. Much helped by Ros, we successfully assembled such old friends and allies as John Huston, Sybil Thorndike, the Peters Ustinov and Bull, Sewell, Mort Gottlieb from New York and, best of all for the family, my brother was flown from Sydney, where he had already started his own management. That party was the last really good one before people started to disappear abroad or, worse, forever.

By now Robert had discovered another new treat: the book-signing tour. He had been writing his *Punch* and *Tatler* columns for long enough to have accumulated several hundred thousand magazine words, and the publisher Jeremy Robson began to issue these at roughly two-yearly intervals under such anthology titles as *A Musing Morley*, *More Morley*, *Morley Matters*, *Morley Marvels* and ultimately, of course, *The Best of Morley*. Each time one of these trouble-free volumes was about to hit the bookstalls, Robert would set off gleefully across the country to any branch of W. H. Smith that could run to a signing session, or better yet to an author's lunch, at which he would scoop the pool, being usually the most experienced and amusing post-prandial speaker present, which often was not saying a lot.

My old Oxford friend and journalist contemporary Christopher Matthew followed him on one of these tours, and wrote memorably about it for the *Oldie* just after Robert died:

In all the years I knew him, I can't remember ever being bored with Robert. Whatever the current scandal, you could guarantee his views on the subject would always be completely original. He arrived once for lunch on a day when the papers were bursting with outrage about the theft of some rare osprey eggs from a secret nest in the Highlands. 'I'm so glad, aren't you?' he said. 'Such nasty birds. I once had an aunt who wore osprey feathers. I never much cared for her, or the feathers.' Perhaps the most surprising thing about him was his shyness. To conceal his nerves he would often be talking as he entered the room, sometimes even before. He had an insatiable curiosity about other people's lives, and was forever getting into conversation with total strangers in the hope that they might tell him something odd or funny or touching. And very often they did. He was unfailingly courteous to anyone who accosted him in the street, and I never once saw him refuse an autograph.

Unlike, it has to be interpolated at this juncture, Alistair Sim, who had a fetish about autographs and used to deliver a ten-minute lecture on the evils of autograph-hunting to anyone unwise enough to ask him for one. In earlier days, it was Robert's and Willy Hyde-White's great delight on movie sets to bribe small boys with half-a-crown to go and demand Alistair's signature, only to watch their little faces glaze over with boredom before Sim was half way through the lecture.

'Travelling with Robert,' continues Matthew,

was not unlike travelling with royalty, and I was the one usually expected to provide the pen. Over the years I acquired a deep sympathy and respect for ladies-in-waiting. In 1975 he invited me to join him on a short jaunt which was to include an engagement at a country-house hotel in Yorkshire, where celebrities would join the diners over liqueurs and coffee, tell stories and engage them in light conversation. The customers that evening were obviously delighted to discover that he was just as they had imagined him: flamboyant, theatrical, larger than life. Few, if any, could have guessed how nervous he was, but he was soon into his stride, telling them about his childhood and early days in the profession, about Marie Tempest and Louis B. Mayer and John Barrymore and Bernard Shaw and his beloved mother-in-law, Gladys Cooper. For over an hour the stories tumbled out, sometimes sad, often touching, always funny.

'Is this the sort of thing you want, dears?' he asked the audience at the end of a story about Greta Garbo. 'Would you like to ask some questions, perhaps?'

'I have a question,' said a man in the front row. 'Why are your fly buttons undone?'

'I had rather hoped', Robert replied, calmly adjusting his dress, 'that it added to the general air of informality.'

What did he think of Yorkshire? 'The important thing', he replied, 'is what Yorkshire thinks of me.'

What were his favourite luxuries? 'Not having to be directed by Peter Brook. A really good new sponge. A chocolate Bath Oliver, followed almost immediately by another.'

What did he think of Malcolm Muggeridge? 'It is inconceivable that he would not bore God.'

How did he get on with young directors? 'I usually give them a week to find out if they know more than I do, and if not I take over myself.'

Did he enjoy entertaining people? 'As long as I am entertaining myself. I love hearing my own opinions, even if I don't always agree with them.'

What did he think of people who live abroad to avoid British taxes? 'I was born a pauper', said Robert, 'and I shall almost certainly die a pauper. If a man is fool enough to want to go and live in Jersey or the Isle of Man and take it all with him, then in my view he deserves everything he gets there.'

'Mr Morley, you claim to be a socialist . . . ' One sensed that this was the moment he'd been waiting for all evening. There was nothing Robert relished more than the opportunity to lower his head and snort and stamp and make spirited passes at any smug Tory unwise enough to show him the red mantilla. But then suddenly the anger subsided, and the fire went out of the eyes to be replaced by mocking self-doubt. 'Darlings, I'm just a well-travelled actor with muddled ideas, like everyone else.'

The following day we drove on to Newcastle, where he was due to speak at the Royal Institute of British Architects (Northumbrian Branch) annual dinner. It was a boisterous, beery occasion and in the middle of a Norma Shearer story, he suddenly lost his patience with them and launched into a blistering attack on architects, planners, one-way streets, shopping centres, tower blocks, office blocks and the whole ghastly muddle of modern city life.

'This is the best country in the world,' he shouted at the astonished gathering. 'Why must you ruin it with your hideous buildings and your terrible schemes?' He sat down to applause that was polite rather than heartfelt, turned to me and pulled a face. 'Have I gone too far this time?' he asked, then added, 'Actually, I've got a bit of a cold coming on.'

Accustomed as Robert was to public speaking, he even found a way of making money at it when not actually book-selling. An agency called Associated Speakers, run then, as now, by the redoubtable Dabber and Paddy Davis, would from time to time despatch Robert, Bully, me and several dozen like us – journalists, actors, broadcasters and other layabouts with a certain gift of the gab – for anywhere up to £1,000 a speech (though in my case more usually around £250) to ladies' luncheon clubs the length and breadth of the land. Then we would gather back at headquarters, usually the weekly *Punch* lunch, to compare notes, fees and horror stories. Basil Booth-royd always had the worst, of going to a lunch club in Cornwall run by a vicar for several of his female parishioners. As Basil ploughed on through his turn, he noticed out of the corner of his eye the vicar removing one of the ladies from the back of the hall to a kind of ante-chamber, returning her after about ten minutes and repeating the process with her neighbour, until about half of the audience had been thus removed and returned.

Being driven back to Truro station by the vicar afterwards, Basil cautiously enquired what had been going on between him and his ladies. 'Ah, so you noticed,' apologised the vicar. 'I was hoping you wouldn't, but you see we only have these lunches once a month, and when I do manage to get my ladies together, I like them to have their feet done, so the chiropodist comes around and sits outside and . . . '

Basil seldom spoke in public again and not long afterwards the whole luncheon circuit collapsed. 'It's a matter of economics,' Dabber explained sadly to Robert over the phone. 'With rising prices, the ladies were told they would have to choose between a speaker and a pudding, and I fear that in many clubs they went for the pudding.'

Undeterred – a word that should appear on his memorial plaque, if ever we put one in the Covent Garden actors' church – Robert went to Acapulco in Mexico to give away the awards at the International Balloonists' Association, just one of the perks of his new-found British Airways fame. Then, since the run A Ghost on Tiptoe had ground to a halt after nearly eighteen months at the Savoy, he had to reconsider his position as an actor.

He was in no mood to retire, firstly because, although the British Airways income was lovely, it was by no means secure, and secondly because he still had a certain lingering love for getting out there in front of a live audience. But in what? His French boulevard farces were clearly a thing of the past, and his experience with Ayckbourn suggested that Robert was unlikely to be able to come to terms with many other young playwrights of the future. On the other hand, as a dramatist himself, he faced a lack of inspiration. He had only got away with A Ghost on Tiptoe by the skin of his teeth, trading unashamedly on the nostalgia of local audiences and the new-found interest of American tourists in seeing their 'Mr British Airways' in the flesh – of which there was, Robert's entire life having been a monument to the lack of any involvement in weight-watching, still a very great deal.

However, he had grown so bored of A Ghost on Tiptoe by the end of its run that his stage jokes were outrageous even by his own standards; such old tried-and-true friends and colleagues as Ambrosine Phillpotts had decided at the final curtain that enough was enough, especially as the play itself had been in a permanent state of change during its run. Joyce Carey, packing up her dressing-room on the last night of the run, happened to look down at the script they had started rehearsing more than a year earlier and noticed that scarcely a word of it had been spoken during the final performance.

While he was thinking about what to do next, he and my mother flew to Morocco for a brief holiday on which they were joined by Kenneth Tynan, who had heard that Marrakesh was a good centre for drugs. He would sit at their table, firmly waving his fingers at the local waiters in a smoking gesture only to turn furious when they subsequently brought him several packets of Players No. 6 tipped. Robert then progressed to Leningrad, not this time on a travel writers' jaunt, but to play Old Father Time in a thoroughly eccentric musical film, *The Blue Bird*, which also starred Ava Gardner, Jane Fonda and Elizabeth Taylor.

George Cukor was to direct this inaugural US-USSR co-production, and on the first day of shooting he assembled the company in the Leningrad studio to announce to their Russian hosts how proud his troupe was to be working in the very same studio where, in 1925, Eisenstein had made *The Battleship Potemkin*. 'Yes,' said the head of SovFilms, responding with equal pride, 'and with much of the very same equipment.'

After that Cukor went a bit quiet, and Robert spent most of his time sending despatches from the war front back to his various editors at magazines as diverse as *Punch*, *High Life* and *Playboy*, which had just awarded him their 'comic writer of the year' trophy. He also spent a certain amount of energy trying to convince Elizabeth Taylor to sample Leningrad night life: Liz refused to leave the hotel on the grounds that she might be mobbed by her millions of Russian fans. The only place she ever got mobbed, of course, was in the hotel dining-room by the American tourists who happened to be staying there, but then again, reflected Robert, that was probably why she never went out – except, of course, to make the film, and on balance they would all have been better off not doing that: 'senile and interminable', thought the *New Yorker*.

Returning home in time for the birth of his second grand-daughter (our youngest child, Juliet, born in December 1975), he found his local playhouse, the Theatre Royal in Windsor, in considerable economic trouble and decided to rescue it with a festival of one-man shows. Not just himself but also Emlyn Williams, Micheàl MacLiammòir, Roy Dotrice – all the great experts in monologues would be asked to give about fifteen minutes of their performances on one single Sunday night. Micheàl came to stay at Fairmans for the weekend, appearing for breakfast on the Sunday in full make-up and eyeliner, but having left his toupée on the side of the bath, which somewhat disturbed my great-aunt.

Worse was to come. We had agreed that each of the eight or ten artists would simply offer the opening section of their recitals, but Micheàl was growing forgetful by this time and, once he had launched into his *Oscar Wilde*, he became totally oblivious to the other solo show specialists lined up in the wings. It was only after nearly an hour that, by frantically waving at him from the back of the stalls, we managed to remind him not to go for the full evening.

The experience did, however, reawaken Robert's interest in retrieving his own solo from the bottom drawer of his desk, and he then took it to the Mandarin Hotel, Hong Kong, where they were offering him a bed and a modest sum in return for a nightly show in the restaurant. It was not a success, at least not among jet-lagged international businessmen more accustomed to Shirley Bassey by way of late-night cabaret, and Robert soon moved on to New Zealand, where his younger son toured him in a revival of *How the Other Half Loves*. This was not a great financial success either, but, by the time it ended, there was better economic news on the Australian horizon: Heinz wished to make him their Mr Soup in a series of television commercials, which entailed returning willingly to Australia every January for the next five years or so. And, back in London, he was at long last able to collaborate with one of the greatest of comic dramatists, a writer perfectly in tune with his own theatrical talents, the veteran Ben Travers.

27

Big Ben

1976–1977

I am now sixty-eight and, if I have learnt anything in a long life on the boards, it is that there is not really a very great deal to acting; beyond a certain audacity. I do it mainly for the lolly, but I'm no longer capable of learning new tricks; so directors are stuck with this resolute, elderly comedian. I see it as my job to entertain whoever turns up at the theatre that night, to make sure that everyone is comfortably seated and kept laughing for a couple of hours. It's much like being a waiter, without having to serve the food or worry about the tips: just save the audience from as much agony as possible while they're with you, that's what it's all about, I think.

Having taken over as Robert's principal theatrical manager, it was Ray Cooney who matched him with the eighty-nine-year-old Ben Travers for what was a marriage made in heaven. After long years in the critical and theatrical wilderness, Travers had suddenly burst back on to the scene with a triumphant National Theatre revival of *Plunder* and a new play, *The Bed Before Yesterday*, in which Joan Plowright had scored an immense success at the Lyric. Not since Coward's seventieth birthday seven years earlier had the British so enthusiastically rediscovered a living dramatist and taken him back so firmly to their hearts, guilty perhaps that both men had been so shamefully ignored by the West End for so long.

On this tide of goodwill, Robert went into rehearsal for a revival of Travers's *Banana Ridge*, not seen in London since 1938, when it had run more than 400 performances. This was not one of his classic Aldwych farces from

Banana Ridge: with Geoffrey Burridge and George Cole

the 1920s, but it had none the less proved valuable to Alfred Drayton and Robertson Hare the first time around, and was going to give Robert and George Cole a long run back at the Savoy Theatre. If only, I kept wishing greedily as much on Pa's behalf as Ben's, this Travers Renaissance could have come a few years earlier in both their West End careers: Robert would have been perfectly suited to many of the other Alfred Drayton/Tom Walls roles in big Ben's classic farces, and he in turn was precisely the type of writer to construct a plot sturdy enough and intriguing enough, even after hundreds of performances, to keep Robert strictly on the rails of its dialogue and character.

Most critics recognised this at once ('Vintage Travers plus sparkling Morley makes pure champagne,' wrote Jack Tinker for the *Daily Mail*) and Val May's alert, witty production was sufficiently strong at the box-office that, when George Cole wished to leave after several months, he could be replaced first of all by Julian Orchard and then, when Julian fell mortally ill, by Ray Cooney himself.

Apart from the deep sadness of Julian's death, another of the old gang gone, these were the last of Robert's truly happy times in the theatre; to be playing nightly at his favourite home, the Savoy, with a company he loved in a classic farce was exactly what he had always meant to do with his career. And there was good news at home, too. During the run my sister Annabel married Charles Little and Robert took her down the aisle before hastening on to play the matinée at the Savoy.

Banana Ridge ran right through 1976. When it ended, he went straight into an undistinguished and unmemorable production of *Great Expectations*, originally conceived as a musical, but destined in the end for American television without any songs, and then on to a much classier thriller, *Someone Is Killing the Great Chefs of Europe*, which, like the earlier *Theatre of Blood*, found him in high gothic comedy for a plot largely contained in its title.

It would be unfair and untrue to suggest that it was all downhill from this point on. Robert was to live happily for another fifteen years, to give one more major stage performance in Australia, and to make another dozen film and television drama appearances, of which half at least were distinguished. Yet there was sometimes a distinct chill of autumn in the air around him: a sense that the best of his work had been done, that he was now attending too many memorial services and not enough christenings, that although uniquely blessed with Joan's love and devotion to his well-being, his younger children were setting up lives on the other side of the world, while his own was shrinking to the race course, the typewriter, the chair by the television all winter and by the pool all summer. It was in so many ways a good life, better than most actors ever achieve. Nevertheless there was a faint sense that, if it were not closing down, life was at least closing in: no more sudden trips on the Trans-Siberian Express, no more returns to haunt the casinos of Las Vegas, just gentle routine of Australian visits every January and a wait by the phone after that to see what brief movie roles Ros could line up for the summer.

Also, he was growing considerably deafer and this in his last decade was to become a major source of irritation, especially for my mother, as it meant having the television volume turned up to stadium strength. But his hearing-aid shortly became a useful new social weapon: he was still attending most Wednesdays at the *Punch* table and derived much innocent pleasure from ostentatiously removing the aid from his ear when one of us proved more than usually boring. He could never manage to cope with its batteries, however; these small, circular electronic nightmares would regularly fall out and leave those around uncertain whether he was switched off or merely powerless in the left ear.

Conversation was fine so long as it was face to face, but crowded restaurants or theatre foyers left him unable to focus on where the correct sounds were coming from, and this made him gradually less inclined to follow his old social life to the full. Fairmans was, at the last, beginning to become the focus of his life, and he expected us to find him there rather than continuing to find us wherever we happened to be. In all other respects, though, his health remained pretty good, somewhat to the irritation of the occasional doctor, who felt that a man of eighteen stone who had never taken any exercise unless forced into it by a film director, and who was still smoking as many cigars as ever, ought to be showing greater signs of wear and tear as he moved into his seventies.

His regular London haunts were the dining-tables of *Punch* and the Garrick, where he would also for many years in the 1970s and 1980s chair the Dramatists' Club, a monthly gathering of playwrights who would meet over dinner to compare contracts and grumble about the successes of their rivals. This Robert much enjoyed, especially on those nights when he could set up one of the older, more conservative Shaftesbury Avenue playwrights against some younger, tieless rebel from the Royal Court and then settle back with brandy and a cigar to watch the postprandial fireworks as two generations collided across the silverware.

Other diversions were becoming fewer and further between, but there was still the racing (he was on to his fifth ownership of a horse) and the ongoing British Airways and Heinz commercials to take care of occasional travels. He also tried out the one-man show for a final, brief Brighton and Richmond season before reluctantly deciding that he was never going to be another Emlyn Williams or Micheàl MacLiammòir, especially not now that they had, rather to his irritation, used up the best of Dickens and his beloved Wilde. He did, however, manage to read some of Oscar's fairy tales on to disc and cassette, made a few more lighthearted BBC radio and television chat show appearances, and then found a useful new career as 'the talent' on a cruise liner. For this he and my mother were given a luxurious first-class cabin on a ship sailing around South America, in return for which all he had to offer were a couple of after-dinner chats to the other passengers about his life and movie times, all of which he enjoyed as much as a pioneering trip to DisneyWorld in Miami on behalf of the ever faithful British Airways commercial-makers.

In Australia in the winter of 1977 for Heinz, he found that his younger son had coaxed out of premature retirement a remarkable actor called Gordon Chater and was touring him in *The Elocution of Benjamin Franklin*, a solo show of considerable emotional power about the life of an old transvestite. Suddenly, Robert saw in this theme an altogether different kind of play: a drawing-room comedy for the West End about what would happen if three happily married and otherwise perfectly ordinary middle-aged businessmen turned out to have a thing about getting into their wives' dresses.

Back in London, he invited a comic writer he had always much admired, John Wells, to come in as his co-author, and together the two of them wrote *A Picture of Innocence*. This was, in my recollection and indeed that of John Wells, a good idea which they never managed to get right.

'We first met for lunch at the Hyde Park Hotel,' recalls John, 'and my first memory was of deep embarrassment as Robert boomed down the stairs, "My darling boy, come on up." But from that moment on we got along splendidly. We worked in the hut at the bottom of his Fairmans garden, Robert alternately inventing the dialogue, typing it or telling me to abdicate my film column on the *Spectator* as it was "a perfectly futile thing to do".'

John took the advice and he was very struck by Robert's sense of stage management, of what would and would not work once they got into rehearsal. 'I was already a dramatist, but he taught me a lot I didn't know about exits and entrances, and he was ruthless about cutting. "That'll do for another play," he'd tell me about some of my favourite lines.'

'Then we had to hawk it around the West End a bit, and we finished up with Duncan Weldon and his partner, Louis Michaels, a marvellous man from the garment trade who still had a tailor's vocabulary. I remember Robert asking Louis if he'd actually enjoyed reading the play and Louis saying, "The important thing, Mr Morley, is whether or not you are happy with it." We were, more or less, and took it out on the road to Birmingham and then rather more surprisingly to Toronto, where Robert did begin to make some rather drastic changes. "This psychiatrist", I remember him saying to me one night, "really ought not to be a small German, but a very tall black lesbian." It was that kind of a play. We had the most wonderful beginning, Robert and his wife both arriving on stage in the same dress and saying, "Snap," but alas we never could find an ending. An old lady in Toronto told Robert she was sitting in Stalls G17 and could see right up his legs, and I think after that he began to wonder whether this was really the kind of play he ought to be taking to his faithful audience in the West End.'

On balance they decided it was not, and *A Picture of Innocence* was to fold quietly on the road a few weeks after Robert's seventieth birthday; he was never again to appear in a play in his own country. By now, to his great sorrow, an increasing number of his old friends and colleagues were departing this world, among them Ambrosine Phillpotts. In the course of a fairly lengthy speech at her memorial service he recalled a couple of episodes in their long partnership which perhaps say as much about Robert himself as about Ambrosine:

I always went too far and on too long for Ambrosine. For more than forty years she had found my views, politics, acting and behaviour a source of perpetual embarrassment, but her affection and loyalty never wavered. I remember her coming into the theatre one evening and meeting me on the stage. 'I'm exhausted,' she told me, 'I've spent the whole afternoon defending you.' 'Who from?' I asked. 'Who from?' her eyes widened in amazement. 'From everybody, of course.'

... Our business is something of a Paul Jones in which you only occasionally dance a number of times with the same partner, but I did seven dances with Ambrosine. I suppose because I cheated a bit and waited for her to come around and then clutched her. She got me out of any number of scrapes. I acted as a sort of brake on her career. Whenever she threatened to become too successful, there was a new script ready, waiting to be performed with me. We did a play originally called *The Shop at Sly Corner* which I retitled, rewrote and dragged to its doom, or very nearly its doom, on a provincial tour during the war. Luckily the author took it back just in time and insisted on the original script. It became a great success in the West End with another actor. Business was terrible when I was in charge. I put it down to the air-raids; Ambrosine put it down to my constant rewriting and interfering, and she was proved right when we got to Bournemouth, which had never heard of a bomb and where we did the worst week of the tour.

One evening, when she was supposed to be listening to one of my long speeches, I suddenly noticed I seemed to be alone on stage. At the end of the scene Ambrosine emerged from a sedan chair which the designer had incorporated into the set. When I asked for an explanation, she said, 'I felt so embarrassed for you, dear, I simply had to find some place to hide.' ...

28

Another Country

1978–1987

*For some reason, either because I am deaf or because Mr McMahon was a mutterer, I
failed to hear his disclaimer that he was not a professional banjo-player, as I had
thought, but a man who had only just ceased to be Prime Minister of Australia. I
understood only that he was a banjo-player who had briefly been involved in local
council politics; 'How wise of you to get out and choose some other career,' I told
him, 'especially as they are all so corrupt out here in government.'*

Forever on the look-out for ways to raise money for the National Society for
Autistic Children (NSAC), Robert hit upon a modest gold mine. For years
his profession had been almost entirely populated by actors telling John
Gielgud stories, anecdotes of famous *faux pas* supposedly made by our
greatest living actor. Why not, thought Robert, extend the idea, invite
dozens of celebrities to contribute their own worst moments and publish the
results for charity? The result was two volumes of *Robert Morley's Book of
Bricks*, both of which went straight into the bestseller charts around the
country and stayed there for several weeks, helped by Robert's personal
appearances around the book stores, earning the NSAC tens of thousands
of pounds towards the completion of a new residential care centre in
Ealing.

Meanwhile, in America, *Too Many Chefs* (as *Someone is Killing the Great
Chefs of Europe* had been more economically retitled) was doing tremendous
box-office business, largely owing to a rave review from Frank Rich in *Time*:

In the role of a haughty gourmet magazine editor, Morley puts on a hilarious show. He pats his gargantuan stomach as lovingly as a child might fondle a stuffed teddy bear. He raises his bushy eyebrows so high that one expects them to graze the ceiling. He turns the mere act of getting up from lunch into a dainty comic ballet. Ordered by doctors to lose weight – half his weight, no less – Morley adamantly refuses; 'I have eaten my way to the top,' he announces in his most imperious manner; 'I am a work of art created by the finest chefs in Europe.' Robert Morley is indeed a work of art; how nice to have him back in the movies, after all those years of hawking plane tickets on television.

Other American critics were no less enthusiastic about Robert, several of them indeed (though, alas, not the Academy itself) nominating him for a Best Supporting Actor Oscar. Although the *Chefs* did not win him that, it did open another final, useful avenue of American employment by fixing him firmly in a catering context. When, a year or two later, a cable channel television company was looking for someone to host twenty-six half-hour shows on which celebrities would divulge and cook on air their favourite recipes, Robert was the natural choice. He can still be seen contentedly munching his way through exotic menus as the host of *Celebrity Chefs* deep into the American video night.

A word here about Robert and *haute cuisine*: although a long-serving food critic of *Punch* and the *Tatler* and, as he always described himself, 'a pudding man', my father had remarkably little interest or expertise in the actual process of cooking, unlike my sister, who took to it professionally for a while. Robert's favourite moments on *Celebrity Chefs* usually involved the inciner-ation of the entire kitchen in the course of an elaborate flambé.

What Robert really enjoyed were restaurants: in them, as in theatres and casinos, he always found humanity at its most intriguing and what he ended up reviewing for us at *Punch* was usually the clientele rather than the menu. His life was lived in the conviction that just around the next corner, wherever he found himself, would lie an astonishing and wonderful and hitherto undiscovered restaurant, and it was no good the rest of us glumly pointing out that we had already passed several with Michelin stars, or that if there was one so special, the chances were that by now it would no longer be undiscovered.

It was the search that appealed to Robert, plus the head-waiter test: could we get in, even if there wasn't a spare table, and if so would the sweet trolley live up to all his expectations? Amazingly often we could, and it did.

His success in *Too Many Chefs* led, meanwhile, to his last Hollywood film, an undistinguished and frenetic farce called *The Scavenger Hunt*, and then it was back to London for what should have been a rather classier affair, Tom Stoppard's adaptation of Graham Greene's *The Human Factor*, which Otto Preminger was making with an all-star line-up: Nicol Williamson, Richard Attenborough, John Gielgud, Robert, Derek Jacobi and Ann Todd. Sadly, however, Otto was by this time well over the hill and had not even managed to organise a budget, so that Ros had a long, though ultimately successful, fight on her hands to get Robert his money.

This, if anything, was a sign of the changing times: not to get paid on a Preminger production of a Stoppard script from a Greene novel indicated as clearly as anything else to Robert that the great days of moviemaking on both sides of the Atlantic might well be over, not merely for him, but for the industry itself. From this point on it was going to be catch as catch can.

But there was still one performance that he keenly wanted to give. A few months earlier, in the West End, he had seen Alec Guinness in a play by Alan Bennett called *The Old Country*. The first of what later came to be known as Alan's 'spy sequence', which would end with his plays about Guy Burgess and Coral Browne in Moscow, and Anthony Blunt at Buckingham Palace, this was a thinly veiled account of a Burgess or Maclean figure forced to live on way past the headlines of his defection in an unChekhovian Russian twilight of exile and impotent rage at the impossibility of ever going home.

Its central character is Hilary, but for much of the first act we are not told that the woods seen through the windows of his apparently comfortable country house are those of Russia rather than Reigate. The expatriate Englishman, his rather shrill county wife and a couple of curious neighbours are all we meet at first, though there is the promise of a distinguished brother-in-law coming to lunch. The talk is elegant, elegaic, discursive; would two men called Johnnie Walker constitute alcoholics synonymous? If not in Britain, could this be somewhere like Rhodesia? Possibly: the natives certainly seem unfriendly, and the whites are evidently trapped in their compound. The talk continues to be of England, though it is of an England already lost, the England of Betjeman and Evelyn Waugh, of *Times* obituaries, the awfulness of Elgar and the fact that zoos are full of people from the same nations as the animals. But still we know not where we are. The birds seem not to sing, but there are rabbits to be shot and constant references are made to exile – Willie Maugham at Cap Ferrat, Max Beerbohm at Rapallo, Hilary in this log cabin in the woods regretting and remembering. It is his wife, who, half an hour into the first act, gives the game away, talking about how little Hilary has in common with his neighbours, 'Just that you're all traitors'.

So we are in Russia. Hilary, traditionally trained by Cambridge and the Foreign Office, gave away state secrets and fourteen years earlier had to disappear overnight by train from London to avoid arrest. Since then he has been working as a translator in Moscow: 'I sit behind a desk; occasionally people ask my advice and then ignore it; it's much like the Foreign Office,' and this is their summer dacha. It may not be Surrey, but then is Surrey still Surrey?

Into this desolate landscape erupts Hilary's brother-in-law, a newly knighted bisexual lecturer of considerable distinction, with news that Hilary is to be forcibly swapped for a Russian spy of greater value. But home to Hilary is where the heart is not; a man with an infinite capacity for melancholy and almost none for love, he lives in a permanently derelict stately home of the mind, the precise geographic location of which has become largely irrelevant even to him. It is neither England nor the Soviet Union, but somewhere inhabited exclusively by the survivors of a prewar education which trained them for a non-existent future and flooded them with the memories of an all-too-present past.

As ever, the play is shot through with Bennett's ability to contort the clichés by which we live ('We never entirely mean what we say. Do I mean that? Not entirely') and to provide instant character self-assessment ('I don't bubble over: I have always been at Gas Mark One'). However Hilary's dacha is no Wendy House, and the Russian Woods are no Forest of Arden; we are reminded that men have died for his treachery and that there is a real world beyond the end of the drive, albeit one that Hilary has never quite managed to enter. His idea of a triumphal return home is an appearance on *Desert Island Discs*; his brother-in-law, fractionally more practical, suggests an 'I was a spy' bestseller to finance life after prison. Yet there are muggers now in Malmesbury and the North Thames Gas Board is no easier to negotiate with than the Kremlin. The only world to which Hilary can ever return is the one which ceased to exist almost before he was born.

The Old Country was, Robert decided, the play in which he wanted to make his next and in fact last stage appearance; my brother, by this time thoroughly established as an Australian theatrical manager owing to the repeated success he was having there with revivals of *The Rocky Horror Show*, agreed to set up a production. Robert went out to open it in February 1980 with an otherwise all-Australian cast including Wallas Eaton and an old friend from the *Edward, My Son* and *How the Other Half Loves* tours out there, Bettina Welch.

Reviews were deeply disappointing ('Plummy Pommy Blah' headlined one) and so were Sydney audiences, largely because they had grown accustomed to Robert returning to them every couple of years in a comedy and were not prepared to take him in a drama. This was, however, their loss; luckily it was not mine. Early in the new year I was sent by *The Times* to interview Peter Brook, who was staging *The Ik* at the Adelaide Festival, and naturally took the chance to stop off in Sydney for a few days.

Jetlagged off the plane from London, I went into the half-empty matinée at the Comedy Theatre and saw, with a sense almost of shock, my father give one of his greatest performances I have ever seen in a theatre. Where Guinness in London had offered a rather dry, almost dessicated Hilary, Robert imbued him with a heartbreaking sense of loss and a terrible forlorn gaiety. It was truly a breathtaking performance. I ought perhaps not to have been so surprised, but then I had not been born when Robert last played *Oscar Wilde* on stage, had been only nine when he closed in *Edward, My Son* and, like too many of my London drama-critic colleagues, I had begun to think of him as always playing variations on a theme of Morley. *The Old Country* was nothing like that: it was dazzling and heartstopping, and I had never been so proud of him or impressed by him in my life. Although we never discussed it, even in the remaining decade of his life, I think he always knew that this was to be his last stage appearance and he was characteristically determined to make it a surprise, even to those of us who thought we knew him best.

In much the same way that sixty years earlier Robert had discovered Bernard Shaw and the possibility of an acting career during a matinée of *The Doctor's Dilemma* on the pier at Folkestone, so I at another matinée in Sydney had seen, finally, where that career had led him and why it mattered so much that he had chosen it. It was a revelation.

After Sydney they took *The Old Country* on to Melbourne and Brisbane, not doing much better at the box-office, but Wilton was, wrote Robert to Joan in England, 'being splendid and not showing how worried he really must be at his old father's box-office figures which are, let's face it, not good'. Heinz, however, came to the rescue with some more soup commercials, and so this last Australian theatrical adventure ended more or less level on balance, despite the fact that Robert went down with blood poisoning in his legs towards the close.

Back in England that rapidly healed, and Robert returned to working with his daughter-in-law on another idea for a bestselling anthology, this time not for charity, but for themselves. *Robert Morley's Book of Worries* was a how-to guide for neurotics, subdividing their possible areas of worry into useful alphabetical categories, and it found a ready market in a nation prone to insecurity and self-doubt.

Aware that he had already given the last performance he seriously cared about, Robert was becoming ever less selective about what he took in the way of offers, leaving it to Ros's intuition to rule out the obviously dicy ones where the money might not follow through. He gladly introduced a thirty-minute series of real-life crime stories on ITV, did a *Tales of the Unexpected* or two for Anglia and went on to play opposite the Muppets and Benji the Wonder Dog in wide-screen capers, all in much the same mood of benign, resigned acceptance. If that was what they wished to pay him to do, then that was indeed what he would do, reserving his private strength for journalism and an occasional guest appearance on a chat show here or there. He and Michael Parkinson became adept at a trans-world version of these; the latter had television shows in both London and Sydney, so the two of them could commute from one to the other, neatly avoiding winters in both nations.

Privately, however, the early 1980s proved a sad time for Robert; in quick succession, he lost four of those he most loved. First his sister Margaret, with whom he had maintained a bickering, but affectionate, relationship across seventy years; next his old actor friend Peter Bull, with whom he had started at Perranporth before the war; then, far too young, Ros's husband, Tom Chatto; and lastly his other oldest friend, Sewell Stokes, who had given him his first great success with *Oscar Wilde*. In some ways it was, I think, Sewell's death which hit him hardest, because for the past twenty years he had been the most constant weekend and Christmas visitor to Fairmans. But it was not until Robert died that we found, put away neatly with his will, a letter of farewell to Sewell which indicated the depth of sadness at his passing:

He always came to us at Christmas, bringing the champagne and the cigars, and obediently placed them on the pile under the tree ... We were hardly ever invited to go to him, only twice was I ever admitted into his flat high opposite the British Museum. I sometimes used to wonder what it was that always brought him to us, always by train and always on Christmas Eve, to share in the ritual of noise and crackers, turkey, plum pudding, decorations, excitement and love. I told myself it was love, but it was also of course custom. Sewell was a creature of custom, the custom all of his life of reading and writing and spending hours in the Reading Room of the Museum and on buses to visit Bully in the King's Road, or sometimes to more mysterious friends in Hampstead whom we were never allowed to hear about, because he didn't really believe in mixing his friends.

Crime always fascinated him, but punishment repelled; in the war he had turned Probation Officer, and became an expert on court and prison life. 'I wonder', one judge asked him, 'if, when you have to know your opposite number on the bench a little better, you could possibly just ask her to shave?' He would go to Brixton or Wormwood Scrubs to listen to prisoners and talk to Governors: was it pity or fascination? A mixture of both, I suppose.

In earlier years he wrote for popular magazines about celebrated authors and actors, and from time to time he would collect these pieces and publish them as books: I hold one in my hand, and marvel at an index which starts with Maud Allen and finishes with Oscar Wilde; he also wrote about Thomas Burke and Gordon Selfridge and Edmund Gosse and Baden-Powell, and of course Mary Pickford.

The cinema might have been invented for Sewell, and he never forsook the National Film Theatre, going back there over and over again to view *Orphans of the Storm* or the early Fatty Arbuckle. It was not a taste I ever really shared with him, but sometimes I would accompany him and always fail to share his delight in the silent, fading, flickering world of Constance Talmadge.

What on earth am I doing here, I would ask myself, and the answer was just to be in his company. There are some men, and Sewell was one, whose company is sought because it is a supreme gift. This year, for the first time, we have Christmas without him and I can't decide what to do: to put his present under the tree, open in vain his bedroom door and look for his Gladstone bag, for he never really totally unpacked? Better just perhaps to write about him this Christmas Eve, and put away the letter along with the will and the birth certificate for others one day to read, particularly my elder son who was also his godson and so loved him as did we all who just now miss him so very much.

Sewell, Bully, Margaret, Tom – all gone within a year or two of the mid-1980s, leaving Robert with what? An aching sense of loss, certainly, but never defeat. Annabel and Charles presented him with another grand-daughter, Daisy, and then another grandson, Jack. They were visited annually in Australia, and Wilton, who continued to thrive in the increasingly precarious world of touring theatre, while in England there were still movies to be made, albeit fleetingly, and television shows to talk on, and restaurant columns to be written. Sometimes, to general amazement and disbelief, he would announce a form of retirement: 'I am seventy-five,' he told the *Sunday Times* in 1983, 'and I should have gone years ago. Usually when people retire they get a gold watch or find someone sitting at their desk. I have just trodden on a sea anemone in Sydney Harbour and I think it's the sign to quit. I think retirement might suit me, as long as Heinz and British Airways don't cut off my pension in commercials altogether.'

Eventually, of course, they did, because no advertisement can last forever; but Ros still found him film roles, and in these years he managed a couple of thrillers (*Loophole* and *The Deadly Game*), a caper quest (*High Road to China*), and a distinguished Stuart Burge BBC television serialisation of Angus Wilson's *The Old Men at the Zoo*. It was not bad for someone who frequently announced his retirement.

In truth, he grew bored if work did not come, and then he became quite quickly bored with the work itself. Treats seemed to happen less often, though he animatedly pottered off to Harare in Zimbabwe to open a wine festival, and then, in still more adventurous spirit, went off with his younger son on the long march to Peking, a journey Wilton abandoned half way through on the grounds that even Brisbane on a wet Monday was more exciting than China.

Robert travelled on, undeterred, finishing back in Hollywood for a last, horrendous television musical of *Alice in Wonderland*, in which he played the King of Hearts opposite Carol Channing as the Queen. This valedictory visit also allowed him to bid farewell to his old friend Willy Hyde-White, about whom he later wrote a superlative epitaph for *The Times*:

He, like me, came of a generation of actors who often, and let us admit sometimes mistakenly, had no great respect for playwrights or directors. Willy and I always preferred our own interpretations of the mood of the evening; we would both stand down stage, staring moodily out into the auditorium in search of a friendly face and a laugh. On the other hand, there were times when my old friend gracefully conceded, and acted the play for all he was worth: he was worth a great deal. Who will ever forget him in *The Reluctant Debutante*, or dancing with Rex Harrison in the film of *My Fair Lady*?

He once made a brief and necessary appearance in the Bankruptcy Court, where even the Official Receiver fed him his best lines. 'If', he said, 'you cannot inform the court how you managed to spend so large a sum in so short a time, perhaps you could tell us what will win the Gold Cup at Ascot this afternoon?' 'Of course, my dear fellow,' Wilfrid rejoined, and rather surprisingly managed to name the winner. 'But only have a small bet, M'Lud,' he cautioned, 'we don't want to have to change places, now do we?'

A sense of departure was already in the air, especially on the locations for *The Old Men at the Zoo*; as Robert noted: 'Marius Goring, Andrew Cruick-shank, Maurice Denham – we were all very relieved to see each other back every morning for rehearsal. At our age, no tantrums: we were more likely to be bickering over the crossword than the lines, or indeed managing to learn them accurately. Then we all had to stop for Ralph Richardson's memorial service. Another one gone.'

Other films, other locations: a Donald Sutherland thriller (*The Trouble With Spies*), New York to start on his *Celebrity Chefs* television series, a trip with Joan around the Norwegian fjords as the guest lecturer on a Viking cruise liner. As he approached eighty, he certainly was not slowing down, though sometimes slightly uncertain where he was supposed to be going next and whether any of his old friends would still be there to keep him company on the journey.

29

A Basher to Travel

1988–1992

I will soon be eighty: what have I done to achieve such longevity? Woken up each morning and tried to remember not to wear my hearing-aid in the bath. It doesn't seem quite enough, but I am blessed with an outer frame which doesn't like exercise, tolerates rich food and alcohol, and which I rest as often as possible . . . Once, on a film-studio floor, I heard an electrician in need of a spotlight on wheels call out, 'Give me a Basher to travel,' and I told myself it should have been the title of my autobiography.

Towards the end, the work began to perk up again: a few scenes in *Little Dorrit*, Christine Edzard's classic Dickens film, and then a major role as the Dimblebyesque war correspondent in *War and Remembrance*, an epic fifteen-hour American television sequel to Herman Wouk's *The Winds of War*, which gave Robert almost a year of work on locations from Singapore to Hawaii and a spectacular death scene in the desert, where he was blown up on a tank.

Along the way he also found time to play Twiggy's father in a peculiar fiasco called *Istanbul Keep Your Eyes Open*, mercifully only ever released into very small video shops, and had a rather better time in Greece making *The Wind* for Nico Mastorakis. For his eightieth birthday we took over a restaurant near Fairmans and gathered as many as we could of the remaining clan. Not long afterwards, in the summer of 1988, he was back at the Fairmans typewriter, again working with Margaret, on a volume entitled *The Pleasures of Age*, then on a travel book, *Around the World in Eighty-One Years*, and finally on a possible television series about life in the office of a theatrical agent not too many miles removed from his own.

But, in truth, he was slowing down quite considerably, though Joan, Margaret and Ros entered into a wonderful, unconscious conspiracy never to make him aware that he was not likely to work again. There were still the Berkshire grandchildren, our three, to lead on expeditions to Windsor races and all nearby Chinese restaurants. My one regret is that in these last and generally, I think, very happy years of his life, I rather lost touch with him, having moved to London as my marriage ended. He never entirely approved of this, but our relationship suffered nothing much worse than a faint distancing. I continued to go to see him on Sundays and we still sat around the pool in summer like a couple of water buffalo, wondering if we ought to be doing anything active and deciding on the whole probably not.

He remained puzzled by my choice of career, wondering how anyone could bear to go on reviewing plays, films, television programmes and books for the whole of a lifetime. Sometimes I hesitantly tried to explain that it was probably no more peculiar a life than that of an actor, if perhaps rather less creative, but that I had the occasional biography to remind me that I was a writer as well as a journalist. He seemed to believe this and was, I think, in some ways grateful that none of his children had ever really been too much trouble to him, except for the infrequent and usually shortlived emotional or financial crisis. It was only after he died that I found, to my huge delight, in a letter he had written from Australia to my mother several years earlier, a line about how much he had admired a hardback collection of my theatre reviews, which I had given him to help him sleep on the plane.

He was also now, in his anecdotage, a regular celebrity guest at theatrical lunches and prizegivings, at least until the notorious occasion of the Olivier Awards in the year when Michael Crawford looked like a runaway winner for his performance in the musical *Barnum*.

Indeed so convinced was Robert of Crawford's supremacy that, when asked to give the award for Best Actor in a Musical, he went up on stage and announced it to be Michael Crawford without even bothering to open the envelope or check the judges' decision, something he only got around to doing after Crawford suggested that it might be a good idea, in case their verdict disagreed with that of my father.

Reluctantly Robert opened the envelope, and discovered that the judges had agreed with him: some ashen moments later, I asked him backstage what he would have done if a different name had been inside the envelope. 'Ignored it, dear boy', Robert said, 'because the judges would obviously have been wrong'.

He was seldom asked to announce a theatrical award again.

In the summer of his eighty-first year, the *Observer* asked him to describe a typical Morley Sunday:

At my age now there is a fatal temptation to count one's days: sometimes, playing with someone else's pocket calculator, I find myself trying to work out the number of seconds during which I have survived. I have, needless to say, never yet made the sum come out satisfactorily, but I do seem to have spent approximately 40,000 Sundays on earth. For the first 1,000 or so I went to church, only to be told that I was a miserable sinner, though I was usually only miserable at having to be there. For the last 39,000 or so Sunday for me has meant luncheon rather than church.

Sometimes my father and I would share a lunch of potted meat sandwiches; towards the end of his life he had an arrangement with his bank, whereby he was allowed to draw out a specified sum on Monday mornings, which he would then distribute during the week to selected bookmakers, dog-track totalisers and a small poker school. The arrangement kept him remarkably happy towards the end, as luckily he was very fond of potted meat. He had a lot in common with a brother-in-law who lived opposite, until being banished to Australia.

I, too, now have one son in Australia, but luckily he comes home from time to time to shop for plays; sometimes fortune smiles on him, at others it is rather well hidden in the clouds. Recently he telephoned to tell us he was thinking of getting out of the theatrical management business: so many thing to go wrong, he complained. There's always an election, or a train strike, or the weather is too hot, or there is a panic on the stock exchange. Joannie was already resigned to his discovery: she had, after all, been hearing much the same from her husband and her mother for the best part of seventy years.

My daughter and her family have also moved from Shepherd's Bush to Bondi Junction, which leaves a considerable gap around the Sunday lunch table in Berkshire, though we do still have my elder grandchildren to share the roast beef and the apple pie or the ice cream. I have always believed in a choice of sweets, have indeed all my life been something of a pudding man, training my family from an early age in how to behave when the sweet trolley comes around, only glancing at one's plate with mock astonishment when the waiter has already filled it with a selection of at least three different desserts. For me two of the most awful words in the English language have always been 'just coffee'.

In the summer, when the weather is fine, we spread a white cloth on the long table in the garden and do our best to recreate the Courvoisier advertisement featuring that huge French family outside their chateau. Not that we have an actual chateau, you understand, but the cottage is painted white and has stood up well to the forty years since we bought it. It's a rehabilitated gamekeeper's cottage, added to modestly over the years, but now of course with far too many empty bedrooms. But today there will be several grandchildren and their parents to lunch, and I must remember to wear my hearing-aid so as to catch some at least of what is going on with them and their lives.

My eldest grandson, Hugo, is already a theatre buff like his father and grandfather, but the rest of them don't yet seem to have caught the bug, which is probably a good thing. Grandchildren provide a quite different euphoria from that of a full house on a Saturday night. My youngest, Jack, has now almost stopped biting his sister, who seems to be going in for serious attacks of chicken pox. My daughter, who once ate broken glass and told us she was too young to die, has been totally changed by being a mother herself. There is no trace now of the despairing cook who once broke the plates when her cake refused to rise, nor of the schoolgirl who once padlocked herself to the front door with a bicycle chain and maintained she had swallowed the key, saying, 'Now perhaps you'll believe me when I say I hate school.' Today she is responsible, caring, unflappable; I suppose it comes to all of us in the end.

My eldest grandson will doubtless finish up somewhere backstage, while his elder sister is struggling with exams and his younger one merely determined to have it all her own way, whatever it all may turn out to be. All too soon, after tea, the garden will go quiet again; no more children racing across the lawn into the pool, or climbing perilously on chairs to reach the tins of chocolate that Joannie hides in the cupboard in a vain attempt to get us all a bit thinner. Our hostages to fortune have left us alone, until the next Sunday lunch.

Time still, though, for another cigar by the pool in the early evening, maybe even a swim with his dauntless old friend Mary Cook, and then time to start reading another of his beloved yellow-jacketed crime novels from Gollancz. Time still, in the week, for a trip to London, lunch with Ros to see if there might be a day or two of filming on the horizon and then, if there was, a brief celebratory stop at the Knightsbridge casino on the way home.

There were other diversions too: visits from Sally and Robert Hardy, divorced by this time, but frequent visitors to Fairmans, as were Gladys's step-daughter Ros Young and the Hardy daughters, Emma and Justine, and of course Catherine and David Barham, Robert's beloved niece and her husband, on their trips up from Kent. In addition there would be the occasional ceremonial outing, such as the honorary doctorate he was given by his local university at Reading in 1988. This was an honour he much enjoyed, especially the red robes and the lunch at which, seated next to one of the faculty wives, he asked her how he had come to be selected for such a distinction, given his shaky educational background. 'Oh,' she said dismissively, 'we usually give it to people who live in the area and who haven't caused too much political or social trouble.'

Sometimes there would be a chat show to do: he and I once did an entire *Parkinson*, which ended with him reciting the whole of Kipling's *If* from memory quite breathtakingly, and on another occasion, his last in front of a live audience, we turned up together for a platform performance on the Cottesloe stage of the National Theatre to sell a couple of our books and generally flip back through the years. This was at the end of September 1991 and suddenly, there, backstage at the National, where he was simultaneously about to make his debut and his farewell, I noticed for the first time how thin he was beginning to be and, to my amazement, even fragile. He was worried that his hearing-aid would not work or would whistle, as it so often did in theatres, and that he would not be able to catch the questions from the audience. I told him that of course I would repeat them to him on stage, that the Cottesloe was full of friends and fans, and that it was simply wonderful to see him there, but he seemed oddly unreassured, frightened almost of doing what he had done so many times before without even thinking about it. For the first time, that night, I realised that he really did not want to be in public any more.

Not that he went into anything like total retreat: he still came to London from time to time, sharing with me the rare delight I had in having written *Noel and Gertie* and seeing it (thanks entirely to Patricia Hodge and Simon Cadell, and their director Alan Strachan) become a West End hit for six months at the Comedy Theatre. He came to the opening of that, went to support other old friends on other celebratory occasions, made the speech at his oldest surviving friend Llewellyn Rees's ninetieth birthday, and kept in close touch with Ros, her partner Michael Linnit and his family, the Tomlinsons, my old Oxford friends, Chris Matthew and Nigel Frith, and their families, and such others as were still able to gather around him at Fairmans over the weekends.

He continued to lead the parade at Wargrave village festivals, often driving through the high street on an open coach in full regalia borrowed from an early movie, and going up the hill to see the Christmas pantomime of the local nursery school. In these last few months his horizons seemed to shrink to the village he had loved for half a century; London began to appear noisy, distant and difficult, and increasingly, when he did write, it was about the past, what kind of life he had enjoyed and what kind of man he thought he had been:

> I'm not sure how I'd rate myself as a father nowadays. Not good, perhaps; much too wrapped up in myself. Loving, certainly, but never much of an influence. My son in Australia once told Alan Whicker on a television programme that he'd really only gone there to escape his father and his elder brother, which shocked us both a bit when we saw it, but I suppose we have both been rather noisy. I also have a daughter now living in Sydney. I'm afraid that if you're an actor and an egomaniac and a show-off, as I am, then perhaps you don't make a perfect parent. But my wife has been a wonderful mother to them all, still is; I think perhaps I was a bit of a bore to them.

On the contrary, he seemed to me an ideal father, generous and funny, and wonderfully undidactic. He never really had the faintest idea what a father was supposed to be or do, which is what made him such a marvellous companion: he was the most unpaternalistic but most genial of parents, and one cannot ask much more than that; at least, I hope my children cannot either.

'No one is actually good enough to deserve a child,' wrote Robert at the time he was thinking of *Edward, My Son*, but some of us seem to have been fortunate enough to deserve him. A lifelong racing and gambling man, he continued to be the luck of our generation. He was also never going to go quietly into that good night. On one of his last American book-signing tours he had almost had himself removed from the air after memorably destroying Bob Hope's defence of the Vietnam War while sitting beside the old comic; and at home he continued to fight lesser campaigns, notably against the destruction of the local Henley cinema and in favour of a golf course being built next to Fairmans by some old farmer friends.

Nevertheless there were signs of mortality at last: 'If life is a party', Robert had told David Lewin towards the end of the last full year of his own life, 'I really should be leaving quite soon. After all, one doesn't wish to outstay one's welcome; I'll just collect my shroud at the door and be off.'

At eighty-two he told the *Evening Standard*:

> One really shouldn't complain about a little diabetes, and luckily the

memory shows, as yet, no sign of Alzheimer's. I keep testing myself out by remembering where I've put my glasses, though I do have trouble now with faces. I spent hours in the Garrick last week talking to Robin Day only to discover much later that he had mysteriously become Donald Sinden. I also don't pick up the jokes in theatres any more, largely because my hearing-aid thinks they should be coming from me. I still average two cigars a day, and have only ever had two operations in my life, tonsils and a rupture. Oh yes, and there was the time I broke my leg, helping Sybil Thorndike out of a taxi. That was really silly.

I love being asleep and, like thousands of others, I dream about having tea with the Queen at Windsor Castle. Just sandwiches and cake, but I'm always a great social success: it makes you feel you have finally reached a proper status in life. My parents both went just before they were eighty, so I feel I've already done a bit better. They give you a blue pill for your heart when you're sixty, you know, and then I have another one now for diabetes, but I don't always remember them both. Originally I had vague thoughts of having myself cremated and having the ashes scattered over the Isle of Man in a high wind, God knows why; now I think I'd just like to settle down in the coffin with my credit cards, in case they are they needed on the other side. One never knows, and I have always found it unwise to travel without them. I've had a charmed life, you know, with Joannie: I found someone who would tolerate me, and thousands wouldn't. I do rather approve of marriage; it gives one a permanent address in life.

By this time, some of my more tactless interviewer colleagues were regularly asking Robert how he would most like to die: 'Watching television, I think,' he mused, 'either the racing or a David Attenborough wildlife programme about giant sloths. I have always rather liked the look of the sloth: such a contented animal, always swims on its back rather like me, though I'm probably not as fast. I think sloth is one of the great virtues: people are always trying to do far too much with their lives.'

Two last, brief professional engagements in 1991: the first was a token guest-star appearance in *The Lady and the Highwayman*, a Lew Grade television costume drama derived from a novel by Barbara Cartland, and the other was rather better: an eight-hour mini-series of *Around the World in Eighty Days*, in which he was able to revive the role of the Governor of the Bank of England, which he had played for the Mike Todd version almost forty years earlier, the only actor now to appear in both versions.

But that really was that. In May 1992 Robert was celebrating his eighty-fourth birthday and, for the first time since my divorce, I was able to gather round the table of a restaurant in Sonning my parents, my children and their mother, and Ruth Leon, with whom I had been sharing my life in London for the past four years. It was a joyous occasion, the first Sunday of summer on which it was possible to eat out of doors, and Pa seemed genuinely delighted to have all the family around him. This meant a great deal to me after an unhappy divorce, so much, in fact, that I think I was eager not to recognise the signs which only later struck me, when I developed the photographs taken over lunch – photographs that show Robert smiling in the sun certainly, but also very grey and very tired and very drawn.

But it was nothing really serious, or so it seemed – not for a man of his age at any rate. A day or two later I went to New York to cover the Tony Awards on Broadway for the arts programme I present every Saturday night on BBC Radio 2. After the show my producers, Stella Hanson and Madeleine Cuming, and I stayed on for a couple of days to do some other interviews in New York, and then we caught the night flight back on the Monday. As we landed early on the Tuesday morning, both Alexis and Ruth were at the airport to meet me, and I knew at once, even before they spoke, why they were there.

On that Sunday, my parents had been due to go to Margaret's for lunch. At around noon Robert said that he felt tired and would therefore happily spend the day in bed with the Sunday papers, but that Joan was to go without him. Over lunch at Margaret's, Joan and Hugo decided that, if Robert were spending the day in bed, then he might like to have the television upstairs with him. Hugo drove back with Joan to carry it to the bedroom. When they arrived, they found Robert slumped across the bed, having suffered a massive stroke. They rang for an ambulance to take him to Dunedin hospital in Reading, and there he died three days later, never having regained consciousness.

Joan, Margaret and Hugo were already at his bedside by the time I arrived – indeed, they had been there all the previous day and most of the night, watching for any sign of movement. That evening I talked to his doctor, who was superbly honest and direct. I had, I told him, a sister in Sydney and a brother living in Tampa, Florida – what should we tell them? 'Tell your brother in Florida', he said, 'that, if he gets on a plane right away, he may just get over here in time. Your sister in Australia has almost no chance, and it would be so much better surely for her and your mother if she were to come a little later, when they will so badly need to be with each other.'

So that was how we arranged it. The following morning, Wednesday, I went to meet my brother at the airport after his overnight flight. We drove straight to the hospital to find that Juliet had come from school and that Pa was still unconscious. Shortly before noon he stirred, as though he knew that as many of us as possible were gathered to say goodbye. Looking just like a baby again, he sighed and died. One of the nurses who had been looking after him covered him with a sheet and laid a single rose on his chest. It was Derby Day, 3 June 1992.

The following morning *The Times* led the obituaries page with the thought that 'few qualities are more likeable than the ability to give the impression that one is enjoying oneself hugely, and few leading actors have integrated this quality more infectiously into their style than Robert Morley.' Pa would have been proud of that, as he would of a headline in my own paper, the *International Herald-Tribune*: 'Robert Morley, British Comic Genius, Dies at 84'. The *Guardian* called him a 'run-of-the-grill Falstaff' and for the *Observer* on the following Sunday Michael Parkinson added: 'If Robert had a mission, it was to emphasise that life was meant to be fun; he was one of the few men I knew who strode through life instead of circum-navigating it. He always seemed to me a complete and fulfilled man, and he died at eighty-four without ever growing old.'

Robert left a wife, three children, five grandchildren, an enormous number of stage and screen memories, several books and plays, and a couple of hundred friends in the theatre, cinema, journalism, publishing, racing and the village, almost all of whom turned up for his funeral and for a gathering afterwards on the lawn at Fairmans; one could look around and see literally his whole life represented by those who were there to see him off. He also left my mother well provided for in Fairmans itself, and just over £74,000; not a lot, someone said, for fifty plays and a hundred movies in a career of sixty years, but then Robert had never expected to do more than draw level with the Inland Revenue at the end, so that was one last triumph, after all.

Another late triumph came a few weeks after his death with the news that his farewell appearance had won an award as the television commercial of its year. There are worse ways to be remembered than as Father Christmas with a recipe for mince pies.

Arnold Holt: Well, ladies and gentlemen, that's how it all happened, more or less . . . Look after yourselves. The way things are in this world, nobody else will.

He lifts his hat and waves cheerily as the curtain falls.

Epilogue
Curtain Call (for Ruth)
1993

'Typical,' she said, returning the typescript, 'absolutely typical, and it's all so bloody English and clenched. You've spent this entire book describing what your father was and did with his life, and still not faced up to the most important issue of all. What he did to you: the fact that everything you are, and worse everything you're not, is because of him, because neither of you ever really bothered to work out your relationship, and now of course it's too late.'

I thought about that for a bit, as one would; we do not take criticism lightly in my family, at least not from those we love. We dole it out on a fairly regular basis, and in my case for a living, but anything less than total blind admiration and enthusiasm in return is regarded by all of us as something of a threat.

Robert for his part did not speak to Godfrey Winn for more than thirty years after Godfrey had unwisely remarked, on seeing me aged five in the street, that I was already decidedly overweight. It was entirely true of course, has been ever since, but somehow not the kind of remark either Pa or I expected to have to listen to. The only trouble with the Winn boycott was that, after about twenty years, Robert began to forget whether it really had been Godfrey, or possibly Cecil Beaton or even Beverley Nichols who had uttered the famous sizist insult, so as a result we had to go around cutting all three of them at cocktail parties in a miasma of vague retroactive indignation.

But was I really paternally challenged, and if so was there anything I could have done about it, even had I wanted to? In America they arrange these things rather differently; a whole nation is still in the therapeutic throes of discovering what their parents did to them, and not caring for the discovery. Like all American trends, this one will soon be with us: indeed even as I write, both Blake Morrison and Jill Tweedie are publishing remarkable voyages of self-discovery which set off from the unsafe harbour of a parent's death.

Why then can't I deliver the filial goods? Why, when I stare in the bathroom mirror every morning and see my father staring back, is he still not telling me anything of great psychological import about either him or me, let alone the two of us together?

'We can be bought,' the great American actor Alfred Lunt once said of himself and his wife Lynn Fontanne, 'but we can't be bored,' and that in essence was also Pa's philosophy: in truth he quite easily got bored of fatherhood. He was the only man I ever knew to catch the Trans-Siberian Railway as an escape from boredom rather than an invitation to ten days of it, and there was I think somewhere deep in him a terror of the family he so loved. Happy enough when leading us into restaurants or watching us splash about in his pool, he would suddenly remember that there was a world elsewhere, and that fatherhood was never going to be quite as much fun as roulette.

Of course he conditioned me. He conditioned me to flee in terror from any really emotional situation; to believe that loving people was the same as looking after them; to know that my only real talent was for living on my wits, and that therefore I had to be careful to keep them about me, not allowing them to be interfered with by those who would wish to get too close. He taught me, by example rather than any conversation, that we were temperamentally observers rather than participants, and that in the end work was likely to be more fun than fun, provided we always found work we enjoyed and then made them pay for that.

But if I never really found Robert psychologically, I also never really lost him except once, when I allowed my emotional life temporarily to paralyse me and he looked on in mild paternal astonishment at the lack of professionalism which had allowed me to put my life in front of my work when there were still children to educate and a family to feed. We never really discussed that of course, but then again we never really discussed anything important for fear that it might lead to trouble or keep us from lunch.

Robert never frightened me, or bored me, or tried to make me anything I hadn't already become by heredity or education or accident or desire. If I disappointed him he never told me, and in our own clenched, curious way we loved each other very much.

But this, as I have noted, is a time for parental revelation, and the one about Robert didn't really come into focus for me until this book was already with the printer. Early in the summer of 1993, I was on a reviewing trip to Broadway and happened upon a remarkable solo show. Called *Shakespeare For My Father*, it has been put together by Lynn Redgrave, who spends a couple of hours alone on stage trying to discover who Michael was by reaching back into his own Shakespearian texts and playing them out, Cordelia to his vanished Lear.

Lynn is eighteen months younger than me; like me, she grew up backstage as the child and grandchild of actors. Unlike me, she has also spent twenty years in America, and is therefore accustomed now to a certain amount of soul-searching: indeed there are moments when her show hovers dangerously between theatre and therapy. But along the way, starting from the appalling and appalled discovery that Michael did not even note her arrival on earth in his detailed daily journal, she does at least begin to define the problem of being an actor's child, for Michael of course was one of those too.

By the time of his last stage appearance at the National, already ravaged by Parkinson's, Lynn had been reconciled to her distant, distanced, dying parent, and told him with some pride that she had located, in Australia, the long-neglected grave of his father, Roy Redgrave. What, she now asked Michael, would he like her to inscribe on it on his behalf? Something about loving father of Michael? After a pause, his hands shaking with the Parkinson's and the emotion, Michael said, 'Just put Roy Redgrave: Actor'.

It's what they all were, you see, just actors. Fatherhood was one of Robert's longer-lasting engagements, but he had to act that, too. I only hope he enjoyed the performance as much as I always did: for I was not only Pa's eldest child, I was always also his travelling audience, and it was a long and very happy tour with maybe a few bad houses here and there, and perhaps just a little trouble with the end of the second act. But nothing that couldn't be fixed in rehearsal, which is where we always were, no matter the country or the town; we were in rehearsal for real life, which luckily only very seldom happened to get in the way.

A Career Chronology

1: Plays in which he Appeared as an Actor:

1928 (debut): *Dr Syn* (Hippodrome, Margate)
1929: *Treasure Island* (Strand)
1930–31: With J. B. Fagan's company, Oxford Playhouse and touring
1932: Touring
1933: With Festival Theatre Company, Cambridge, and touring *Up in the Air* (Royalty)
1934: Touring with Sir Frank Benson's company
1935: *Richard of Bordeaux* (National Tour)
Founder member of Peter Bull's summer theatre at Perranporth
1936: *Oscar Wilde* (Gate) and Perranporth season
1937: Alexandre Dumas in *The Great Romancer* (Strand and New)
Henry Higgins in *Pygmalion* (Old Vic) and Perranporth season
1938: *Oscar Wilde* (Fulton, New York) and Perranporth season
1939: Perranporth season
1941: Decius in *Play with Fire* (Brighton and national tour)
Sheridan Whiteside in *The Man Who Came To Dinner* (Savoy)
1943: *The Man Who Came To Dinner* (national tour)
1944: Charles in *Staff Dance* (national tour)
1945: The Prince Regent in *The First Gentleman* (New and Savoy)
1947: Arnold Holt in *Edward, My Son* (His Majesty's)
1948: Arnold Holt in *Edward, My Son* (Martin Beck, New York)

1949–50: Arnold Holt in *Edward, My Son* (Australia and New Zealand tour)

1950: Philip in *The Little Hut* (Lyric)

1954: Hippo in *Hippo Dancing* (Lyric)

1956: Oswald in *A Likely Tale* (Globe)
Panisse in *Fanny* (Drury Lane)

1958: Sebastian in *Hook, Line and Sinker* (Piccadilly)

1960: Mr Asano in *A Majority of One* (Phoenix)

1961: Mr Rhodes in *Mr Rhodes* (Theatre Royal, Windsor)

1962: The Bishop in *A Time to Laugh* (Piccadilly)

1966–67: *The Sound of Morley* (solo show on UK and Australian tours)

1967: Sir Mallalieu FitzButtress in *Halfway up the Tree* (Queen's)

1970: Frank Foster in *How the Other Half Loves* (Lyric) (also Canada 1972 and Australia 1973)

1974: Barnstable in *A Ghost on Tiptoe* (Savoy)

1976: Pound in *Banana Ridge* (Savoy)

1978: George in *A Picture of Innocence* (British and Canadian tour)

1980: Hilary in *The Old Country* (Australian tour)

2: Plays Written or Co-written:

1935: *Short Story*

1937: *Goodness, How Sad*

1944: *Staff Dance*

1947: *Edward, My Son* (with Noel Langley)

1953: *The Full Treatment* (with Ronald Gow)

1954: *Hippo Dancing* (after André Roussin)

1957: *Six Months' Grace* (with Dundas Hamilton)

1958: *Hook, Line and Sinker* (after André Roussin)

1974: *A Ghost on Tiptoe* (with Rosemary Anne Sisson)

1978: *A Picture of Innocence* (with John Wells)

3: Solo Shows:

1966: *The Sound of Morley*

1977: *Robert Morley Talks to Everybody*

(Also cabaret: Café de Paris, 1957;
Mandarin Hotel, Hong Kong, 1976.)

4: Plays Directed:

Several at Perranporth 1936–9
1953: *The Full Treatment* (Kew)
1957: *The Tunnel of Love* (Her Majesty's)
1959: *Once More, With Feeling* (New)

5: Books Published:

1966: *Robert Morley, Responsible Gentleman* (with Sewell Stokes)
1974: *A Musing Morley* (anthology of journalism)
1976: *Morley Marvels* (anthology)
1978: *More Morley* (anthology)
1980: *Morley Matters* (anthology)
1982: *The Best of Morley* (anthology)
1983: *Robert Morley's Book of Bricks*
1985: *Robert Morley's Second Book of Bricks*
1986: *Robert Morley's Book of Worries*
1988: *The Pleasures of Age*
1991: *Around the World in 81 Years*

6: Films and Television Films:

(dates refer to first British release or screening)

1938: *Marie Antoinette*
1940: *You Will Remember*
1941: *Major Barbara*
1942: *This Was Paris*
      The Big Blockade
      The Foreman Went to France
      The Young Mr Pitt
1945: *I Live in Grosvenor Square*
1948: *The Ghosts of Berkeley Square*
1949: *The Small Back Room*
1951: *An Outcast of the Islands*

1952: *The African Queen*
Curtain Up
1953: *The Final Test*
The Story of Gilbert and Sullivan
Melba
Beat the Devil
1954: *The Good Die Young*
The Rainbow Jacket
Beau Brummel
1955: *Quentin Durward*
1956: *Loser Takes All*
Around the World in Eighty Days
1958: *Law and Disorder*
The Sheriff of Fractured Jaw
1959: *The Journey*
The Doctor's Dilemma
Tales from Dickens (ITV television film)
Libel
1960: *The Battle of the Sexes*
Oscar Wilde
1961: *Joseph and his Brethren*
The Young Ones
1962: *Go To Blazes*
Road to Hong Kong
The Boys
1963: *Nine Hours to Rama*
Murder at the Gallop
Ladies Who Do
The Old Dark House
1964: *Take Her, She's Mine*
Hot Enough for June
Of Human Bondage
1965: *Topkapi*
Genghis Khan
1966: *Those Magnificent Men in their Flying Machines*
A Study in Terror
The Alphabet Murders
1967: *Life at the Top*
The Loved One
Hotel Paradiso

Way, Way Out
Tendre Voyou
1968: *Finder's Keepers*
The Trygon Factor
Woman Times Seven
Hot Millions
1969: *Some Girls Do*
Sinful Davey
1970: *Twinky*
Doctor in Trouble
Cromwell
Song of Norway
1972: *When Eight Bells Toll*
1973: *Theatre of Blood*
1974: *Great Expectations*
1976: *The Blue Bird*
1978: *Someone is Killing the Great Chefs of Europe*
1979: *Scavenger Hunt*
1980: *The Human Factor*
O Heavenly Dog
1981: *The Great Muppet Caper*
Loophole
1982: *The Deadly Game* (BBC Television)
1983: *High Road to China*
The Old Men at the Zoo (BBC Television)
1984: *The Trouble with Spies*
1985: *Alice in Wonderland*
1986: *The Wind*
Little Dorrit
1987: *War and Remembrance*
1989: *Istanbul: Keep Your Eyes Open*
1991: *The Lady and the Highwayman*
Around the World in Eighty Days (television remake)

7: Radio and Television and Recordings:

Robert made his radio debut in New York in 1937 and his television debut in Britain early in the 1950s, appearing from then onwards regularly in both media on chat shows and live dramas, a tradition he continued in Britain, America and Australia throughout the rest of his life. He was also a regular panellist for quiz shows, notably *What's My Line?* and *Call My Bluff*, and wrote and starred in three television situation comedy series: *Not in Front of the Children* (1952), *If The Crown Fits* (1961) and *Charge!* (1969), as well as an episode of *Alfred Hitchcock Presents* (1965).

In the early 1970s he read several of Oscar Wilde's fairy tales for long-playing records, and was on television a regular guest of Jack Paar, Johnny Carson, David Frost, Terry Wogan and Michael Parkinson. He also hosted *Sunday Night at the London Palladium* in the late 1950s, appeared as a patient on *Emergency Ward 10*, as a guest of *Morecambe and Wise* and hosted several talk shows of his own for BBC radio and television. In America during the 1980s he was the host of a cable television cookery show called *Celebrity Chefs*, and made more than a hundred commercials, principally for British Airways and in Australia for Heinz Soups.

Index

Names of plays, films etc are to be found by categories under the name of Robert Morley and also in the Chronology.

231